THE
LAST PILLARS
of
DARWINIAN
EVOLUTION
FALSIFIED

FURTHER EVIDENCE PROVING
DARWINIAN EVOLUTION WRONG

Jerry Bergman, Ph.D.

WESTBOW
PRESS®
A DIVISION OF THOMAS NELSON
& ZONDERVAN

WestBow Press books may be ordered through booksellers or by contacting:

WestBow Press
A Division of Thomas Nelson & Zondervan
1663 Liberty Drive
Bloomington, IN 47403
www.westbowpress.com
844-714-3454

ISBN: 978-1-6642-6296-6 (sc)
ISBN: 978-1-6642-6297-3 (e)

Library of Congress Control Number: 2022906305

Print information available on the last page.

WestBow Press rev. date: 5/7/2022

Books by Jerry Bergman

Teaching About the Creation/Evolution Controversy. Bloomington, IN: Phi Delta Kappa Educational Foundation.

Understanding Educational Measurement and Evaluation. Boston, MA: Houghton Mifflin Co.

The Criterion: Religious Discrimination in America. Richfield, MN: Onesimus Publishing Co.

"Vestigial Organs" Are Fully Functional: A History and Evaluation of the Vestigial Organ Origins Concept. Terre Haute, IN: Creation Research Society Books.

Ward's Science Lab Safety Manual. Rochester, NY: Ward's Natural Science Est., Inc.

Persuaded by the Evidence. Green Forest, AR: Master Books.

Hitler and the Nazi Darwinian Worldview: How the Nazi Eugenic Crusade for a Superior Race Caused the Greatest Holocaust in World History. Kitchener, Ontario, Canada: Joshua Press.

Slaughter of the Dissidents: The Shocking Truth About Killing the Careers of Darwin Doubters. Southworth, WA: Leafcutter Press.

The Darwin Effect: Its Influence on Nazism, Eugenics, Racism, Communism, Capitalism & Sexism. Green Forest, AR: Master Books.

Transformed by the Evidence. Southworth, WA: Leafcutter Press.

The Dark Side of Darwin. Green Forest, AR: New Leaf Press.

C.S. Lewis: Anti-Darwinist: A Careful Examination of the Development of His Views on Darwinism. Eugene, Oregon: Wipf & Stock Publishers.

Silencing the Darwin Skeptics: The War Against Theists. Southworth, WA: Leafcutter Press.

Evolution's Blunders, Frauds, and Forgeries. Atlanta, GA: CMI Publishing.

Fossil Forensics: Separating Fact from Fantasy in Paleontology. Tulsa, OK: Bartlett Publishing.

How Darwinism Corrodes Morality: Darwinism, Immorality, Abortion, and the Sexual Revolution. Kitchener, Ontario, Canada: Joshua Press.

Censoring the Darwin Skeptics: How Belief in Evolution is Enforced by Eliminating Dissidents. Southworth, WA: Leafcutter Press.

Darwinism is the Doorway to Atheism: Why Creationists Become Evolutionists. Southworth, WA: Leafcutter Press.

God in President Eisenhower's Life, Military Career, and Presidency. Eugene, OR: Wipf & Stock Publishers.

The "Poor Design" Argument Against Intelligent Design Falsified. Tulsa, OK: Bartlett Publishing.

Science is the Doorway to Creation: Nobel Laureates and Other Eminent Scientists Who Reject Orthodox Darwinism. Southworth, WA: Leafcutter Press.

Useless Organs: The Rise and Fall of the Once Major Argument for Evolution. Tulsa, OK: Bartlett Publishing.

Apes as Ancestors: Examining the Claims About Human Evolution. Tulsa, OK: Bartlett Publishing, co-authored with Peter Line, Ph.D., and Jeffrey P. Tomkins, Ph.D.

Darwinian Eugenics and The Holocaust: American Industrial Involvement. Ontario, Canada: Involgo Press.

How Great Evil Birthed Great Good: The True Story of Two Families. Bloomington, IN: WestBow Christian Publishing.

Endorsements

Just like a Greek temple that its builders centuries ago thought would stand resolute forever by support from three pillars, only to be subsequently ravaged by war, earthquakes, and eventually collapse, Dr. Bergman has very adeptly, and in his inimitable style, identified the three "pillars of evolution" and toppled all three of them into a heap. The fairytale of evolution thus has ended up in a pile of rubble, having nothing left to stand on. This book will help to shine a spotlight on the bankruptcy of evolution and the affront it is to intelligence, reason, wisdom, and, incidentally, verified science.

Bryce Gaudian, Hayward, Minnesota

This book is the most definitive refutation of Darwinism I have ever read. Professor Bergman demolishes the core evidence for evolution, abiogenesis, natural and sexual selection, and mutations. If any one of these pillars of evolution is demolished, the theory fails. In this book Bergman managed to demolish all three pillars. Many evolutionists recognize that problems exist with all of these major pillars but have not been able to find a satisfactorily naturalistic replacement. How do they deal with this conundrum? They recognize the only feasible alternative is theism, an alternative most leading Darwinists cannot accept, regardless of the evidence. This conclusion is supported by a recent survey of AAAS members that found 99 percent were evolutionists and 93 percent were atheists. The 6 percent fill in the holes in Darwinism with God, a very problematic solution. Bergman shows his conclusion is not based on a 'God of the gaps' explanation, but rather is based on clear scientific evidence.

Wayne Frair, Ph.D., Professor Emeritus of Biology, The King's College, New York

I look forward to every new book by Jerry Bergman, because he writes about critically important topics, and has a wealth of information from his nine college degrees (including two PhDs) and his decades of experience as a professor, author, and speaker. What could be more momentous than collapsing the pillars of evolution? Our whole intellectual culture rests on this foundation of sand, supported by three basic ideas: life originated from unguided chemicals, natural selection caused the development of all higher organisms, and the raw material for natural selection is random mutations.

Challenge any one of these and evolutionism teeters and falls. Bergman challenges all three in a coup-de-grace that leaves secular materialists with nothing left to support their worldview, an ideology that has had devastating effects in all aspects of society, as he has documented in his previous books. This book deftly wields scientific evidence—not religious arguments—to expose the sham that is Darwinian evolution. I can't think of anything more urgent for changing secular culture than demolishing the pillars that seem to give this hideous ideology an illusion of scientific respectability.

David Coppedge worked at JPL (Jet Propulsion Laboratory) in Pasadena, CA, as a system administrator for the Cassini Mission to Saturn from 1997 to 2011, and was Team Lead System Administrator for nine of those years.

As a peptide chemist, I carefully reviewed Dr. Jerry Bergman's new book with much interest. He thoroughly reviews the history and status of the three core secular arguments for Darwinian macroevolution with almost 1,000 references. His thorough review of the peer-reviewed literature shows every one of the three pillars to lack credibility. The presented conclusions are logical and should satisfy any person with an open mind, but will not impact others because Darwinism is based on a belief in a worldview that forces one to ignore or reject the clear evidence that falsifies it.

Kenneth W. Funk, Ph.D., Organic Chemist

Dr. Jerry Bergman has done it again! He has taken on the juggernaut of entrenched evolutionary dogma and has overturned its false narratives by doing the heavy lifting—the digging, the dissecting, and the documenting of the truth—that his readers have come to expect . . . and deserve. If you thought that Darwinian naturalism is supported by the evidence from "convergent evolution" or "homology," think again! If you have been taught that "co-option," "pseudogenes," "molecular clocks," or even "endosymbiosis" has proven evolutionism with genius genetics and cellular science, then it's time to be reschooled by Professor Bergman's tremendous tutelage! After all, you deserve a factual education based on empirical science and updated evidence. Class is in session. It's truth time!

David V. Bassett, M.S. (Secondary Science Educator for over 31 years)

I am convinced that a proper training in science requires that undergraduates are confronted by the problems of contemporary science. Only then can they see science as an activity, and not as a body of received doctrine.

John Maynard Smith, Oxford University Press, *Evolutionary Genetics*, 1989, p. v.

CONTENTS

Acknowledgments xiii

Introduction by Kirk Toth, M A. (Biology) xv

Author's Introduction xvii

Foreword by Professor Norman Geisler xxiii

1	The Taxonomy Crisis in Defending Neo-Darwinism 1
2	Convergent Evolution Theory Fails 30
3	Homology Provides Evidence Against Evolutionary Naturalism 64
4	Irreducible Complexity: A Major Problem for Darwinism ...97
5	Co-option Fails to Explain the Evolution of Complex Features 132
6	Pseudogenes —Junk DNA or Intelligent Design? 151
7	Antibiotic Resistance and Macroevolution 185
8	Matter, Energy, and Entropy 213
9	The Failure of Endosymbiosis to Bridge the Gap Between Eukaryotes and Prokaryotes 223
10	Summary 247

ACKNOWLEDGMENTS

I gratefully acknowledge the assistance of Dave Decker, Roger Lovell, Frank Vosler, Ken Funk, Ph.D., Tim Wallace, M.A., Bert Thompson, Ph.D., Wayne Frair, Ph.D., Bryce Gaudian, Clifford Lillo, M.A., and John Woodmorappe, M.A., for their comments on earlier drafts of this book. In addition, I wish to thank Ted Siek, Ph.D., Mary Ann Stuart, M.A., Nathaniel Jeanson, Ph.D., Todd Elder, Jody Allen, R.N, Jean Lightner, DVM, M.S., John UpChurch, Kevin Anderson, Ph.D., David Demick, M.D., John Woodmorappe, M.A., Clifford Lillo, M.A., David V. Bassett, M.S, and several anonymous reviewers for their comments on earlier drafts of this book.

INTRODUCTION
BY KIRK TOTH, M A. (BIOLOGY)

In his first book in this series, titled *The Three Pillars of Evolution Demolished*, Dr. Bergman delivers a lethal blow to any attempts to support the nineteenth-century ideas of Darwinian evolutionary theory using reason or science. The entire Darwinian view of macroevolution today rests on three ideas, 1) the appearance of life from non-life (abiogenesis), 2) the adequacy of natural and sexual selection to account for the incredible variety of life-forms we see today and in the fossil record, and 3) the power of genetic mutations to provide all the raw material for selection to act upon. Dr. Bergman demonstrates conclusively that none of these three ideas are supported by the scientific evidence, and in fact, the science argues against their acceptance. All students of biology should be exposed to Dr. Bergman's thoroughly researched and comprehensive critique of naturalistic evolutionary theory.

In the second volume, entitled *The Last Pillars of Darwinism Falsified*, Dr. Bergman deals with problems presented to secular evolutionary theory. These insurmountable problems include the seemingly ubiquitous nature of irreducible complexity, the observed consequences of the principle of entropy, and problems in taxonomy. The evolutionary ideas of "convergence" and "co-option" are shown to be wholly inadequate to explain biological reality. The idea of endosymbiosis is explained and refuted as well.

These two volumes are meticulously and exhaustively researched, argue from a purely scientific perspective, and provide the intellectual "knock-out punches" to the Darwinian evolutionary worldview which those with an open mind have all been expecting.

AUTHOR'S INTRODUCTION

My previous book titled *The Three Pillars of Evolution Demolished* has documented in detail the fact that the main pillars of evolution have been refuted by the peer-reviewed scientific literature. This book shows that the rest of the commonly used pillars to defend evolution have also been refuted by the peer-reviewed scientific literature. This project has been for me a lifelong study for which this book is a summary. It is the culmination of four decades of research on the issue of evolution, 41 years of teaching life science at the college level, and over 1,700 publications in 2,400 college libraries in 65 nations and 13 languages.

Chapter 1: The Taxonomy Crisis in Defending Neo-Darwinism

What this chapter is about:

Evolutionists have concluded that orthodox biological Neo-Darwinism (crossing the major dividing lines between the Genesis kinds) is proven by documenting that an organism has evolved into an entirely new species, involving a study called taxonomy. Consequently, taxonomy is critical in demonstrating evolution. A species is commonly defined as those within a population with the ability to interbreed, and two animals that cannot interbreed are considered two separate species. A major purported proof of evolution is biological change to the degree that interbreeding between two animals is no longer possible. Darwinists claim that, when this is achieved, evolution has been proven. This chapter shows that this and other definitions of a species are all very problematic for many reasons, indicating major unsolved difficulty for the common evolutionary claim.

Chapter 2: Convergent Evolution Theory Fails

What this chapter is about:

Convergent evolution is a failed attempt to support Darwinism by attempting to deal with the fact that life as a whole does not physically look anything like it evolved from a common ancestor. The theory of convergent evolution postulates that the remarkable biochemical and anatomical similarities existing in very different life-forms that could not have had a recent common ancestor are due to different organisms independently evolving very similar solutions to common problems. For example, animal eyes are postulated to have separately evolved nearly 60 times. Convergent evolution is also used to support major organ and biochemical similarities in cases where certain morphological differences are so great, such as between insects and humans, that a recent common ancestry is not in the realm of possibility. The difficulty with the evolutionary convergence theory is that convergence claims are often just-so stories lacking empirical or scientific support. They are, in short, a very weak attempt to explain what is unexplainable by Darwinism.

Chapter 3: Homology Provides Evidence Against Evolutionary Naturalism.

What this chapter is about:

Homology is the theory that macroevolutionary relationships can be proven by illustrations comparing the anatomy and physiology of different animals. The most common example is comparisons of arm bones found in most introductions in various biology books. This theory has been commonly cited in textbooks as a major proof for evolution since Darwin. A review of the literature on homology has indicated the theory does not provide evidence for evolutionary naturalism, and that the common examples of homology can be better explained by Intelligent Design. Furthermore, increased knowledge about the genetic and molecular basis of life has revealed many major exceptions and contradictions to the theory which, as a result, largely have invalidated the evidence of homology as a proof of Darwinism.

Chapter 4: Irreducible Complexity: A Major Problem for Darwinism

What this chapter is about:

The Irreducible Complexity concept is central to the Darwinism controversy. Irreducible Complexity refers to any machine, system, or symbol that requires two or more parts in order to function. Examples include molecules, proteins, mousetraps, organelles, and organisms such as humans. The irreducible complexity concept has been used by a wide variety of academic disciplines for centuries to understand the details of structure and function. It is also a major problem for evolution. The levels of irreducible complexity, such as the irreducible core and its mode of function, are also discussed. Some of the major objections to irreducible complexity, such as the junk DNA theory and the scaffolding argument, are reviewed in some detail. The major argument against irreducible complexity, co-option, is covered in the companion chapter. Examples of irreducible complexity in both the biological and non-biological worlds document the conclusion that the common objections do not falsify the concept.

Chapter 5: Co-option Fails to Explain the Evolution of Complex Features

What this chapter is about:

The co-option argument is the most common method of attempting to refute the concept of Irreducible Complexity. This argument attempts to explain how irreducible complexity can be achieved through natural means by utilizing existing parts to construct a new biological part, machine, or structure. Problems with the co-option argument include the fact that this claim does not explain the origin of the parts, nor does it explain the origin of the design or proper assembly for the new arrangement of parts formally used for other projects.

Chapter 6: Pseudogenes—Junk DNA or Intelligent Deign Pseudogenes

What this chapter is about:

Pseudogenes are genes that ostensibly lack the transcription or translation machinery required to produce protein. They are often used by Darwinists as evidence for the wasteful process that resulted from the evolution of the genome and, indirectly, as evidence for common descent because they appear to be evolutionary leftovers of past evolutionary life-forms. Recent research indicates that many, or even most, pseudogenes have a function, and several examples are discussed.

Chapter 7: Antibiotic Resistance and Macroevolution

What this chapter is about:

The antibiotic resistance issue often is presented both as a modern example of evolution by mutations and clear evidence for Darwinism. However, in nearly all cases the acquisition of resistance is not due to mutations, but a result of complex, built-in genetic and molecular biological defense systems. Those few examples that are due to mutations are in nearly all cases not a gain of genetic information, but loss mutations that cause damage to a structure or loss of the structure.

Chapter 8: Matter, Energy and Entropy

What this chapter is about:

This chapter describes the tendency of the universe to "wind down" over time, eventually leading to a state of complete entropy. This shows that the universe must have had a beginning, when it was "wound up." Evidences are presented that argue against the universe always existing.

A discussion of the inertia of matter shows that there must have been a "first mover" to initiate matter and the forces that act upon it. This chapter explains why the universe must have been created by an outside force, a "first cause," and that it must be continually sustained by organizing and ordering energy from outside itself.

Chapter 9: The Failure of the Endosymbiosis to Bridge the Gap Between Eukaryotes and Prokaryotes

What this chapter is about:

All cells can be divided into two major types: **prokaryotic**, cells without organelles, and **eukaryotic**, cells with them. An enormous gap exists between the two basic cell types that has not, and cannot, be bridged by transitional forms. The most popular effort to bridge the gap is the theory of endosymbiosis popularized by Lynn Margulis. This theory postulates that some of the eukaryote organelles evolved from other organisms which took residence in primitive prokaryotic cells. Many major problems with this hypothesis are reviewed, leading to the conclusion that this theory is widely accepted not because of empirical evidence, but by default because it is the only somewhat plausible *evolutionary* hypothesis.

Chapter 10: Summary

FOREWORD
BY PROFESSOR NORMAN GEISLER

An important topic in the biological origins controversy is the evolution of humans. This subject is important not only among creationists and Intelligent Design supporters, but also among evolutionists themselves. The issues presented in this book carefully document the fact that the Darwinian worldview can, and often does, cause scientists to naively accept conclusions based on very flimsy evidence. This is a much-needed book that, unlike many others published in the field, is one work that objectively evaluates the evidence for the Darwinian origins belief. Bergman documents that the peer-reviewed science overwhelmingly refutes the major pillars for Darwinism and its various offshoots. The fact is, few evolutionists bother to research the other side of the common evidence for evolution and this is one reason why these pillars are uncritically repeated in the literature. This observation is well illustrated in this important new work by a noted college biology professor and prolific author. Highly recommended.

Dr. Norman Geisler is a long-time professor and author of some 80 books, many of which are on the creation-evolution issue, including *Origin Science, Knowing the Truth about Creation*, and the definitive book on the history of the creation-evolution debate titled, *Creation & The Courts: Eighty Years of Conflict in the Classroom and the Courtroom.*

PORTRAIT OF CARL LINNAEUS, ALSO KNOWN AFTER HIS ENNOBLEMENT AS CARL
VON LINNÉ (1778). LINNAEUS WAS A SWEDISH BOTANIST, PHYSICIAN, AND
ZOOLOGIST CREDITED WITH FOUNDING THE FIELD OF TAXONOMY. COURTESY OF
THE WELLCOME COLLECTION. LONDON.

CHAPTER 1

The Taxonomy Crisis in Defending Neo-Darwinism

Introduction

Darwinists believe that the crossing of the dividing line between what they refer to as microevolution (changes *within* Genesis kinds) and macroevolution (orthodox biological neo-Darwinism, i.e., changes *between* Genesis kinds) is documented by the science of taxonomy. Taxonomy is a system for classifying and identifying organisms first developed by Carolus Linnaeus in the 18th century. Taxonomy is critical for evolutionists to demonstrate that one species evolved into another entirely new species.

Macroevolution is often defined as evolutionary divergence of two life-forms beyond the species level. Although no single universally accepted definition of a species exists, it is commonly defined as the ability to interbreed: If two life-forms cannot normally interbreed, they are defined as two separate species. Evolutionists use this definition to "prove" macroevolution by obtaining evidence that a member of an isolated gene pool has changed (evolved) sufficiently so that it can no longer interbreed with a member of its parent-population pool. The implication is that isolation and natural selection can eventually lead to a new population so different that they can no longer breed with the original parent-population and, therefore, a new species has evolved. Evidence of this event is commonly exploited by Darwinists as definite proof of macroevolution. However, this chapter shows conclusively that the definition of a species is so problematic that it cannot be used as a proof of evolution. Genetics professor Steve Jones notes, when classifying species,

> opinion, the enemy of science, creeps in. Is one kind of bird really unlike another? How different does it have to be to count as distinct? What, indeed, is a "species" in the first place? Does it have a scientific definition, or is it all in the eye of the beholder? The question is at the center of the theory of evolution.[1]

As we will document, classifying animals is no easy task.

The term *species* is from the Latin word *specere*, meaning "to look at" or the "appearance of" a new "kind" of animal, a term obviously borrowed from the Creation account in Genesis where God is said to have created the various kinds of animals. Which life-forms belonged to a certain species was once determined by comparing the purely morphological features of two animals, a branch of biology called *taxonomic systematics*. As more and more animal kinds were discovered and named, this classification system became increasingly problematic. As a result, the criteria used to classify life became more complex and, many feel, very inconsistent and confusing.

For example, animals that were very similar morphologically, such as the African and Indian elephant, were classified as belonging to separate species based on relatively minor differences, such as adult size.[2] In this case, only someone fairly knowledgeable about elephants could tell the difference. Yet the single domestic dog species (*Canis familiaris*) contains animals (i.e., dog breeds) that are drastically

---

[1] Jones, 2000, p. 41.
[2] Silverstein, et al., 1998

different in size, temperament, and many other traits. Conversely, as Jones[3] notes, "most members of most species do not look much different" from each other:

> Any fruit fly is much like another .... In spite of
> some exceptions—the colorful snails or butterflies
> that come in dozens of forms and ... share a Latin
> name imposes, almost by definition, a certain
> uniformity upon those who bear it. That comforts
> both creationists and experts on taxonomy. They like
> to see existence as a set of neat ideals, each filled with
> some pure Platonic essence. However, a great deal
> is hidden within even the most uniform creature.
> Genetics shows that no one ... can any longer suppose
> that all the individuals of the same species are cast in
> the very same mold.[4]

An example of the problem in classifying human and ape fossils given by the senior editor of *Nature*, Henry Gee, is that "almost every time someone claims to have found a new species of hominin, someone else refutes it. The species is said to be either a member of *Homo sapiens*, or a pathological example, or an ape."[5] He then gives several typical, now well-known, examples.

The Subjectivity of Taxonomy

Taxonomy, a field more recently known as systematics, is the science of classifying and naming both living and extinct organisms. Classification for most of history was based on the animal's morphological

---

[3] Jones, 2000, p. 44.
[4] Jones, 2000, p. 44.
[5] Gee, 2011, p. 34.

relationships with other life-forms.[6] Although taxonomy as an avocation dates back to before the time of Aristotle, the taxonomic system used today was developed only in the 1700s by Swedish biologist Carolus Linnaeus. His system is called the *binomial nomenclature* method because it uses two names to classify an organism. The assigned two-word Latin name (such as *Homo sapiens*) designates the first word, which is always capitalized, as the (*gener*ic) genus, and the second word, never capitalized, as the (*specific*) species.

Biologists now classify all life on Earth into a hierarchy of groups of related organisms called *taxa* (singular, *taxon*). From the most to the least inclusive, the taxa are: *Domain, kingdom, phylum* (plural, *phyla*), *class, order, family, genus* (plural, *genera*), and *species* (see Table I for the human taxonomy). Intermediate taxonomic levels can be created at any taxonomic level by using one of three prefixes, *super-*, *sub-*, and *infra-*.

TABLE I: TAXONOMY OF MODERN HUMANS

Taxonomic Level	Name	Distinguishing Feature
Domain	Eukarya	Nucleated Cell/Organelles
Kingdom	Animalia	Animal
Phylum	Chordata	Spinal cord
Subphylum	Vertebrata	Segmented backbone
Superclass	Tetrapoda	Four limbs
Class	Mammalia	Suckles young
Subclass	Theria	Live birth
Infraclass	Eutheria	Has a placenta
Order	Primates	Highly developed
Superfamily	Hominoidea	Humanlike
Family	Hominidae	Two-legged
Genus	*Homo*	Human
Species	*sapiens*	Modern human

---

[6] Turner, 2003.

Many inconsistencies with this tidy system soon became obvious to both biologists and professional taxonomists. A good example was illustrated by the fact that, in the 1800s, humans were once classified by the leading evolutionist in Europe after Darwin, Ernst Haeckel, into four different genera and 12 different species.[7] Another, more modern example of this problem is that a new approach to the study of spiders has resulted in radical changes in their classification. The result is that "families once thought to be distantly related are now considered very close, and vice-versa."[8]

The focus of this review is on evaluating the taxonomic criteria and methods used to classify animals at the genus and species level, as well as to show that classification of life is very problematic. Those who group a large variety of animals into one species are called "lumpers" and those who tend to form many new species are called "splitters." This results in scientists increasingly coming up with

> more and more, new and (some say) improved species definitions; yet each also brought its own new complications. Like sailors in a leaky dinghy, taxonomists and biologists have found their boat forever sinking, as each tried endlessly to patch his or her own or someone else's deflating definition, to what everyone would agree has been absolutely no good end … Taxonomists … could not agree on how the world was ordered, how particular groups had evolved and come to be, how to decide to order or name life. They couldn't even agree on what a species was.[9]

---

[7] Haeckel, 1911, p. 436.
[8] Preston-Mafham, 1996, p. 32.
[9] Yoon, 2009, p. 108.

Problems with the Interbreeding Definition

Classification of animals based on their morphological distinctions can be useful, but this system is very problematic for many reasons. One of these reasons is the fact that the major taxonomic classification system is both inconsistent and contradictory because "the whole idea of 'species' is a totally artificial one, devised by biologists before they understood evolution."[10] The most common definition of a species, the ability to interbreed, will be evaluated first. If two animals can interbreed to produce viable, fertile offspring, they are considered the same species; if not, they are considered different species.[11] Harvard professor Ernst Mayr championed the "Biological Species Concept" which holds that reproductive isolation is sufficient to separate species.[12]

Although "interbreeding" is a very useful definition, so many exceptions exist that using it for definitive purposes is far less-than-perfect, even for sexual animals.[13] Furthermore, the differentiation of species based on interbreeding applies *only* to sexually reproducing organisms. Sexual compatibility cannot be measured in the absence of sexual behavior.

Asexual organisms, such as many mushrooms, often cannot even be cultured to determine sexual compatibility. Consequently, many asexual species cannot be classified by this method, and this number may increase dramatically in the next few decades because some microbiologists estimate only one to five percent of all existing bacterial species have been classified.

Organisms that reproduce asexually include not only bacteria, but aphids, aspens, spider plants and even some lizards.[14] Classifying all single-celled organisms, all of which reproduce by the cell splitting into two daughter cells, is also problematic because biologists use the term

---

[10] Clegg, 2012, pp. 274-275.
[11] Cole, 1984, p. 30.
[12] Mayr, 2014.
[13] Hey, 2001; Shaw, 2002.
[14] Yoon, 2009, p. 107.

'species,' which in this case is used only as an analogy to how the term is applied to more complex organisms: "In practice, species of single-celled organisms are differentiated from each other by their biological niche, by the way they generate energy, and by the way the cell is put together."[15] Furthermore, many animals, such as most Platyhelminthes (flat worms) and many round worms (nematodes) are hermaphroditic, making it very difficult to determine the range of life within which the life-form can reproduce. Hence, other definitions of species have been developed, creating conflicts among Darwinists.

The method usually used by botanists, zoologists, and all other biologists to assign organisms to a species category is "based on morphology: the overall appearance and behavior of bodies. ...Bacteriologists ... employ a different rule of thumb: If two kinds of bacteria share 85 percent of their measurable traits in common, they are taken to be members of the same species."[16]

Yet another problem in defining clear boundaries between species is the fact that many organisms swap genes, not only from one strain of one species to another strain, but also even across species.[17] This process, now known as "horizontal gene transfer," is a common phenomenon.[18] Two organisms that are *reproductively* isolated but not *genetically* isolated, thus able to freely exchange genes, may be able to achieve the advantages of sexual reproduction without sex. This fact has greatly complicated the dividing line between two species, because many species are "defined by their genomes: Each has its own unique set of genes, distinguishable from those of another species. But the definition breaks down if gene swaps are common."[19]

Many other major difficulties exist when the ability of two groups to interbreed or not is used as the major evidence defining macroevolution. Speciation classification based on interbreeding is complicated by

---

[15] Trefil, 1992, p. 27.
[16] Margulis and Sagan, 2002, p. 142.
[17] Margulis, 1996.
[18] Pennisi, 2004, p. 334.
[19] Pennisi, 2004, p. 335.

situations where species A and C cannot interbreed, but species A can interbreed with species B, and then species B can breed with species C. For example, some animals that are part of the same species, e.g., very large dogs such as the Great Dane and a small dog, such as a Chihuahua, *do not* normally interbreed because of great physical size differences. However, both can be forced to interbreed by various methods, such as by artificial insemination or by interbreeding with a middle-sized animal first. Some animals capable of inbreeding produce offspring that usually are sterile. The most common example, a female horse and a male donkey, can breed, but usually produce a sterile mule.

Other animals historically regarded as different species, such as lions and tigers, cows and buffaloes, camels and llamas, and wolves and dogs, all have been interbred successfully. The no longer active Bryan College website listed almost 3,000 hybrid crosses between animals once classified as different species. Interbreeding studies are required to accurately classify sexual species, but are rarely completed for various reasons:

> The classical definition of a species is that two organisms are the same species if they interbreed. Unfortunately, it isn't always possible to use this definition in practice. Take one example: scientists have identified millions of different species of beetles. Do you suppose they actually tried to breed each of these with all the others? Of course not—they simply looked at the anatomy of the insects and made a judgment based on their experience. Similarly, when species are extinct (like dinosaurs), you can't test the breeding compatibility, even in principle.[20]

One cannot know if two animals are, in fact, physiologically incapable of interbreeding due to genetic incompatibility unless (and

---

[20] Trefil, 1992, p. 36.

until) both genetic studies and breeding experiments of the two groups are completed. This is rarely done because of cost, time, and lack of interest. It is much easier for Darwinism supporters to assume that lack of interbreeding is due to the inability to interbreed, and then classify accordingly. In many instances, such as in the case of Darwin's finches, life-forms were incorrectly assumed to be incapable of interbreeding. In this case, empirical research has found that this species separation claim was invalid. If a population is extensively studied enough, examples of interbreeding are found from time to time.[21]

One potential method that could be used to evaluate the level of species separation is to determine if a sperm type matches the required receptor located on a potential egg. However, this method has so far not been applied to any great extent, partly because it is expensive and time-consuming.

Species classification depends on the definition of species used in a specific case, and not on the actual population changes themselves. As noted, some animals that do not normally interbreed, such as a Chihuahua and St. Bernard, are classified as one species, while the hummingbird family comprises many different species, some of which are almost impossible to tell apart! Thus dogs, regardless of size, color, hair, or habits, are all classified as one species, but hummingbirds with very minor differences are listed as different species.

These examples that illustrate how difficult it is to determine species divisions expose the high level of subjectivity involved in species classification.[22] Even for experts, "distinguishing between different species of closely related organisms can be difficult."[23] This is illustrated by the fact that seemingly very minor differences, such as the size of the nucleus in the animal's blood cells, or the size of the epidermal cells on toe pads, or even the number of nucleoli in eye cornea cells are all used to differentiate species.[24]

---

[21] See Grant, 1998, 2000.

[22] Mousseau, et al., 2000.

[23] Cole, 1984, p. 30.

[24] Cole, 1984, p. 30.

Margulis and Sagan, after noting that "many millions of words have been written on the definitions of species," suggest a new testable idea to define species, namely an "organism (A) belongs to the same species as another organism (B) if and only if A and B have precisely the same cellular ancestors, that is, they are descended from the same genomes, and the relations between these genomes are the same."[25]

Nongenetic Barriers to Interbreeding

Interbreeding limits are often *not* a result of a biological inability to breed, as the species concept would imply. Breeding that normally occurs between animals of a single species is often prevented by mechanical factors, not genetic limits, such as a major disparity in physical size, as noted above with dogs. Another factor to consider is that two animals that might breed in captivity or in a lab, will not do so in the wild. Others will breed in the wild, but not in a lab, or even in captivity.[26] Two animals often will not normally interbreed due to a variety of rather minor, even trivial, barriers. For example, breeding often depends on mating cues such as scent, to which, for example, dogs and horses respond. Placing a commercial camphor-menthol compound on the nostrils of horses prevents all breeding.

If breeding cues are visual, such as with many birds, slight coloring differences that would not interfere with, for example, dog or horse breeding, can cause a female to refuse a male, or the male to be uninterested in a female. Some animals, such as hummingbirds, use optical cues to select mates. Slight song differences, such as exist among the Greenish Warbler, can also prevent interbreeding.[27] This is why factors differentiating animals are sometimes so subtle or innocuous that humans have difficulty recognizing them.

Most living populations can be subdivided and placed in separate

---

[25] Margulis and Sagan, 2002, p. 58.
[26] Yoon, 2009.
[27] Collinson, 2001.

locations or environments so that they will interbreed only with each other. In a small, isolated gene pool, recessive traits can emerge to become the hallmark of that particular species. For this reason, forming a "new species" by design (or accident) is often not a difficult task. In other cases, geographical, chronological, or other nongenetic boundaries can limit interbreeding.

Slight seasonal cue differences are one reason why the "ring species" type of frog, found from Northern to Southern United States, will breed with the immediate North and South neighbors, but will not with frogs located too far north or south. The seasonal mating cues in this case are too different.[28] This example also illustrates the fact that taxonomic separation into two species can be arbitrary—even herpetologists are not sure where to draw the line between two frog species.[29] Ring species are important in evolutionary biology because the

> evolutionary divergence of a single species into two *has never been directly observed in nature*, primarily because speciation can take a long time to occur. A ring species, in which a chain of integrating populations encircles a barrier and the terminal forms coexist without interbreeding, provides a situation in which variation in space can be used to infer variation in time.[30]

Conditions can change that allow two *different* species within one ring to merge into one breeding population.[31] A good example is the fact that different species of Darwin's finches have been found to produce hybrids.[32] Further research, mostly in the area of genetics, has also blurred this once clear concept.[33]

---

[28] Irwin, et al., 2001a, pp. 223-243.

[29] McKey, 2000.

[30] Irwin, et al., 2001, p. 333, emphasis mine.

[31] Bowen, et al., 2001, p. 1029.

[32] Lamichhaney, Sangeet, et al., 2018, pp. 224-228.

[33] Liebers, et al., 2004; Pereira, et al., 2011; Joseph, et al., 2008; and Irwin, et al., 2001.

The claim that macroevolution occurs as a result of "new" species being created by microevolution is very problematic for many other reasons. As noted, the species label is very useful in classifying life, but sharp lines rarely can be drawn.[34] A major difficulty is that the definition and criteria used to define a species, genus, etc., generally are skewed by most taxonomists to favor an evolutionary interpretation of the data.

Taxonomists frequently create a new species according to their understanding of how evolution proceeds (i.e., how microevolution supports macroevolution). Taxonomic classification may result in ten species of finches, even if evidence exists that these ten do not legitimately separate into ten species. This error is especially the case if the putative "speciation" that occurs is solely a result of minor genetic information loss, genetic shuffling, and/or various genetic combinations.

Taxonomists often reject breeding experiments performed in artificial environments, such as exist in captivity, unless they demonstrate an *inability* to produce fertile offspring.[35] Cole admits this rule makes it very difficult in many cases to determine if two groups of organisms belong to the same species. The example Cole gives is freshwater fish and crustaceans living in ponds or in separate drainage systems have a limited capacity for dispersal. Consequently, there may be no useful evidence bearing on whether individuals from different populations could interbreed and produce fertile offspring in nature. In addition, our ignorance of geographic distribution and variation of many terrestrial organisms is so great that often we do not know whether distinct populations are in fact interbreeding or capable of it.[36]

In these cases, taxonomists often use morphology alone to classify into separate species—referred to as the "morphological species

---

[34] Hey, 2001; Shaw, 2002.
[35] Cole, 1984, p. 30.
[36] Cole, 1984, p. 30.

concept."[37] A handicap of this method is that new information can result in species reassignment. For example, Linnaeus classified mice as a single species but, by 1940, almost 150 species were claimed, each with its own Latin name. By around 1990, the mice were all again lumped into a single species with around a dozen subspecies.[38] The newest trend is to group mice into about seven separate species. For this reason, Jones notes that wherever a

> species may be (and they are not what birders or governments hope), they are not fixed. Instead, their boundaries change before our eyes. What is a mere variety to some is granted its own identity by others. Quite often, animals that are similar on the surface differ in their genes.[39]

Genetic analysis may solve the species classification problem, but several lifetimes would be required to sequence the genomes of all life-forms. For all these reasons, some biologists now use the working definition of species as a

> group of organisms, minerals, or other entities formally recognized as distinct from other groups. A taxon of the rank of species; in the hierarchy of biological classification, the category below genus; the basic unit of biological classification ... we suggest that organisms with the same kinds and numbers of integrated genomes in common are members of the same species.[40]

---

[37] Cole, 1984, p. 30.
[38] Jones, 2000, p. 50.
[39] Jones, 2000, p. 53.
[40] Margulis and Sagan, 2002, p. 207.

Classifying Extinct Life-Forms into Species

A significant problem in demonstrating transitional forms is to document trans-species and family levels of evolution. Achieving this goal depends on the specific definition of species that one elects to use, which we noted is a difficult task. Determining if two sexually reproducing animals are part of the same species also requires knowledge of their interbreeding abilities, and this cannot be determined for extinct life-forms. Why it is difficult to conclude much about trans-species evolution from the fossil record was well put by Professor Trefil who wrote: "My favorite question when I want to annoy my paleontologist friends: if you had the fossils of a Chihuahua and a St. Bernard, would you identify them as the same species? About half of them say no."[41]

Because scientists cannot carry out interbreeding studies with fossils, they must rely totally on bone and teeth evaluations and, occasionally, external morphology. Only rarely does evidence of internal morphology exist to aid them in making adequate comparisons. The problem of using morphology was illustrated by a London University biologist when he noted, if a mammologist were to evaluate modern dog breeds on morphology alone, he would classify them into "at least a score of ... well defined species."[42]

A strong tendency also exists to "split" taxa into different species based on relatively trivial differences in order to obtain credit for discovering a new species, or to provide evidence of evolution. The genus rank is typically much better-defined, but less common. As a result, a great deal of debate exists over the classification of extinct animals.

Many examples exist of fossil vertebrate species defined almost exclusively by an evaluation of dentition or feet, both of which are useful, yet very limited, for classification. As a result, minor differences can be amplified by a researcher into a species-defining character. An

[41] Trefil, 1992, p. 36.
[42] Jones, 2000, p. 25.

example is the mosasaurs, large (10- to 50-plus feet long) marine lizard-like reptiles that traveled by flippers instead of legs and feet.

One of the larger genera, *Mosasaurus*, includes the following different species *M. hoffmani* (the first discovered), *M. conodon*, *M. dekayi*, *M. maximus*, and *M. missouriensis*.[43] Of these, *M. maximus* has recently been placed in with *M. hoffmani*. The differences between these different species are all based on relatively minor morphological differences. *M. dekayi* was identified only by its teeth, and even the original specimen (a single tooth) has now been misplaced!

The identification criteria for this species were based on the presence of several prisms around the tooth. This was presumed to be sufficiently distinctive because the other species of mosasaurs do not have prismatic teeth, rather their teeth tend to be conical and smooth. This is only one example of many which illustrate the fact that determining a species can be based on very little evidence. Even *M. dekayi* is considered somewhat suspect, but the species has for now been retained until more data exist.

Leading ancient DNA researcher Svante Pääbo, after decades of research agreeing with this conclusion, wrote that the many "examples of convergent evolution was to me a strong message that morphology is often an unreliable indicator of relatedness among organisms. It seemed that almost any body shape or behavior could evolve independently."[44] He added that "taxonomy.... is a sterile academic exercise, particularly when discussing extinct human forms... Another reason.... [is that taxonomy] has a tendency to elicit scientific debates that have no resolution."[45]

---

[43] Russell, 1967.
[44] Pääbo, 2014, p. 66.
[45] Pääbo, 2014, p. 238.

Numerical Taxonomy

Discouragement over existing taxonomic methods motivated the development of a radical new system based on using the tools of math and statistics. The classic determinate of a species, namely the ability to interbreed, was discarded by the numerical taxonomist. The rules were: weighting of morphological traits was not allowed, use every feature that could be measured, every feature is given an equal value regardless of its use, or lack thereof, and the more features used the better.[46] The numerical taxonomists soon had produced countless trees and appeared to have a scientific, objective, quantitative method void of the subjective judgment Linnaeus used.

Traditional taxonomy used weightings to determine which traits were most important in their taxonomic system, such as the presence of mammary glands, which were determined to be a critical trait in classifying an animal in the category now called mammal. Thus bats, whales, humans, and dogs were all classified as mammals.

The new system threw out weighting of each trait that was selected, which was itself a source of bias. The originators of the numerical system first used bees to research their system. For example, Professor Sneath used a single number to describe each of 122 traits he identified for each of the 97 species of bees, producing 11,834 data points. The species that shared the greatest number of similarities, irrespective of the traits' assumed importance, would be clustered together in the same genus.

They then used the *Pearson r* correlation coefficient to determine how close two different life-forms were. A high *Pearson r* value indicated that two life-forms were evolutionarily close, and a low *Pearson r* value indicated that two life-forms were very dissimilar. The deviation from the mean (x-x⁻) was used to obtain a z score, which was then utilized to calculate the *Pearson r* correlation coefficient.

In the numerical taxonomic system, if the correlation they

---

[46] Sokal and Sneath, 1963.

completed was close enough—even if the evidence indicated that interbreeding was impossible--they were grouped together in one group.

One factor that has spurred on the development of this new system was an evaluation of bacteria. One major criteria used in bacterial taxonomy was to divide those that had one flagellum (plural, flagella) in one group and those that had two lateral flagella in another group.[47] This criterion was discarded when taxonomist Peter Sneath, while researching the flagella on a *Chromobacterium*, "realized that a bacterium could actually change from having one kind of flagellum to the other ... It was like basing a taxonomy on an organism's moods," a worthless system.[48] Another problem was that the more researchers looked, the more trouble they saw in bacteria taxonomy:

> It seemed that every bacteriologist had a different idea about which features of a bacterium were the best to use to divide them up into species and genera. Yet hardly anyone, it seemed, had bothered to describe ... the rationale behind the choice of their particular favorite key feature, much less defend that rationale.[49]

The problem was that bacteria, even when seen through a microscope, are remarkably featureless. In addition, it

> was equally futile to apply the evolutionary taxonomist's method of trying to infer the evolutionary history of a group to attempt to order it, that is, to try to decipher which organisms evolved from which different lineages. This approach, already extremely difficult even in organisms about which taxonomists already had very strong senses and inclinations and

---

[47] Yoon, 2009, p. 196.
[48] Yoon, 2009, p. 196.
[49] Yoon, 2009, p. 196.

about which so much of the biology was very well known, was essentially useless with the microbes.[50]

Another general problem was that many traits were too difficult to measure, (such as many hair traits), or could not be visualized, (such as behavioral traits). The new system "did not, and did not claim to, speak to Darwin's demands" because

> the [phylogenetic] trees produced by numerical taxonomists did not reflect the underlying evolutionary relationships that taxonomists knew were their ultimate goal. To get at the evolutionary history ... would require rather those same old subjective judgments ... based on other expert knowledge. It would require going to places that the numerical taxonomist in making his tidy tree was not willing to go. And that meant... that while numerical taxonomy might produce an ordering that was objective and repeatable, it was, in some ways, as useless as ... ordering by size, as it had nothing to do with the evolutionary tree of life.[51]

Furthermore, not the least among the serious problems with the system was "one of the method's main selling points," namely, its claimed objectivity. The reality was, as

> any taxonomist knew all too well, choosing characters—picking out of all the myriad features of a bee the pattern of coloring on its rear end as one of your coded items—was in itself subjective. The characters, however numerical, were highly biased by what was most obviously visible to the researchers.[52]

---

[50] Yoon, 2009, p. 197.
[51] Yoon, 2009, p. 210.
[52] Yoon, 2009, pp. 210-211.

In short, the numerical taxonomy system failed to achieve what it was designed to achieve.[53]

Phylogenetic Systematics (Cladistics)

Cladistics (from ancient Greek κλάδος, klados, meaning branch) is a taxonomical technique used to arrange organisms according to how they supposedly branched off of the currently accepted evolutionary tree of life. Organisms are grouped based on using one or more shared unique characteristics that come from the group's putative last common ancestor. Cladism was developed by Willi Hennig who recognized that the main problem of basing taxonomy on evolution was that the cladists were forced to select some traits and ignore others to determine the phylogeny of what evolutionists were trying to determine — "the true evolutionary tree of life."[54] Furthermore, Hennig arrogantly believed that he was "unlike all other taxonomists in history, because he knew which similarities ... were" critical to develop an evolutionary taxonomy.[55]

Already a problem existed — Hennig assumed that he knew the common similarities shared by the descendants of some animals, and no other group. The obvious problem is that the whole system is based on the standard evolutionary tree. Assuming that birds evolved from dinosaurs, the cladist taxonomic naming was based on this assumption. Nonetheless, he was confident in his conclusions because all one had to do was to identify the traits of their common descendants, then determine those that were similar to, in this example, dinosaurs and birds. To do this, Hennig had to "identify the similarities that were shared uniquely by those descendants and no other groups." He also

---

[53] Vernon, 1988.

[54] Yoon, 2012, pp. 212, 242.

[55] Yoon, 2009, p. 242.

realized that the similarities they would share would be of exactly one type — traits that were new and unique that had evolved in that ancestor and were then passed down. These similarities would serve as identifying membership badges for all descendants. Complete groups of relatives could be recognized by evolutionary novelties unique to each particular lineage. This was Hennig's brainchild: Use only shared evolutionary novelties to identify groups of evolutionary relatives.[56]

In one example, the first bird had evolved a feathered wing supported by a specific bone structure, thus all animals with that design had evolved from the first bird, and consequently were part of the bird family. In response to this taxonomy method, Mayr wrote he could "barely.. contain his disgust… 'I am very delighted that the cladists speak of birds as avian dinosaurs because it shows how idiotic their whole scheme is!'"[57]

The main problem with their system was that the criteria cladists' used were very subjective, which was the same problem that existed with all previous taxonomic systems including lineages.[58] In determining the classification, cladists could select the wing structure, the presence or absence of feathers, or the ability to fly. The cladists' "use of evolutionary novelties alone to create orderings and groupings was a violation of…objectivity."[59]

[56] Yoon, 2009, p. 242.
[57] Mayr, 2002, p. 960; see also Simpson, 1964.
[58] Yoon, 2009, p. 260.
[59] Yoon, 2009, p. 260.

Baraminology Research

Research comparisons using baraminology in many cases have also produced mixed results for many of the same reasons. One baraminology approach compares selected traits using the Pearson correlation coefficient to estimate the relative similarity of birds and dinosaurs.[60] Comparing 187 characters of 42 taxa found a positive distance correlation between all birds in the sample and deinonychosaurians. No bird in the sample was found to share a positive distance correlation with any non-deinonychosaurian coelurosaur.[61]

This type of analysis must first select the traits to compare, assume each trait should be given equal weight, and also select the bird and dinosaurs or other taxa with which to make comparisons.[62] This requires very subjective judgments that could produce either positive or negative correlations, depending on the animal taxa and the traits selected.[63] This is what Wood found, namely that "using Senter's set of taxa and characters supports his conclusions of morphological continuity, but other sets with more characters do not."[64] Wood added "Any baraminology study can be disputed, and none can be considered truly definitive."[65] Non-statistical methods of baraminological research include morphology, cladistics, and especially hybridization data.

The Genesis Kind

The "Genesis kind" does not usually refer to species, but is more comparable to the modern systematic classification, such as the cat, dog, or human families.[66] Wide genetic variation within each animal

---

[60] Wood, 2011, p. 915.
[61] Wood, 2011, p. 916.
[62] Senter, 2010.
[63] Yoon, 2009.
[64] Wood, 2011, p. 914.
[65] Wood, 2011, p. 917.
[66] Froman, 2016; Mehlert, 1995.

kind allows breeding of many species from one pair of the originally created kinds, and many of the various forms within the Genesis kind, or even within a taxonomic family, are cross-fertile.[67]

No variation, though, has been clearly shown to cross the Genesis kind boundary, and animals from different "kinds" or families have never been able to "cross breed" to reproduce. Breeding experimentation has created many types of "new" animals, but has not yet achieved hybridization with a different family kind, such as breeding cats and mice. Nor have animals that are clearly morphologically "in-between," for example, a domestic cat and an amphibian, or even a cat and a chicken, have ever been produced. Clear limits of interbreeding exist that cannot be bridged, and locating these limits requires much research and study.

Conclusion

This chapter has briefly reviewed why no single definition of species has of yet "satisfied all naturalists." A major reason is that

> every naturalist knows vaguely what he means when he speaks of a species. The amount of difference considered necessary to give to two forms the rank of species is quite indefinite. One text on evolution reviews seven statements of what the mythic word might mean and—as does every attempt to impose order on the chaos of life—fails.[68]

In retrospect, in the over 150 years since Darwin published his *On the Origin of Species*, we know now that his work

---

[67] Berndt, 2001; 2004.
[68] Jones, 2000, p. 53.

had shaken the foundations of science, philosophy, religion, and politics; he had changed Humanity's view of its place in the universe. But somehow, even after a full century, his work had not made any significant dent in the workings of taxonomy, a field to which his discoveries were fundamental.[69]

The species concept is an imperfect and problematic method used to classify all life. As Yale-trained taxonomist Carol Yoon wrote, the species classification was the "gray area of the field" and, more problematically, "it was a moving target."[70] For this reason Mayr concluded, "There is probably no other concept in biology that has remained so consistently controversial as the species concept."[71] And medical and science writer T. DeLene Beeland wrote that the "species problem ... refers to the centuries old struggle of biologists to define exactly what species are. No current definition works when applied across all taxonomic kingdoms."[72] She then discusses why this is such an enormous problem.

Although necessary and useful, the species concept has clear limits that disallow its use to document macroevolution. Changes within a species that are sufficiently large to prevent interbreeding do not provide evidence for macroevolution. Even the much-touted ring species cases are rare and problematic.[73] Neo-Darwinism requires evidence of changes much greater than simply the prevention of interbreeding between two very similar life-forms.

When Watson and Crick discovered the structure of DNA, they did not know they were correct because they took a poll, or because they had the support of a long list of Nobel Laureates. They knew they were right because the X-ray diffraction images they obtained in the

---

[69] Yoon, 2009, p. 109.
[70] Yoon, 2009, pp. 104-105.
[71] Mayr, 1982, p. 251.
[72] Beeland, 2013, p. 26.
[73] Irwin and Irwin, 2002, p. 596.

lab supported the double helix molecular structure and nothing else. Ultimately, any scientific theory is true based not on who believes in it, but on the scientific empirical evidence supporting it. As *CSI*'s fictional forensic scientist Gil Grissom says, "It's all about the evidence." In short, "classification of anything biological is notoriously ambiguous."[74] The result of the problems outlined above was that "it became very difficult, eventually impossible, to defend the workings of evolutionary taxonomy as a science, as a reasonable and rational endeavor."[75]

---

[74] Rosebury, 1969, p. 210.

[75] Yoon, 2009, p. 203.

References

Anonymous. 2004. *A Survey of the Fossil Record*. http://www-rohan. sdsu.edu/-rhmiller/fossilrecord/bio.htm.

Beeland, T. Delene. 2013. *The Secret World of Red Wolves*. Chapel Hill, NC: The University of North Carolina Press.

Berndt, Chard. 2001. "The Fundamental Unit of Biological Taxonomy." www.creationbydesign.com/articles.

_____. 2004. "Biblical Classification of Life." www.creationbydesign. com.

Bowen, B.W., A.L. Bass, L.A. Rocha, W.S. Grant, and D.R. Robertson. 2000. "Phylogeography of the trumpet fishes (Aulostomus): Ring species complex on a global scale." *Evolution* 55(5):1029-1039.

Clegg, Brian. 2012. *The Universe Inside You*. New York, NY: MJF books.

Cole, Charles J. 1984. "Taxonomy: What's in a Name?" *Natural History* 93(9):30-33.

Collinson, Martin. 2001. "Greenish Warbler, 'Two-barred Greenish Warbler,' and the speciation process." *British Birds* 94(6):278-283.

Froman, Craig (editor). 2016. *How Many Animals Were on the Ark?* Green Forest, AR: Master Books.

Gee, Henry. 2011. "Craniums with Clout." *Nature* 478(7367):34, October 2011.

Grant, Peter R. 1998. *Evolution on Islands*. New York, NY: Oxford University Press.

Haeckel, Ernst. 1911. *History of Creation*. New York, NY: D. Appleton.

Hey, Jody. 2001. *Genes, categories, and species: The evolutionary and cognitive causes of the species problem*. New York, NY: Oxford University Press.

Irwin, Darren E., Staffan Bensch, and Trevor D. Price. 2001. "Speciation in a ring." *Nature* 409:333-337.

Irwin, Darren E., Jessica H. Irwin, and Trevor D. Price. 2001a. "Ring species as bridges between microevolution and speciation." *Genetica (Dordrecht)* 112-113(1):223-243.

Irwin, Darren E., and Jessica H. Irwin. 2002. "Circular overlaps: Rare demonstrations of speciation." *Auk* 119(3):596-602.

Joseph, L., G. Dolman, S. Donnellan, K. Saint, M. Berg, and A. Bennett. 2008. "Where and when does a ring start and end? Testing the ring-species hypothesis in a species complex of Australian parrots." *Proceedings of the Royal Society B: Biological Sciences* 275(1650):2431-2440, https://royalsocietypublishing.org/doi/10.1098/rspb.2008.0765.

Jones, Steve. 2000. *Darwin's Ghost: The Origin of Species Updated.* New York, NY: Random House.

Lamichhaney, Sangeet, et al. 2018. "Rapid Hybrid Speciation in Darwin's Finches." *Science* 359(6372): 224-228.

Liebers, D., P. Knijff, and A. Helbig. 2004. "The herring gull complex is not a ring species." *Proceedings of the Royal Society B: Biological Sciences* 271(1542):893-901, doi: 10.1098/rspb.2004.2679

Margulis, Lynn. 1996. "Archaeal—eubacterial mergers in the origin of eukarya: Phylogenetic classification of life." *Proceedings of the National. Academy of Science, USA* 93(3):1071-1076.

_____, and Dorion Sagan. 2002. *Acquiring Genomes: A Theory of the Origins of Species.* New York, NY: Basic Books.

Mayr, Ernst. 1982. *The Growth of Biological Thought.* Cambridge, MA: Harvard University Press/Boston, MA: Belknap Press.

_____. 2002. Interview with Ernst Mayr. *Bio Essays* 24(10):960-973.

_____. 2014. "Numerical Phenetics and Taxonomic Theory." *Systematic Zoology* 14(2):73-97.

McKey, Doyle B. 2000. "*Leonardoxa africana* (Leguminosae: Caesalpinioideae): A complex of mostly allopatric subspecies." *Adansonia* 22(1):71-109.

Mehlert, A.W. 1995. "On the Origin of Cats and Carnivores." *CEN Tech. J.* 9(1):106-120.

Mousseau, Timothy A., Barry Sinervo, and John A. Endler (editors). 2000. *Adaptive Genetic Variation in the Wild*. Oxford, NY: Oxford University Press.

Pääbo, Svante. 2014. *Neanderthal Man: In Search of Lost Genomes*. New York, NY: Basic Books.

Pennisi, Elizabeth. 2004. "Researchers Trade Insights about Gene Swapping." *Science* 305(5682):334-335.

Pereira, R., W. Monahan, and D. Wake. 2011. "Predictors for Reproductive Isolation in a Ring Species Complex Following Genetic and Ecological Divergence." *Evolutionary Biology* 11(1):194, doi:10.1186/1471-2148-11-194.

Preston-Mafham, Ken, and Rod Preston-Mafham. 1996. *The Natural History of Spiders*. Ramsbury, Marlborough, England: Crowood Press.

Rosebury, Theodor. 1969. *Life on Man*. New York, NY: Berkley Medallion Books.

Russell, D.A. 1967. "Systematics and Morphology of American Mosasaurs." *Peabody Museum of Natural History, Yale University. Bulletin* 23:138-141.

Senter, Phil. 2010. "Using creation science to demonstrate evolution: Application of a creationist method for visualizing gaps in the fossil record to a phylogenetic study of coelurosaurian dinosaurs." *Journal of Evolutionary Biology* 23(8):1732–1743.

Shaw, Kerry L. 2002. "Do We Need Species Concepts?" *Science* 295(5558):1238-1239.

Silverstein, Alvin, Virginia Silverstein, and Laura Silverstein. 1998. *Evolution.* Brookfield, CT: Twenty-First Century Books.

Simpson, George Gaylord. 1964. "Numerical Taxonomy and Biological Classification." *Science* 144(3619):712-713.

Sokal, Robert, and Peter Sneath. 1963. *Principles of Numerical Taxonomy.* San Francisco, CA: W.H. Freeman & Company.

Trefil, James. 1992. *1001 Things Everyone Should Know About Science.* New York, NY: Doubleday.

Turner, George. 2003. "How Are New Species Formed?" *New Scientist,* June 14, pp. 36-37.

Vernon, Keith. 1988. "The Founding of Numerical Taxonomy." *The British Journal for the History of Science* 21(2):143-159.

Wood, Todd. 2011. "Using creation science to demonstrate evolution? Senter's strategy revisited." *Journal of Evolutionary Biology* 24(4):914-918.

Yoon, Carl Kaesuk. 2009. *Naming Nature: The Clash Between Instinct and Science.* New York, NY: W.W. Norton & Company.

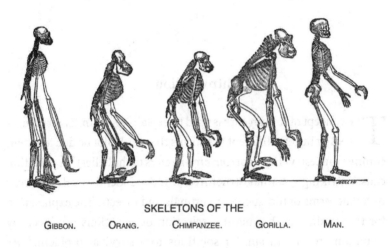

SKELETONS OF THE

GIBBON.   ORANG.   CHIMPANZEE.   GORILLA.   MAN.

AN EXAMPLE OF CONVERGENT EVOLUTION OF PRIMATE BONES. THE GIBBON AND GORILLA WERE NOT DRAWN TO THE SAME SCALE AS THE OTHER PRIMATES. FROM FRONTISPIECE OF THOMAS HUXLEY *EVIDENCE AS TO MAN'S PLACE IN NATURE.* 1863. NEW YORK, NY: D. APPLETON.

CHAPTER 2

Convergent Evolution Theory Fails

Introduction

The concept of *convergence* is used to explain very similar structures existing in very different life-forms that could not be due to recent common ancestry. The term *convergent* refers to the belief that evolution causes strikingly similar structures to independently evolve in very different forms of life, such as mammals and insects. The explanation for this finding is that natural selection of variations produced by mutations results in similar solutions to a survival problem.[76] As University of California Professor William Clemens wrote, the term "convergent evolution" is used to describe body organs and structures where two groups of distantly related organisms "evolve to look very much like one another."[77]

Professor Losos defined convergent evolution as the event where two different orders of higher animals or plants independently evolve very similar structures to adapt to similar environmental conditions.[78] For this reason, it is concluded that two structures that look strikingly similar in two very different distinct life-forms must have evolved

---

[76] Werner, 2009, p. 62.
[77] Clemens, 1968, p. 1.
[78] Losos, 2011.

separately. For example, flight has evolved separately in birds, insects, reptiles, and even mammals (bats), and many similarities exist, such as illustrated by the major similarities of many wing structures, including wing bones which are labeled homologs.[79]

The classic textbook example of evolutionary convergence is the presence of wings in both birds (class Aves) and bats (class Mammalia). Their flying structures are postulated to be similar by evolutionists, not due to common descent, but rather because the forces of selection evolved very similar structures, in this case wings, by very different pathways. Actually, much better examples of "convergence" exist, because bat wings are very different in several ways from bird wings, even though both function as highly effective flight organs.

The most well-known convergence example is between placentals and marsupials which, even though evolutionists claim they have evolved separately, nevertheless have developed "some striking similarities of form."[80] Evolutionist professor Stanley Rice defines convergent evolution as follows:

> Convergence occurs when similar adaptations evolve in separate lineages of organisms. Convergent adaptations have evolved separately (by *convergent evolution*), rather than being inherited from a common ancestor. Convergence can often be recognized because the organisms evolve the adaptation in different ways.[81]

Futuyma defines the term by noting some of the many examples of convergence that exist "such as the eyes of vertebrates and cephalopod mollusks, in which functionally similar features actually differ profoundly in structure."[82]

---

[79] Rice, 2007, pp. 91-92.
[80] Rice, 2007, p. 91.
[81] Rice, 2007, p. 89.
[82] Futuyma, 2005, p. 49.

Cambridge University paleontologist Conway Morris defines evolutionary convergence as the "recurrent tendency of biological organization to arrive at the same 'solution' to a particular 'need,'" producing the widespread pattern in nature in which evolutionarily unrelated organisms possess nearly identical anatomical, physiological, biochemical, or behavioral characteristics.[83]

Morris documents numerous examples of evolutionary convergence in which it is claimed that different species independently evolved very similar designs, even though their last common ancestor was postulated to have existed many millions of years earlier. Morris concludes that these examples also illustrate what evolution predicts, namely the trend toward greater complexity in life.[84]

Some Definitions

When similar structures in two or more species, such as the limb bone structure existing in all vertebrates, are judged to be a result of evolution from a common ancestor, evolutionists label them "**homologous.**" Conversely, when similar structures are believed by evolutionists to have arisen *independently*, they are called "**convergent.**" Some examples that appear to be due to convergence are actually "**analogous,**" meaning structures that have a common function, such as butterfly and bird wings, but not a common design.[85] In the end, the main way evolutionists differentiate analogous from homologous structures is through the filter of evidence for their theory of common ancestry.

A similar concept, **homoplasy**, occurs when two taxa possess similar characteristics that were not present in their last presumed common ancestor. Homoplasy encompasses both convergence and parallelism, and can exist in both closely related organisms, and in

---

[83] Morris, 2007, p. xii.
[84] Morris, 2007.
[85] Shute, 1970, p. 147.

organisms from different phyla. Convergence is proposed as one possible explanation for homoplasy, but other explanations exist, and the recency of the putative common ancestry is not part of the homoplasy determination.

Another example is very similar echolocation systems in animals that have very different phylogenies, such as bats, South American oil birds, southeast Asian swiftlets, Gymnarchus fish, porpoises, and other cetaceans including dolphins.[86] Evolutionists do not claim that bats, birds, fish, and mammals have a recent common ancestor, but that they evolved their very similar modern forms by separate evolutionary paths many thousands of years ago.

They also separately evolved remarkably similar echolocation systems. The fact is, "Convergent evolution is a process that has occurred throughout the tree of life, but the historical genetic and biochemical context promoting the repeated independent origins of a trait is rarely understood," and, as we will show, is an attempt to explain a major problem for evolution.[87]

Eye Convergence Claims

Many examples exist of two or more very different life-forms, such as insects and cephalopods, that share some very similar physical or biochemical traits but where major differences preclude a recent common ancestry. One of the most cited examples of convergence is eye evolution. Salvini-Plawen and Mayr concluded that one of the most complex body organs, the eye, evolved independently by convergent evolution over 60 times.[88] Specifically, the "independent evolution of light-detection organs in 40 separate animal lineages, and the probable independent origination of light detection organs in 20 additional

---

[86] Lissmann, 1963, p. 50; Grundfest, 1960, pp. 115-124.

[87] Huang, et al., 2016, p. 10,613.

[88] Salvini-Plawen and Mayr, 1977, p. 247.

lineages ... [brings] the total to 60 separate convergences" of seeing eyes.[89]

Most evolutionists believe all vertebrates evolved the camera eye by convergence, an idea compounded by the fact that an enormous variety of life-forms have a very similar eye design. All of the major eye structure parts of humans, vertebrates in general, and squids in particular, are almost identical, yet none of their theorized last common ancestors possessed eyes. Thus, evolutionists postulate they must have separately evolved very similar eyes from eyeless ancestors.

Morris cites the eye as one of "the most compelling examples" of convergence.[90] He claims the camera-like eye alone "has evolved independently at least six times" in different totally unrelated species, due to convergent evolution.[91] For instance, both the human and the octopus possess camera eyes that, although in most ways are very similar, have certain differences.

The major basic eye types (compound eye, corneal lens eye, apposition compound eye, etc.) all utilize visual information, but in very different ways. Most cephalopods have "simple" eyes, but the squid and octopus have eyes that are designed very much like the human eye. The squid and octopus are animals that evolutionists believe shared a very ancient common ancestor with humans many millions of years ago.

Professor McGhee adds that the "independent evolution of complex camera eyes in the chordates (human and our kin) and in the mollusks (the octopus and their kin) is a classic case of amazing convergent evolution, oft cited along with the convergent evolution of wings in tetrapods."[92]

For evolutionists, the convergence solution is superior to any other hypothesis that attempts to explain the similarity problem: "It requires little persuasion to become convinced that the lens eye of a vertebrate

---

[89] McGhee, 2011, p. 67.
[90] Morris, 2007, p. 151.
[91] Morris, 2007, p. xii.
[92] McGhee, 2011, p. 70.

and the compound eye of an insect are independent evolutionary developments."[93] However, in reality, many very primitive, so-called simple life-forms, also have very complex, advanced eye organs. For example, the complex camera eye is also found in some worms, spiders, and even jellyfish, causing major problems for the entire evolutionary tree.[94] Spiders, in contrast to most other arthropods, have a lens eye very similar to that of vertebrates.[95]

Convergent evolution means that "the great similarity in the design of the eye in vertebrates and cephalopods and the profound parallelism between the cochlea in birds and mammals ... although very striking, *do not imply any close biological relationship.*"[96]

Another example, (among hundreds of others), is the remarkable similarity of the human ear and that of some insects. One study of the "functional and anatomical aspects of hearing in humans finds extraordinary similarity in the ear of a rainforest katydid" which is explained as a result of "two phylogenetically remote organisms, katydids and mammals, [that] have evolved a series of convergent solutions to common biophysical problems, despite their reliance on very different morphological substrates."[97]

Other Putative Examples of Convergence

Another striking example of convergence is the panda's thumb. Besides the five normal vertebrate fingers, all pandas have an extra "finger" on their forelimbs. This extra finger is actually a modified wrist bone that enables pandas to hold on to bamboo shoots while eating them. There are two families of pandas known, the giant panda and the red panda.

---

[93] Salvini-Plawen and Mayr, 1977, p. 210.
[94] McGhee, 2011, p. 70.
[95] Rice, 2007, p. 90.
[96] Denton, 1986, p. 178; emphasis in original.
[97] Hoy, 2012, p. 895; Montealegre-Z, et al., 2012, p. 968.

Both share this extra thumb design and, although one would assume they are evolutionarily closely related, they are not.

After decades of discussion, biologists now classify them into two very distinctly different histories: the red panda is placed in the raccoon family, the giant panda is placed in its own family and, consequently, their peculiar "thumb" design is now interpreted as yet another example of convergence.

Shute adds to this list of convergent features spinal tracts, ears, the placenta, sweat glands, electric organs, kidney function, the manufacture of breast milk, brown fat, and fern vessels.[98] Even bird plumage traits are considered examples of convergent evolution.[99]

Convergence of Body Plan

Many other examples of convergence include ichthyosaurs (a reptile), sharks (a fish), dolphins and whales (mammals), all possessing very similar body forms. All four of these life-forms also have a dorsal fin, a pectoral fin, and a finned tail.[100] Furthermore, similarity exists between the whale flipper's bone structure and that of an ichthyosaur, (somewhat analogous to the mole's forelimbs and the general design of the mole cricket insect).[101] Evolutionists conclude that the shark has "not changed much in the last 400 million years,"[102] and thus the modern shark is considered an ancient fish, (known as a "living fossil"). Conversely, evolutionists conclude that the dolphin evolved only 10 to 12 million years ago,[103] and is therefore considered a modern mammal.

Evolutionists believe that the nearly identical body plans of Mesozoic animals (those with differentiated tissues), and aquatic reptiles, sharks, fish, and dolphins, all evolved independently by

---

[98] Shute, 1969, p. 147.
[99] Mundy, et al., 2004.
[100] Anonymous, 1998.
[101] Denton, 1986, p. 178.
[102] Katsenelinboigen, 1997, p. 184.
[103] Kalman, 2003, p. 8; Klinowska, 1991, p. 5.

convergent evolution.[104] They all display a remarkably similar external physical resemblance, even though they obviously do not have a close evolutionary relationship.

Then consider the very similar type of intelligence existing in mammals, including dolphins, birds, and other totally evolutionarily unrelated animals.[105] The separate emergence of a degree of human-like intelligence in species as different as dolphins and whales also illustrates the claim of Darwinists that "nature abounds in examples of convergence."[106]

Biochemical and Genetic Convergence

Convergence theory has been applied not just to organisms, but also to organs, cells, organelles, and even biochemicals. In many cases where the animals' morphological similarity is greatly different, many features, such as the biochemical pathways used, are virtually identical.

Many identical, or nearly identical, complex genetically produced structures supposedly evolved independently across the living world. Actually, the most striking examples of claimed convergence are in biochemistry. A common example is the alcohol dehydrogenase enzyme, which is manufactured in a wide variety of organisms, from the very primitive unicellular life-forms in kingdom Protista to life as evolutionarily advanced as humans.[107]

A gene named Distalless is involved in controlling limb development in animals as different as mice, butterflies, sea urchins, fruit flies, and two species of unrelated worms. Distalless is not homoplastic, but a homologous gene that codes for analogous structures. The same gene is found in an almost identical form in many other species that are not even remotely related to each other. In all of these cases, this gene is

---

[104] Rice, 2007, p. 92.
[105] Emery and Clayton, 2004; Kalman, 2003.
[106] Denton, 1986, p. 178.
[107] Hjelmqvist, et al., 1995.

involved in controlling limb development, even of limbs that are not evolutionarily homologous.[108]

Certain female hormones, once thought to be synthesized only in certain mammals such as primates, have even been detected in some plants. Shute lists several scores of examples[109] and many thousands of other examples exist. Another example is a specific enzyme called *cytochrome P450 dependent monooxygenase*, which is hypothesized to have separately evolved in a wide variety of life-forms, from lycophytes (such as club moss), to angiosperms (flowering plants).[110] This phenomenon is one of many examples evolutionists describe as functional convergence of non-homologous enzymes. In this case, the similarity is strictly functional and *not* in the amino acid sequence or the protein's structure.

Plants that belong to very divergent branches of the evolutionary tree are known to use many very different biochemical pathways to produce the familiar chemical called caffeine. For example, the different plants that produce coffee, tea, cocoa, oranges, and guarana all manufacture caffeine using different enzymes and substrates, a finding the authors attempt to explain by convergent evolution.[111]

The first comprehensive phylogeny of the acanthomorphs (spiny-rayed fish), a group that includes close to a third of all living vertebrate species, was completed in 2013. To construct their phylogenic tree, researchers compared ten genes from more than 500 fish species representing most spiny-rayed fish families. The results confounded traditional phylogeny, concluding that tuna fish are more closely related to seahorses than to swordfish or barracuda, and puffer fishes are closely related to anglerfish, the only known modern fish whose bodies are wider than they are deep.[112] Applying the evolutionary convergence theory by concentrating on shared genes among the acanthomorphs

---

108 Wells, 2000, pp. 74-76.
109 Shute, 1969, pp. 135-138.
110 Nelson, et al., 1993.
111 Huang, et al., 2016, p. 10,613.
112 Near, et al., 2013.

has destroyed the traditional phylogeny, a fact that renders all attempts to produce an evolutionary tree problematic.

Many other biochemicals, such as certain proteins, enzymes, and other structures existing in very different kinds of life, are strikingly similar, or even identical. For example, at a low resolution, the quaternary structural level of the myosin 2 motor protein is identical in turkeys and scallops, even though evolutionists claim the common ancestor of these life-forms goes back over 600 million years.[113]

In what has been called a "remarkable example of convergent evolution.... insect species spanning 300 million years of divergence have evolved identical single-amino-acid substitutions that confer resistance to plant cardenolide toxins."[114]

Darwinists had long assumed biochemical research would support convergence theory, but the "last few years have seen an explosion of research into the genetic basis of convergent evolution, with many studies finding that convergent phenotypes have been produced through similar changes at the genetic level, but other [studies] discovering convergent phenotypes resulting from different genetic changes."[115] This statement illustrates the fact that Darwinists' attempts to explain reality from an evolutionary worldview involves a great deal of guesswork.

Bioluminescence is found in many different animal classes from bacteria to insects to fish, yet the bioluminescence chemistry in all known animals is remarkably similar.[116] Yet another example is photoperiodism, a means of seasonal adaptation found in a wide variety of organisms that is "one of the most remarkable examples of convergent evolution [known], being universal in both plants and animals."[117]

Another case involves tunas and lamnid sharks having "very

---

[113] Knight, 2008; Jung, et al., 2008.
[114] Whiteman and Mooney, 2012, p. 376.
[115] Losos, 2011, p. 1872.
[116] Lima-de-Faria, 1988.
[117] Porter, and Collins, 1984, p. 8.

similar biomechanical schemes for movement" even though sharks are not bony fish, as is the tuna.[118] This example illustrates the major problem of the biochemical evolutionary convergence explanation, namely that the

> evolutionary convergence between them is so striking that in many ways these distantly related groups resemble each other more than they resemble their own close ectothermic relatives. Such similarity is more remarkable considering that these features evolved independently, long after the ancestors of bony and cartilaginous fishes diverged more than 400 million years ago. The shared characteristics in these distantly related groups... distinguish them from virtually all other fishes.[119]

Only two evolutionary theories for the origins of close biochemical composition are possible, and both are extremely unlikely. One theory is convergent evolution. The other theory is that many proteins have not significantly changed in what Darwinists estimate is over 600 million years. This condition, called *structural conservation,* confounds molecular dating techniques which are used to estimate evolutionary time scales from comparisons of DNA and/or protein sequences. This is one more example of research that has found the "molecular clock" dating technique seriously flawed.[120]

Highlighting the dichotomy between "convergent evolution" verses "structural conservation" are the genes isolated and sequenced from the blind cavefish, *Astyanax fasciatus,* which were found to be homologous to human red and green visual pigment genes. Both fish and humans have one red-like visual pigment gene and multiple green-like visual pigment genes. By comparing the DNA sequences of human

---

[118] Shadwick, 2005, p. 524.
[119] Shadwick, 2005, p. 524.
[120] Tompkins and Bergman, 2015; Welch and Bromham, 2011.

and fish visual pigment genes, scientists have concluded that the red pigments in humans and fish independently evolved from the green pigment by identical amino acid substitutions existing in only a very few key positions in the protein.[121]

However, one cannot empirically determine if protein similarity is due to conservation (meaning "preserved by homologous/common ancestor relationship") or convergence. In one case, Yokoyama and Yokoyama argued for conservation, but in another case, in a very similar situation, they argued for convergence. This confusion is common, and thus Doolittle noted: "Convergence as a phenomenon in molecular evolution is an issue that confuses many discussions."[122]

Embryological Convergence

Among the many examples of embryological convergence include the two basic types of germ-cell formation. One is by *preformation*, where the cell inherits the internal signals located in a region inside of their own cell structure, and the second is by *epigenesis*, where the signals that direct primordial germ-cell formation come from the surrounding tissues outside of the germ cell. The two very different modes of germ-cell formation do not cluster together in separate sections of the evolutionary tree as evolution requires. Instead, "they are distributed haphazardly among various phyla on different branches of the tree."[123]

This problem is explained by a convergent evolution view that postulates that the two types evolved, then de-evolved, and lastly, re-evolved hundreds, if not thousands, of times. Such mental gymnastics are very revealing about the entire convergent idea that attempts to explain away significant problems of evolution.

---

[121] Yokoyama and Yokoyama, 1990.
[122] Doolittle, 1994, p. 15.
[123] Meyer, 2013, p. 129.

Convergence in Plants

Many examples of convergence also exist in plants, such as their complex chemical scents.[124] Evolutionists believe that the succulent water-storage system and Crassulacean acid metabolism (CAM) photosynthesis system have evolved separately in several very different plant families, such as the cactus and lily families in North American deserts, and the spurge plant family existing in South African deserts.

Serpentine soil tolerance is postulated to have evolved at least seven different times in plants.[125] The photosynthesis system involving 4-carbon metabolism is speculated by evolutionists to have evolved over 30 separate times. Several very different plant lineages are thought to have separately evolved the ability to grow in toxic soil due to high concentrations of heavy metal ions.[126]

Claims of Convergence Widespread

Convergence is so widespread in the living world that paleontologist Simon Conway Morris calls this fact outright eerie.[127] Morris' list of a few examples of evolutionary convergences alone takes up five pages.[128] Rice personifies evolution by insisting convergence happens "so frequently that it constitutes one of the major features of evolution … even though there may be an almost infinite number of possible biological adaptations, there are only a limited number of strategies that work, and evolution keeps finding these strategies over and over."[129]

Convergence is so common that Professor McGhee documents hundreds of examples in the animal and plant worlds as well as in ecosystems, organic molecules including proteins and enzymes, tissues,

[124] Pichersky, 2004.
[125] Patterson and Givnish, 2003, p. 261.
[126] Rice, 2007, p. 89.
[127] Morris, 2007.
[128] Morris, 2007, pp. 457-461.
[129] Rice, 2007, p. 93.

and even behavior, as well as embryological and fetal development.[130] Fazale Rana and others have documented thousands of examples of putative convergent evolution in both plants and animals.[131]

A Review of the Most Common Example of Convergence Evolution: Marsupials

The "most astonishing example of convergence is the similarity between some species of marsupial mammals and some placental species."[132] A case in point is that the morphological similarity between the placental canis wolf and the marsupial Tasmanian wolf is much closer than between, for example, St. Bernard and Chihuahua dogs. Yet another example is the "marsupial flying phalanger which looks and behaves just like the flying squirrel of the new world. Marsupial moles, with their tiny eyes and big burrowing claws, are dead ringers for our placental moles."[133] The marsupial-placental example meets Darwin's criteria of falsifiability, namely that "If it could be demonstrated that any complex organ existed, which could not possibly have been formed by numerous, successive, slight modifications, my theory would absolutely break down."[134]

Most mammals are placentals, but many mammals in Australia are marsupials. Although marsupials and placentals are often morphologically very similar, they are in many ways so strikingly different that it is recognized they could not have evolved from the same biological order. For this reason, these mammals are divided into two very different groups, eutherians (placental mammals) and metatherians (marsupials), which are believed to have diverged in

[130] McGhee, 2011.
[131] Rana, 2008.
[132] Coyne, 2015, p. 142.
[133] Coyne, 2015, p. 142.
[134] Darwin, 1859, p. 189.

North America from a common ancestor very early in evolutionary history.[135]

The Contrast Between Eutherians and Metatherians

The critical reproductive differences that exist between marsupials and placentals are so enormous that it is clear they could not have evolved from a recent common ancestor. The main difference between the two is that marsupial embryos develop mainly in a pouch and placental embryos develop entirely in a uterus or womb. Marsupial embryos leave the womb while still very immature and crawl up to a specially designed pouch to complete their remaining embryonic and fetal development. In contrast, placental mammal embryos complete their development in the mother's womb and are born live.

Marsupials use one of three different pouch types called *marsupiums*, and no placental mammal requires any part of the pouch system. Marsupials do not develop a placenta; rather they create what is called a uterine yolk sac. The marsupial gestational period is very short compared to that of placentals, requiring their embryonic offspring to climb from the uterine yolk sac to the pouch where their mother's teats are located, a feat that is impossible for placental mammal embryos unless numerous major significant structural variations occur.

The opossum, a marsupial, gestates its young for about 13 days, while a similar-sized placental animal, the skunk, requires close to 65 days.[136] The opossum weighs about 0.2 grams when it leaves the womb; a skunk about 33 grams when it leaves the womb, or 150 times that of the opossum. To aid their offspring's survivability, some marsupials can actually suspend their embryo's growth until environmental conditions improve.

To succeed in its womb-to-pouch journey, a marsupial embryo precociously develops forelimbs and claws. When it reaches the

---

[135] Mikkelsen, et al., 2007, p. 167.
[136] Austad, 1988, p. 102.

pouch, the mother's nipples swell, sealing the embryo to its mother for as long as two months. The embryo then releases itself from the nipple and wanders longer and longer distances from its mother until weaning. Then, depending on the marsupial, it is either on its own (e.g., opossums) or travels in herds (e.g., kangaroos).

Some placentals, such as the wolf, ocelot, anteater, flying squirrel, ground hog, and mouse, all have remarkably similar marsupial counterparts, yet are believed by evolutionists to have radically different evolutionary lineages. The similarity involves not only major outward appearance, but also significant skeletal structure and internal organ similarity (see Table I for the corresponding placental and Australian marsupials). The similarities between placentals and marsupials are so great that they are called mammal twins. Paleontologists normally rely on morphological similarities to construct evolutionary trees, but, in the case of mammal twins, this approach has totally failed.

The convergent theory is the hypothesis that these very different mammalian orders independently evolved striking similarities for hundreds of traits in response to environmental similarities. In other words, mutations and natural selection caused them to evolve along very similar lines due to adaptations to similar environments, and not due to recent common ancestry. For this reason, placentals and marsupials each constitute a single monophyletic group, even though evolutionists still assert that they diverged from a common ancestor that lived far back in the early Cretaceous period.[137]

Table I. Morphologic correspondence of different orders living in Australia

Placentals	Marsupials
Wolf (*Canis*)	Tasmanian Wolf (*Thylacinus*)
Ocelot (*Felis*)	Native Cat (*Dasyurus*)
Anteater (*Myrmecophaga*)	Anteater (*Myrmecobis*)

---

[137] Janke, et al., 1994, p. 243.

Flying Squirrel (*Glaucomys*)	Flying Phalanger (*Petourus*)
Groundhog (*Marmota*)	Wombat (*Phasolmys*)
Mouse (*Mus*)	Mouse (*Dasycercus*)
Placental Mole (*Talpidae*)	Marsupial Mole (*Notoryctidae*)
Lemur (*Strepsirrhini*)	Spotted Cuscus (*Spilocuscus maculates*)
Saber tooth placental (*Similodontidae*)	Saber tooth marsupial (*Thylacosmilidae*)

Other Differences Between
Marsupials and Placentals

Many other major sexual differences exist between marsupials and placentals. All marsupials, male and female, have an epipubicor or marsupium bone, a structure that no placental mammal possesses. Male marsupials have a bifid or forked penis, and the marsupial male genitalia are also reversed so that the scrotum is anterior to the penis; no placental mammal has either of these characteristics. The female marsupial, unlike female placentals, has a reproductive tract that almost completely doubles in size just prior to birth when an independent birth canal forms.[138]

Another difference is that marsupials have a much smaller, and usually narrower, brain case than exists in similar-sized placentals. Marsupial brains also lack a corpus callosum, the broad thick connection between left and right brain hemispheres. Contrasts between marsupials and placentals include not just soft tissues, but also certain major skeletal differences. A skilled mammologist can often determine if an animal is a marsupial and not a placental from the skull alone. A Tasmanian wolf (thylacine) skull, when examined carefully and compared side by side, can be seen to be distinctly different from a North American wolf skull, even though many of their major skull traits and their overall shape are almost identical.

Another skeletal difference is that most marsupials have a

---

[138] Szalay, 1999.

fenestrated palate, which no placental possesses. Most marsupials have an inward-jutting angular jaw process that placentals lack. Marsupial dental patterns also differ from that of placentals in several major ways, including in some cases the number of lower and upper jaw teeth. The skeletal difference has been used to locate evidence for their divergence from a common ancestor and their convergent evolution, but research has so far failed to make even a reasonable case for their macroevolution. These many differences are why evolutionists believe the placental's and marsupial's common ancestor lived far back in deep time, and the only way they can explain the many profound similarities is by claiming convergent evolution.

The Many Other Problems with Convergence Theory

Many biologists have effectively argued against the convergent evolution theory for very good reasons. The main problem is that it is a *post-hoc* armchair explanation that is not based on evidence. It is used in an attempt to explain away a problem, namely how could two animals that are so far apart on the evolutionary tree be so similar in so many critical ways?

Another problem with the theory is that, as a result of studying fossils, scientists have difficulty determining

> whether organisms shared a characteristic because they inherited it from a common ancestor, or because they evolved it separately by convergence. This sometimes makes reconstructing fossil history difficult. Sometimes in the fossil record a species appears to have become extinct then reappears. Is it because the species was rare for a long time, then reappeared in greater abundance (what paleontologist David Jablonski calls *Lazarus taxa*, because they appeared to rise from the dead), or because another

lineage evolved similar features by convergence, and
it just looked like a reappearance (what paleontologist
Douglas Erwin calls *Elvis taxa*).[139]

The theory of convergence not only lacks evidence for a mechanism,
but is at times used to explain a wide variety of similarities better
explained by other theories. Doolittle concluded convergence claims
are confusing for several reasons, one of which is that often "not
enough care is taken to state exactly what kind of convergence one has
in mind." He adds, "Functional and mechanistic convergence are both
common, and some structural convergence has probably occurred, but
a convincing case for genuine [genetic] sequence convergence has yet
to be made."[140] Although claims of convergent evolution are common,
even ubiquitous, their identification, interpretation, and explanation
are controversial, and valid alternative explanations often exist.[141]

To summarize the major problem: how could random mutations
and natural selection repeatedly generate the same complex designs,
sometimes several scores of times? An alternative explanation is that
*this similarity is indicative of an intelligent designer using the same
design in different contexts.* Svante Pääbo, after decades of research,
wrote that convergence creates major problems for taxonomy, writing
that the many "examples of convergent evolution was to me a strong
message that morphology is often an unreliable indicator of relatedness
among organisms."[142]

Professor Lima-de-Faria, in an extensive study of convergent
evolution, concluded that the striking similarities between two very
different life-forms, which convergence theory attempts to explain,
is a major "puzzling fact" of evolution that is not only unexplained
by Darwinism, but is also a major problem for the theory.[143] Simpson

---

[139] Rice, 2007, p. 93.
[140] Doolittle, 1994, p. 15.
[141] Losos, 2011.
[142] Pääbo, 2014, p. 66.
[143] Lima-de-Faria, 1988, p. 271.

stressed that "the phenomenon of evolutionary convergence...
is a source of disquiet and precaution to paleontologists and other
biologists."[144]

Another major problem with convergent evolution as an
explanation is that many of the examples, such as the American wolf
and the Tasmanian wolf mentioned above, are *far too similar* to have
evolved separately from an ancient common ancestor during the
early Cretaceous, as convergent evolution theory postulates. Many
convergent evolution examples are often so similar in so many ways
that only someone who carefully studied the difference could interpret
the data to make the appropriate distinctions.[145]

The Tasmanian wolf and the North American wolf have almost
identical body morphology, including even their jaw structure and
dentition pattern. Both the behavior and lifestyles of the North
American wolf and the Tasmanian wolf are very similar. Their skeletal
structures, especially their skulls and teeth, are so similar that, unless
compared side by side and labeled, only someone who has previously
studied the difference can distinguish between them.[146] The close
similarity is used as part of a museum exhibit in Australia to illustrate
the fact that there are fewer differences between the Tasmanian wolf
and *Canis lupis* than between many dog breeds. Yet, due to significant
differences in their reproductive systems, the wolf is a placental
classified with the dog, and the Tasmanian wolf is a marsupial classified
with the kangaroo.

As part of their final exam, zoology students at Oxford were
required to identify 100 zoological specimens. A "dog" skull that
actually was the Tasmanian Wolf *Thylacinus*, successfully fooled many
students until they caught on to the ploy.[147] The examiners then placed
an actual dog skull in their laboratory exam, which again confused the
students. Dawkins noted that the main "way to tell the difference is by

---

[144] Simpson, 1980, pp. 12-13.
[145] Simpson, 1980.
[146] Denton, 1986, p. 178.
[147] Dawkins, 2004, p. 229.

the two prominent holes in the plate bone, which are characteristic of marsupials generally."[148]

Yet another problem with the convergent theory is the claim that living in similar environments and experiencing similar selection pressures can produce convergent evolution.[149] This is called the adaptationist theory of convergence, and new research on the adaptationist and constraint perspectives on convergent evolution evaluated

> the more fundamental question about the predictability of evolutionary change. More generally, convergent evolution has long been taken as evidence of adaptation, but some recent workers have questioned the ability of evolutionary biologists to infer the operation of natural selection from the phylogenetic pattern.[150]

This theory of convergence adaptation is problematic because often the environments of two animals believed to have very similar traits due to convergence are often very different. Except for opossums and their relatives, marsupials are now found only in Australia and New Zealand. The environments of North America and Australia are very different in climate, terrain, and, especially, in the life-forms inhabiting the land.[151]

Furthermore, no reason exists to believe similar environmental demands could commonly evolve two very different animals with so many very similar traits. Nor does any direct evidence exist that very similar environments will evolve different animals to increasingly resemble each other until they become, not just superficially identical, but in many ways close to physiologically identical as well.

---

[148] Dawkins, 2004, p. 229.
[149] Milner, 1990; Losos, 2011.
[150] Losos, 2011, p. 1,872.
[151] Johnson, 1955, p. 489.

Labeling Does Not Explain Lack of Evidence

The *post hoc* convergent evolution explanation lacks direct evidence, and simply naming an event does not explain it. For example, one author explains two different genes as a "striking case of convergent evolution," yet no evidence is provided for the evolution of the new genes. The fact that no record of its evolution exists is explained away by asserting

> that "genes emerge and evolve very rapidly, generating copies that bear little similarity to their ancestral precursors" because they are apparently "hypermutable." Finally, when all else fails, scenarios invoke the "*de novo* origination" of new genes, as if that phrase—any more than the others just mentioned—constitutes a scientific demonstration of the power of mutational mechanisms to produce significant amounts of new genetic information. ... What causes new genes to evolve so rapidly? Their "hypermutability" or perhaps their ability to undergo "rapid, adaptive evolution." How do we explain the origin of two similar genes in two separate, but otherwise widely disparate lineages? Convergent evolution, of course.[152]

Examples of this major problem for convergent evolution include the presence of two very "similar genes in two separate, but otherwise widely disparate genetic lineages." The problem of convergent evolution is compounded by

> the improbability of finding even one functional gene in sequence space, let alone the same gene arising twice independently. No one knows exactly [why], but

---

[152] Meyer, 2013, p. 228.

perhaps it was a "fortuitous juxtaposition of suitable sequences," or "positive selection," or "*de novo* origination." Need to explain two similar genes in more closely related lineages? Try "gene duplication," or "chimerical gene fusion," or "retropositioning," or "extensive refashioning of the genome," or some other scientific-sounding combination of words.[153]

Scientific sounding words are not science, nor an explanation, but only appear to explain a problem which they, in fact, do not explain.

Darwinists argue that very similar biochemistry and anatomical structures exist in a wide variety of organisms because natural selection independently and repeatedly evolved certain structures to facilitate survival. Thus, the theory argues, the eye independently evolved as many as 60 times due to the fact that vision is critical not only to locating food and mates, but also avoiding predators, and communicating and bonding with other animals, such as in herds and packs.[154] Lastly, it is well recognized that evolution of close-to-identical structures is very unlikely. This was best expressed by Stephen Jay Gould when he wrote, in reference to the human mind, that "our origin is the product of massive historical contingency, and we would probably never arise again even if life's tape could be replayed a thousand times."[155] The same point is valid for all other organs and organisms.

Convergence: A Problem for Darwinism

This concept is so important to Darwinism that Oxford University Professor George wrote that evolutionary theory would be falsified if significant evidence was found against the view that two very similar organisms could gradually evolve from very different ancestral lines.

---

[153] Meyer, 2013, p. 228.
[154] Salvini-Plawen and Mayr, 1977.
[155] Gould, 1989, pp. 233-234.

George concluded this evidence would cast serious doubt on evolution even though "Darwin [himself] believed firmly in the law that 'nature never repeats herself,'" meaning distinct animal structures can evolve only once because the likelihood of their evolving at all is so unlikely that evolving them twice is close to zero.[156] Thus, humans could not have evolved separately along very different lines several times in history, yet, as we will show, this is exactly what convergence claims.

The fact is, both George's and Darwin's conclusions are ignored by evolutionists because they must claim convergence in order to explain the hundreds of examples of "nature repeating herself" in the real world. Darwinists assume that evolutionary convergence *must* have occurred in modern organisms because, despite major external differences, many organisms have profound similarities that they must have achieved by evolutionary convergence; this is the only explanation that evolutionists have been able to postulate to retain their theory in the face of powerful evidence against it.[157] This is why University of Chicago Professor Jerry Coyne concluded that: "Convergence is one of the most impressive features of evolution, and it is common: there are hundreds of cases."[158]

The Creation Explanation for Convergence

Creation and Intelligent Design argue convergence is primarily a result of design constraints. Thus DNA (or RNA in retroviruses) is common to all known life-forms, and employs an almost universal amino acid code to produce all of the required protein conformations (physical shapes) for enzymes, and structural and transport proteins because, given the many existing constraints and choices, it is the best possible design. Likewise, ATP is the main transmitter of energy used in life-forms ranging from bacteria to plants, to animals, to humans because

---

[156] George, 1982, p. 146.
[157] Rice, 2007, p. 93.
[158] Coyne, 2015, p. 142.

it is the most effective molecular design for short-term storage and transfer of the right-sized energy packets.

An analogy in the human-designed world is the computer chip, which is found in everything from watches to stoves, washers and dryers, phones, televisions, automobiles and, of course, I-pads and computers. The basic chip design is modified for each specific use. Likewise, all those examples claimed to be a result of convergence use the same basic design modified for use in a specific organism.

Likewise, similarly designed eyes are found in a wide variety of animals because the basic eye design is the most effective design for life in a wide variety of environments. The basic design is modified to meet the needs of the specific organism and the specific environment it is designed to inhabit.[159] Furthermore, the eyes of very different life-forms, such as mammals and octopuses, are very similar, even though evolutionists would propose that eyes must have evolved along very different animal lines.

When the Darwinian tree of life is examined, we find that highly developed traits, which are expected only in highly evolved life-forms, are scattered throughout the Darwinian phylogenetic tree, and not just located in the highly evolved animals.

Conclusions

The convergence "just-so stories" attempt to explain the fact that life-forms located on very different parts of the evolutionary phylogenetic tree, that do *not* have a recent common ancestor, have many remarkably similar organs and structures. Darwinists are forced to conclude these must have evolved independently, thus the convergent evolution theory. Many animals with homologous structures clearly could not have descended via the same evolutionary branch, such as fish and

---

[159] Hamilton, 1987.

birds, yet homology is used as proof of common descent. In short, Werner states the problem as follows:

> Scientists who oppose evolution ask how similarities can be used as evidence for evolution if so many "unrelated" animals also have similarities. How can you have it both ways? You cannot claim that similarities in animals are evidence for evolution in the face of unrelated animals also possessing similar features.[160]

Evolutionists deal with this major contradiction by postulating convergence as the evolutionary explanation for this problem. A review of convergence theory finds thousands of claimed examples, but little or no documented empirical evidence exists for the evolutionary convergence claim. It is an arm-chair post-hoc explanation that attempts to explain away those life-form traits which appear to be very closely related to other life-forms, but these same life-forms manifest major differences so great that a close branch of common ancestry must be ruled out.

The fact that many central physiological differences exist between the two major subclasses of mammals, placentals and marsupials, that externally appear to be very similar, has created major problems for Darwinists' attempts to support evolution. The idea that animals such as marsupials and placentals have "convergently" evolved many striking similarities on top of their profound differences, often lacks both a mechanism and a rational explanation.[161] As a whole, the many examples Darwinists attempt to explain by the theory of convergence are far better explained as a result of design limitations.[162]

Furthermore, the convergent theory has close to zero support in the fossil record. The main example explored in this chapter, marsupials, illustrates both the rationale and the problems with the theory, which is a just-so story lacking empirical evidence of even plausible convergent

---

[160] Werner, 2010, p. 62.
[161] Losos, 2011.
[162] Rana, 2008; ReMine, 1994.

evolutionary steps. Lastly, as Morris admitted, "we do not understand ... how organisms assemble. .[into] exceedingly complex functional entities, nor why they repeatedly navigate to convergent solutions."[163]

Spetner's notation that mammals and katydids "have evolved to hear in a markedly analogous way" is an example. Spetner then shows this "notable case of convergence" is problematic for many reasons, one of which is that while genetic plasticity may account for a few examples of convergence, it does not account for very similar hearing systems in life-forms located on drastically different parts of the putative evolutionary tree.[164]

The convergence problem was accurately summed up by Cambridge University Ph.D. Steven Meyer, who wrote that "the repeated need to posit convergent evolution (and other related mechanisms) casts further doubt on [the attempt to achieve evolutionary] ... phylogenetic reconstruction. Invoking convergent evolution negates the very logic of the argument from homology, which affirms that similarity implies common ancestry, except... in those many, many cases when it does not. Repeatedly invoking convergence negates the assumption that justifies the method of phylogenic reconstruction in the first place, namely that similarity is a reliable historical signal of common ancestry."[165]

In essence, the convergent evolution hypothesis requires the "reinvention of the wheel" hundreds or even thousands of times. The eye alone is hypothesized to have evolved independently as many as 100 different times.[166] Given the very small probability of the evolution of a single eye or even organism, the likelihood of it occurring numerous times is indefensible. As quoted above, Gould noted that even if evolution were repeated a thousand times, it probably would not produce the human mind again.[167]

---

[163] Morris, 2010, p. 141.
[164] Spetner, 2014, p. 90.
[165] Meyer, 2013, pp. 133-134.
[166] Land, and Nilsson, 2002; Fernald, 2001, pp. 2-4.
[167] Gould, 1989, pp. 233-234.

References

Anonymous. 1998. "Sharks and Camels ... Cousins?" *Creation* 21(1):7.

Austad, S. 1988. "The Adaptable Opossum." *Scientific American* 258(2):98-104.

Coyne, Jerry. 2015. *Faith vs. Fact: Why Science and Religion are Incompatible.* New York, NY: Viking Press.

Clemens, W. 1968. "Evolution." *International Journal of Organic Evolution* 22(1):1-24.

Darwin, Charles. 1859. *The Origin of Species.* London, UK: John Murray.

Dawkins, Richard. 2004. *The Ancestor's Tale. The Dawn of Evolution.* Boston, MA: Houghton-Mifflin.

Denton, Michael. 1986. *Evolution: A Theory in Crisis.* Bethesda, MD: Adler & Adler Publishers, Inc.

Doolittle, R. 1994. "Convergent Evolution: The Need to be Explicit." *Trends in Biochemical Sciences* 19(1):15-18.

Emery, N., and N. Clayton. 2004. "The Mentality of Crows: Convergent Evolution of Intelligence in Corvids and Apes." *Science* 306:1903-1907, December 10.

Fernald, R.D. 2001. "The Evolution of Eyes." *Karger Gazette*, no. 64, pp. 2–4, January.

Futuyma, Douglas. 2005. *Evolution.* Sunderland, MA: Sinauer Associates.

George, Wilma. 1982. *Darwin.* Glasgow, Scotland: Fontana Paperbacks.

Gould, Stephen Jay. 1989. *Wonderful Life: The Burgess Shale and the Nature of History.* New York, NY: W.W. Norton & Co.

Grundfest, H. 1960. "Electric Fishes." *Scientific American* 203(4):115-124.

Hamilton, H.S. 1987. "Convergent Evolution—Do the Octopus and Human Eyes Qualify?" *CRSQ* 24(2):82-85, September.

Hjelmqvist, L., M. Metsis, H. Persson, J. Hoog, J. McLennan, and H. Jornvall. 1995. "Alcohol Dehydrogenase of Class I: Kiwi Liver Enzyme, Parallel Evolution in Separate Vertebrate Lines, and Correlation with 12S rRNA Patterns." *FEBS Letters* 367(3):306-310, July 3.

Hoy, Ronald R. 2012. "Convergent Evolution of Hearing." *Science*, 338(6109):894-895, November 16.

Huang, R., A.J. O'Donnella, J.J. Barbolinea, and T.J. Barkmana. 2016. "Convergent Evolution of Caffeine in Plants by Co-option of Exapted Ancestral Enzymes." *Proceedings of the National Academy of Science* 113(38):10,613–10,618.

Janke, A., G. Feldmaier-Fuchs, W. T. von Haeseler, and S. Pääbo. 1994. "The Marsupial Mitochondrial Genome and the Evolution of Placental Mammals." *Genetics* 137(1):243-256.

Johnson, D.H. 1955. "The Incredible Kangaroo: Australia's Famous Marsupial Sits on Its Tail, Fights Like a Man, Bounces Like a Steel Spring, and Graces a Coat of Arms." *The National Geographic Magazine* 108(4):487-500.

Jung, H.S., S.A. Burgess, N.Billington, M.Colegrave, H.Patel, J.M. Chalovich, P.D. Chantler, and P.J. Knight. 2008. "Conservation of the Regulated Structure of Folded Myosin 2 in Species Separated by at Least 600 Million Years of Independent Evolution." *PNAS* | 105(16):6,022-6,026, April 22.

Kalman, B. 2003. *A Dolphin's Body.* New York, NY: Crabtree Publishing Company.

Katsenelinboigen, A. 1997. *Evolutionary Change: Toward a Systemic Theory of Development and Maldevelopment.* Amsterdam, The Netherlands: Gordon and Beach.

Klinowska, M. 1991. *Dolphins, Porpoises, and Whales of the World*. Gland, Switzerland: International Union for the Conservation of Nature & Natural Resources.

Knight, P. 2008. "Ancient protein offers clues to killer condition." Leeds, West Yorkshire, England: University of Leeds (press release).

Land, M.F., and D.-E. Nilsson. 2002. *Animal Eyes*. Oxford, England: Oxford University Press.

Lima-de-Faria, A. 1988. *Evolution without Selection: Form and function by Autoevolution*. Amsterdam, The Netherlands: Elsevier.

Lissmann, H.W. 1963. "Electric Location by Fishes." *Scientific American* 208(3):50-59.

Losos, J.B. 2011. "Convergence, Adaptation, and Constraint." *Evolution* 65(7):1,827-1,840, March 11.

McGhee, G. 2011. *Convergent Evolution: Limited Forms Most Beautiful*. Cambridge, MA: The MIT Press.

Meyer, Stephen C. 2013. *Darwin's Doubt*. New York, NY: HarperOne.

Mikkelsen, T.S., M. Wakefield, B. Aken, C. Amemiya, J. Chang, S. Duke, M. Garbe, A. Gentles, L. Goodstadt, A. Heger, et al. 2007. "Genome of the marsupial *Monodelphis domestica* reveals innovation in non-coding sequences." *Nature* 447(7141):167–177.

Milner, R. 1990. *The Encyclopedia of Evolution*. New York, NY: Facts on File.

Montealegre-Z, F., T.Johnsson, K.A. Robson-Brown, M. Postles, and D.Robert. 2012. "Convergent Evolution Between Insect and Mammalian Audition." *Science* 338(6109):968-871, November 16.

Morris, Conway. 2007. *Life's Solution: Inevitable Humans in a Lonely Universe*. Cambridge, MA: Cambridge University Press.

_____. 2010. Evolution: Like any other science it is predictable. *Philosophical Transactions of the Royal Society B* 365(1537):133-145, January 12.

Mundy, N.I., et al. 2004. "Conserved Genetic Basis of a Quantitative Plumage Trait Involved in Mate Choice." *Science* 303(5665): 1,870-1,873, March 19. Summarized by Hopi E. Hoekstra and Trevor Price. "Parallel Evolution is in the Genes." *Science* 303(5665):1,779-1,781, March 19.

Near, T., and ten other authors. 2013. Phylogeny and tempo of diversification in the superradiation of spiny-rayed fishes. *Proceedings of the National Academy of Science* 110(31):12,738-12,743, July 30.

Nelson, D., T. Kamataki, D. Waxman, F.P. Guengerich, R.W. Estabrook, R. Feyereisen, F. Gonzalez, M. Coon, I. Gunsalus, O. Gotoh, O. Kyuichiro and D.W. Nebert. 1993. "The P450 Superfamily: Update on New Sequences, Gene Mapping, Accession Numbers, Early Trivial Names of Enzymes, and Nomenclature." *DNA and Cell Biology* 12(1):1-51, January-February.

Pääbo, Svante. 2014. *Neanderthal Man: In Search of Lost Genomes.* New York, NY: Basic Books.

Patterson, T.B., and T.J. Givnish. 2003. "Geographic Cohesion, Chromosomal Evolution, Parallel Adaptive Radiations, and Consequent Floral Adaptations in *Calochortus* (Calochortaceae): Evidence from a cpDNA Phylogeny." *New Phytologist* 161(1):253-264, January.

Pichersky, E. 2004. "Plant scents - Mediators of inter-and intraorganismic communication." *American Scientist* 92:514-521.

Porter, R., and G.M. Collins. 1984. *Photoperiodic regulation of insect and molluscan hormones.* London, UK: Pitman Publishing.

Rana, Fritz. 2008. *The Cell's Design.* Grand Rapids, MI: Baker Books.

ReMine, Walter. 1994. "The Biotic Message—An Introduction." *Proceedings of the Third International Conference on Creation.* Pittsburgh, PA: *Creation Science Fellowship,* pp. 433-444.

Rice, Stanly. 2007. "Convergence," pp. 89-93 in *Encyclopedia of Evolution.* New York, NY: Facts on File.

Salvini-Plawen, L., and E. Mayr. 1977. "On the Evolution of Photoreceptors and Eyes."

In *Evolutionary Biology,* Vol. 10. New York, NY: Plenum publishing Corp. Edited by M. Hecht, W. Steeve, and B. Wallace.

Shadwick, R.E. 2005. "How Tunas and Lamnid Sharks Swim: An Evolutionary Convergence." *American Scientist* 93(6):524-531.

Shute, Evan V. 1969. "Square Pegs in Round Holes or Ridiculous 'Convergence'." *CRSQ* 5(4):135-138, March.

_____. 1970. "Puzzling Similarities." *CRSQ* 7(3):147-151, December.

Simpson, George. 1980. *Splendid Isolation: The Curious History of South American Mammals.* New Haven, CT: Yale University Press.

Spetner, Lee. 2014. *The Evolution Revolution - Why Thinking People are Rethinking the Theory of Evolution.* Brooklyn, NY: Judaica Press.

Szalay, F.S. 1999. "Marsupials," pp. 703-714, in *Encyclopedia of Paleontology. Volume 2: M-Z.* Chicago, IL: Fitzroy Dearborn Publishers. Edited by Ronald Singer.

Tompkins, Jeffrey P., and Jerry R. Bergman. 2015. "Evolutionary Molecular Genetic Clocks--A Perpetual Exercise in Futility and Failure." *Journal of Creation* 29(2):26-35.

Wells, Jonathan. 2000. *Icons of Evolution.* Washington, D.C.: Regnery Publishing.

Welch, J., and L. Bromham. 2011. "Molecular dating when rates vary." *TRENDS in Ecology and Evolution* 20(5):320-327.

Werner, C. 2009. *Evolution: The Grand Experiment.* Green Forest, AR: New Leaf Press.

Whiteman, N., and K. Mooney. 2012. "Insects converge on resistance." *Nature* 489(7416):376-377.

Yokoyama, R. and S. Yokoyama. 1990. "Convergent Evolution of the Red- and Green-Like Visual Pigment Genes in Fish, *Astyanax fasciatus,* and Human." *Proceedings of the National Academy of Science, U.S.A.* 87(230):9,315-9,318.

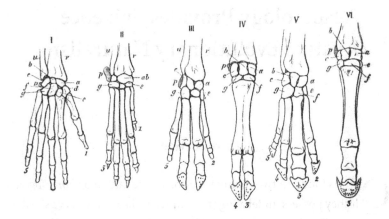

An example of homology. From Carl Gegenbaur: *Elements of Comparative Anatomy*. London, UK: Macmillan. Page 483, Figure 268. Homology of the hand to forelimbs, 1878. Shown are 1. Human Hand; 2. Dog leg and foot; 3. Pig leg and foot; 4. Ox leg and foot; 5. Tapir leg and foot; 6. Horse leg and foot. Similarities exist due to design constraints but, nonetheless, major differences exist. Why the human hand was compared with the leg and feet of other animals was not stated except this comparison shows homology better than comparing all legs and feet.

CHAPTER 3

Homology Provides Evidence
Against Evolutionary Naturalism

Introduction

Organs found in two distinct life-forms are said to be *homologous* if they possess underlying structural similarity and serve similar functions. The human arm and the seal flipper, for example, have similar internal bone structures, even though they function in very different environments—for humans the air, and for seals, the water. Macroevolutionists believe these homologous organs resulted from divergent evolution from the common ancestor from which both humans and seals descended. They assume that the human arm, the dog leg, the whale flipper, and the bat forelimb are all organically related.[168] Conversely, homologous organs fit with the concept that the Designer reused certain plans in constructing many animals because a particular scheme was efficient or utilitarian. Homologies support the design interpretation because they are evidences of basic patterns or plans.

Extensive comparisons of skeletons, muscles, nerves, body organs, cell ultrastructure, and biochemistry of different animals have

---

[168] Hall, 1994.

confirmed that a great deal of similarity exists in both their structure and function. By arranging or classifying large sets of anatomical structures according to the similarity of selected traits, evolutionary naturalists have attempted to demonstrate evidence for a long, gradual line of progressive animal changes terminating in the most-evolved organism, humans. Evolutionists then argue these comparisons prove the concept that all life evolved from a hypothetical putative "common ancestor" protocell that they believe lived about 3.5 billion years ago. Called *homology* or the homology theory, (*homo* means 'the same,' *ology* means "the study of"), this view has been presented as a major evidence of macroevolutionary theory since Darwin. An example of this reasoning is as follows:

> If you look at a 1953 Corvette and compare it to the latest model, only the most general resemblances are evident, but if you compare a 1953 and a 1954 Corvette, side by side, then a 1954 and a 1955 model, and so on, the descent with modification is overwhelmingly obvious. This is what paleontologists do with fossils, *and the evidence is so solid and comprehensive that it cannot be denied by reasonable people.*[169]

Homology is not used as just a minor "proof" of evolution, but instead has been widely cited by evolutionists as one of the *most compelling* lines of evidence that exists as proof of their theory.[170] Bill Nye proclaimed that "homology is one of the absolutely most compelling indicators of the process of evolution."[171] Homology was so critically important that Darwin recognized the *"major* source of evidence for common descent is the concept of homology." Darwin's theory of common descent concluded that

---

[169] Berra, 1990, p. 117; emphasis in original.
[170] Denton, 1986, p. 143; Jones, 1981.
[171] Nye, 2014, p. 149.

the structures that we call homologies represent characteristics inherited with some modification from a corresponding feature in a common ancestor. Darwin devoted an entire book, *The Decent of Man and Selection in Relation to Sex*, largely to the idea that humans share common descent with apes and other animals . . . Darwin built his case mostly on anatomical comparisons revealing homology between humans and apes. To Darwin, the close resemblances between apes and humans could be explained only by common descent.[172]

Darwin reasoned that members of the same class of animals resemble each other in the general plan of their design, and this resemblance is often described by the term homology.

What can be more curious than that the hand of a man, formed for grasping, that of a mole for digging, the leg of the horse, the paddle of the porpoise, and the wing of the bat should all be constructed on the same pattern and should include similar bones in the same relative positions?[173]

An early example of how homology was used to argue for macroevolution is a 1928 biology text which, in answer to the question, "Why do the individuals in a species have all of their parts homologous?", said:

The obvious answer is, that they all *descended from the same ancestors* . . . Biologists carry this answer a step further and say that since homology within the species is the result of common ancestry therefore *all*

---

[172] Hickman, et al., 1996, pp. 159-160; emphasis mine.
[173] Darwin, 1872, pp. 434-435.

> *homology is due to common ancestry* and the closeness
> of relationship determines the number of homologous
> parts.[174]

Conklin, implying that a design explanation also exists, claimed the only *natural* explanation for homology is evolution. In his words, the fundamental resemblances between embryos, larvae, and adults

> are just as genuine homologies as those between adult
> structures, and the only natural explanation that has
> ever been found for such homologies is inheritance
> from common ancestors . . . These fundamental
> resemblances, or *homologies*, as they are technically
> called, call for some explanation, and the only
> natural explanation that has ever been proposed is
> evolution.[175]

A much more recent quote illustrates how this line of reasoning is still being used today to argue that homology as evidence for the common ancestry of all life is "very strong."

> Why is it that bats and whales have so much in
> common anatomically with mice and men? Why
> do virtually all vertebrate forelimbs have the same
> basic "pentadactyl" (five fingered) design? (This is one
> of numerous examples of "homologous" structures
> exhibited by related species.)[176]

Professor Barr concludes the answer is evolution. He lists homology as the *first* argument on his list of evidences for evolution. As the above quotes show, the same line of reasoning has been used to "prove"

---

[174] Wellhouse and Hendrickson, 1928, p. 147; emphasis in original.
[175] Conklin, 1928, pp. 72, 74.
[176] Barr, 1997, p. 15.

evolution for well over a century. Some evolutionists, though, are more honest. Dobzhansky admitted the following:

> Homology does not prove evolution, in the sense that nobody has actually witnessed the gradual changes in the millions of consecutive generations which led from a common ancestor to a bird on the one hand and to man on the other. But homology suggests evolution; the facts of homology make sense if they are supposed to be due to evolution of now different organisms from a common stock.[177]

The argument from homology has been used in high school and college biology textbooks for generations.[178] A survey by the author of 45 widely used recent college textbooks and 28 high school texts revealed that all of those that discussed evolution except one employed homology as a *major* proof for Darwinism. Most of these discussions were brief and almost identical in content and thrust, even using similar examples such as the limb homology. The following example was typical:

> The seven bones in the human neck correspond with the same seven, much larger, neck bones in the giraffe: they are homologues. The number of cervical vertebrae is a trait shared by creatures descended from a common ancestor. Related species share corresponding structures; though they may be modified in various ways.[179]

---

[177] Dobzhansky, 1959, pp. 227-228.
[178] Jones, 1982.
[179] Milner, 1990, p. 218.

History of the Homology Theory

Homology, as it was originally defined by Richard Owen, had no phylogenetic significance and was used only to document similarities without reference to ancestry.[180] DeBeer actually argued that homology should *not* be used as a guide to phylogeny, noting it is now clear the assumption "that the inheritance of homologous structures from a common ancestor explained homology was misplaced; for such inheritance cannot be ascribed to identity of genes. The attempt to find 'homologous' genes, except in closely related species, has been given up as hopeless."[181]

The comparative anatomy argument called homology probably was first popularized by Huxley in 1863 to argue for human evolution. In his *Man's Place in Nature* he gathered what Milner concluded is "overwhelming evidence for close homologies – muscle for muscle and bone for bone. Huxley's comparative anatomy demonstrated that man is more similar to the apes (gorillas, chimps, orangs) than the apes are to monkeys."[182]

After the spread of Darwin's ideas, the structural similarity in many animals that had been obvious to anatomists for generations as due to design was reinterpreted as evidence for common descent. The concept of homology, which originally meant only that a set of structures was fundamentally similar, was first noted in 1843 by one of Darwin's most informed critics, Sir Richard Owen.[183] Before Darwin, homology observations were explained by a concept called *ideal archetypes*, meaning the Creator used superior-design prototypes throughout His creation. A branch of this worldview is now called

---

[180] Boyden, 1947.
[181] DeBeer, 1971, p. 16.
[182] Milner, 1990, p. 218.
[183] Berry and Hallam, 1987; Boyden, 1947.

intelligent design theory.[184] It was not until after Darwin that homology implied common ancestry.[185]

An Evaluation of Homology Evidence for Evolution

That some similarity exists when certain aspects of select life-forms are compared is obvious. The question with which we are concerned here is, "Does the similarity which exists prove one structure evolved into another and, ultimately, the complex *evolved* from the simple?" The simplest and most obvious explanation for the fact of morphological similarities between bones, sensory organs, lungs, or gills is that the *requirements of life are similar* for similar living things, and some designs are preferred in constructing animals because some designs are superior to other, competing designs.[186]

All automobile, bicycle, and pushcart tires are round because this design shape (round) is superior for the function of most tires. A tire homology does not prove common descent, but common design by engineers throughout history because of the superiority of the round structure for rolling. Likewise, most vertebrate kidneys are structurally very similar because they have an almost identical physiological role in the body and, consequently, must be similar in both structure and function to accomplish that role.

Homology also does not prove a set of animals is related by descent because both similarities and differences exist for any two animal types. Traits often are chosen arbitrarily by evolutionists only because they seem to provide evidence that two animals are related. The only criterion used to select examples of homology usually is, "Does the example support what is assumed to be an evolutionary relationship?" All other examples are ignored or explained away. This fact is so well-recognized, and because examples exist that contradict the explanation

---

[184] Wells and Nelson, 1997, p. 12.

[185] Boyden, 1947, p. 648.

[186] Jones, 1982.

of common descent, that evolutionists have attempted to separate most putative examples of homology into two types: **analogy** and **homology**:

> a distinction must be made between similarity due to common ancestry, or homology, and resemblance which is due solely to similarity of function, known as *analogy*. Thus the forelimbs of humans, horses, whales, and birds are homologous: they are all constructed on the same pattern, and include similar bones in the same relative positions because these are all derived from the same ancestral bones.[187]

Conversely, the wings of birds and insects are analogous because they both

> serve the same purpose, but do not constitute modified versions of a structure present in a common ancestor. The wings of birds and bats are homologous in skeletal structure because of descent from the forelimb of a common reptilian ancestor; but they are analogous in terms of their modification for flight–feathers in birds, skin membranes in bats.[188]

In other words, if a design similarity supports evolutionary assumptions, it is listed as evidence of homology and accepted as evidence for evolution. Conversely, if a design similarity does *not* support evolution, it is called an **analogy**, and it is concluded that the similarity is due not to a common ancestor, but because a certain design is highly functional for a specific body part.

Development of streamlined fins in fish (teleosts) and flippers in dolphins (mammals) are analogous because they function alike, but their underlying structure is very different. "Wings of birds, insects,

---

[187] Berry and Hallam, 1997, p. 82.
[188] Berry and Hallam, 1997, p. 82.

and bats are also analogous: similar in form and function, but with entirely independent evolutionary histories."[189]

Many analogous structures are assumed to exist due to **convergent evolution** (covered in the previous chapter), which is defined as the separate evolution of similar structures due to similar environmental demands.[190] Convergent evolution also is used to explain similar designs that have formed from different embryonic structures or precursors.

Creationists have concluded that *all* examples of homology actually are better explained by analogy, and the resemblance which exists is due *in all cases* to similarity of function and/or design constraints. The forelimbs of humans, whales, and birds are similar because they serve very similar functions and have similar design constraints. Likewise, the foot of a bird and a maple leaf share some similarities due to design ideals, not because birds evolved from maple trees, or that they share a recent common ancestor. The conclusion that two homologous bones are similar because they were "derived from the same ancestral bones" as Barr claims, is not based on direct evidence, but instead on *a priori* conclusions demanded by macroevolution. For this reason, "the evolutionist argument from homology lacks scientific content" which

> strikes at the root of all attempts by evolutionists to give homology an objective basis and distinguish *homology* (similarities due to descent) from *analogy* (similarities *not due* to descent). The only way they can recognize analogous variation, especially when due to convergent evolution, is by criteria (e.g., genetic or embryological) which we now know do not hold for organs of "unquestionable" homology. The evolutionist concept of homology is now shown to be entirely subjective.[191]

---

[189] Milner, 1990, p. 218.
[190] Audesirk and Audesirk, 1999.
[191] Barr, 1982, p. 159.

The late Stephen J. Gould even concluded that "the central task of evolutionary biology is . . . the separation of homologous from analogous likeness," and then emphasized "homology is similarity due to descent from a common ancestor, period."[192]

Although many similarities exist in almost all animal structures, structural variations are the norm. Often the variations found in the animal world seem to exist solely to produce variety, and not for the purpose of conferring a survival advantage to the animal. To argue for macroevolution via comparisons, judging levels of "complexity" also is problematic because an enormous number of exceptions exists. The comparative anatomy argument fails completely when an attempt is made to trace *all* living forms of life from fossils, back to their postulated universal common ancestors. Few modern skeleton, muscle, and brain counterparts exist in any single-celled animals, or in many putative stages afterward.

No biological or logical requirement exists to vary the design of bones, muscles, and nerves needlessly in every living form beyond what is necessary to adapt the animal to its environment. Although variety for the sake of variety is universal in the natural world, variety that interferes with the life process, or an animal's survival, is usually avoided in animal design. Design constraints severely limit the possible variations in an animal's anatomy, and excess deviation from the ideal can interfere with the animal's ability to survive.

The many similarities that exist among members of the animal kingdom also could be the result of the fact that a *single designer* created the basic kinds of living systems, then specially modified each type of life to enable it to survive in its unique environmental niche. Examples of major environments in which organisms must be designed to exist include on land, water, air, or in the case of worms, in the ground. Structures that serve *similar purposes* under *similar conditions* and that are nourished by *similar foods* would possess similarity in both

---

[192] Gould, 1988, p. 26.

design and function. This is illustrated in a critique of Berra's Corvette analogy cited above:

> Berra's primary purpose is to show that living organisms are the result of naturalistic evolution rather than intelligent design. Structural similarities among automobiles, however, even similarities between older and newer models (which Berra calls "descent with modification") are due to construction according to pre-existing patterns, i.e., to design. Ironically, therefore, Berra's analogy shows that even striking similarities are not sufficient to exclude design-based explanations. In order to demonstrate naturalistic evolution, it is necessary to show that the mechanism by which organisms are contracted (unlike the mechanism by which automobiles are constructed) does not involve design.[193]

Convergent Evolution

A major problem with homology theory is that many structures appear similar *superficially,* yet differ significantly in anatomy, physiology, histology, etc. Since such examples are not explained easily by homology, evolutionists have hypothesized an explanation for this problem, called **convergent** evolution, which attempts to explain the apparent analogy. As covered in detail in the previous chapter, convergent evolution is defined as the evolution of similar structures in two or more animals due to similar evolutionary forces operating independently.

The most common examples of convergent evolution include the theorized wing evolution. Wings are believed to have evolved a minimum of four times – in birds, bats (in the order Chiroptera), insects, and reptiles (such as the pterodactyl).

---

[193] Wells and Nelson, 1997, p. 14.

Another example is the streamlined shape of seals (a mammal) and penguins (a bird), the streamlined fins in fish (a teleost), and flippers in dolphins (a mammal).[194] Darwinists conclude that most of the marsupials evolved in convergence with their placental counterparts. Examples include the marsupial mouse glider and the placental flying squirrel, the tiger cat (a marsupial carnivore) and the placental mammal tiger, and the cuscus (a marsupial monkey) and the primate monkey. All these marsupials look remarkably like their counterparts.[195]

Evolutionists have concluded that bird wings did not evolve from fly wings for several reasons. Chief among them is the fact that of the many insect impressions in stone, or the many examples of insects in amber that have been discovered, no evidence exists of insects evolving into birds or any other animal.

Furthermore, in many ways, some insect structures and organs are more complex than comparable parts in reptiles or mammals. Consequently, although the evolutionary progenitors of birds are highly debated among evolutionists, insects are not considered likely candidates. The most common theory of bird evolution suggests that they evolved from coelurosaurian dinosaurs or another reptile. Thus, the wings of birds and insects are labeled, not homologous, but analogous, because powerful evidence exists to refute the idea that birds evolved directly from some insect types. This is one of many examples against homology that evolutionists ignore by claiming that this example does not falsify homology theory because it was caused by **co-evolution**. As will be shown, however, no evidence exists to support the co-evolution theory.

Co-Evolution

Homology is often explained by co-evolution, the theory that two similar structures evolved independently from a recent common ancestor. The

---

[194] Audesirk and Audesirk, 1999.
[195] McFadden and Keeton, 1995.

classic example of co-evolution is the Tasmanian wolf (a marsupial) and members of the dog family (which consists of placental mammals). The two animals appear remarkably alike physically, but evidence from the fossil record militates against the theory that one evolved from the other. For this reason, it has been proposed they evolved independently into two animals so close in physical appearance that a detailed knowledge of the two animals is required to tell them apart!

The suggestion that two animals which look remarkably alike, such as the dog and Tasmanian wolf, evolved independently is untenable and thus is a major problem for evolution. Co-evolution was hypothesized to explain the numerous examples of homology in which the available evidence makes clear that the animals under consideration were not linked by a recent common ancestor. An example of such gratuitous hypothesizing is the following: "Linnaeus's original classification of animals does not distinguish between analogous and homologous structures. Creatures were often put in the same groups by resemblances to an imagined "divine plan" or "design." Since Darwin. . . species are classified to reflect the relative closeness or distance of their common ancestry."[196]

Biochemistry Homology

The homology argument from biochemistry is identical to the homology argument in anatomy. As the study of comparative anatomy has found evidence of anatomical homologies, likewise biochemistry research on different organisms finds much evidence of biochemical homologies. As Kimball admits, "the biochemical similarity of living organisms is one of the most remarkable features of life."[197] For example:

> Cytochrome enzymes are found in almost every living organism: plant, animal, and protist. The enzymes of the citric acid cycle are also almost

---

[196] Milner, 1990, p. 218.
[197] Kimball, 1965, p. 547.

universally distributed. Chlorophyll *a* is found in all green plants and almost all photosynthetic protists. DNA and RNA are found in every living organism and, so far as we can determine, contain the same hereditary coding mechanism.[198]

He then ignores the intelligent design argument, opining that the reality that

> underneath the incredible diversity of living things lies a great uniformity of biochemical function is difficult to interpret in any other way but an evolutionary one. Presumably these molecules were put to their current use very early in the history of life and almost all modern forms have inherited the ability to manufacture and use them.[199]

A good early example of this reasoning from a textbook that is almost 50 years old is as follows:

> Why should all mammals be so similar in their chemical make-up? The pancreas of the pig can supply insulin which serves the same purpose as our own insulin. The thyroid gland of the sheep was long used for supplying thyroxin for our use. The hormones seem to be identical. And why are the digestive enzymes of mammals, in many cases, chemically the same? The answer can again be given by paleontologists. Fossils seem to show that mammals are descended from a common ancestor; they are closely related to each other.[200]

---

[198] Kimball, 1965, p. 547.
[199] Kimball, 1965, p. 547.
[200] Kroeber, et al., 1969, p. 483.

Another example of biochemical homology from one of the most widely used biology textbooks in America over the past thirty years provides insight into *why* the biochemistry of life often is so similar:

> Not only do the classes of vertebrates resemble one another in structure and in development, but there is also a marked similarity in function. For instance, the internal secretions of mammals are alike in many respects. The digestive enzymes are so similar that many commercial products such as *pepsin* have been extracted from cows, sheep, and hogs, and are used successfully in human medicine. *Insulin* and *thyroid* hormone, endocrine products taken from animals, have tremendous use in human treatment. Antitoxins produced by the horse are used in immunity treatments of human diseases such as diphtheria, scarlet fever, and tetanus.[201]

Extensive biochemical research since 1963 has shown this evolutionary reasoning to be incorrect. The simplest reason for biochemical homology is that all life, from the simplest eukaryote to humans, requires very similar inorganic elements, compounds, and biomolecules. Consequently, all life is required to use similar metabolic pathways to process these compounds.

Most organisms that use oxygen and rely on the metabolism of carbohydrates, fats, and proteins must use a citric acid cycle which is remarkably similar in all organisms. Furthermore, the metabolism of most proteins into energy produces ammonia, which is processed for removal in similar ways in a wide variety of organisms. What evolutionists must explain is why billions of years of evolution have not produced major **differences** in the biochemistry of life.

Many biochemical structures/systems in yeasts and other so called

---

[201] Moon, et al., 1963, p. 662.

"primitive life" forms are almost identical to the biochemical families in humans. With some minor variations, all life uses the same minerals, the same sugar and lipid families, the same 20 amino acids, about 14 vitamins, and the same basic genetic code.[202]

Even the complex proteins used in all life often are identical or very similar. If we remove ribosomes from bacteria and "put them in a test tube, they'll translate human messenger RNAs into human proteins – and *vice versa*."[203] The problem for evolutionists is that the biochemistry of all life, even that allegedly separated by millions of years of geologic time, *is far too similar for evolutionary explanations*. Despite the many significant differences between the two basic cell types, eukaryotes and prokaryotes, they are both remarkably similar on the biochemical level:

> Prokaryotes and eukaryotes are composed of similar chemical constituents. With a few exceptions, the genetic code is the same in both, as is the way in which the genetic information in DNA is expressed. The principles underlying metabolic processes and most of the more important metabolic pathways are identical. Thus, beneath the profound structural and functional differences between prokaryotes and eukaryotes, there is an even more fundamental unity: a molecular unity that is basic to life processes.[204]

Although many biochemical similarities exist in life, millions of biochemical differences exist that are inexplicable via evolution. Many, if not most, of these differences do not provide a selective advantage. Creationists suggest such differences exist due to the need for ecological balance, and because of the Creator's desire to employ variety. Also, when one compound in an organism is altered, scores

---

[202] Hoagland and Dodson, 1995.
[203] Hoagland and Dodson, 1995, p. 122.
[204] Prescott, Harley, and Klein, 1990, p. 87.

of other compounds with which it interacts also must be changed so that the entire biological system can function as a harmonious whole.

The Fall of Homology

Homology first led Darwinists to assemble examples that seemed to prove ancestor-descendant relationships which often were quite convincing. As scientists learned more about anatomy, physiology, and especially genetics, the entire concept of homology increasingly came under attack. Eventually it was conceded that we "still do not know the true answer on the phylogenetic descent of tetrapods, as homology concepts tend to fail when it comes to tracing evolutionary novelties."[205] One problem, as noted above, was that examples which seemed to fit evolutionary assumptions often were cited, while the examples that did not fit were ignored. In time, more and more examples were discovered that had to be ignored. In addition, as Professor Milton has observed,

> It is homology that Darwinists rely on to bridge the gaps in the fossil record . . . [and] It is homology that underlies the diagrams drawn up by Darwinists from Haeckel to the present day showing how every living thing is related. Ultimately, however, it is homology that has provided the greatest stumbling block to Darwinian theory, for at the final and most crucial hurdle, homology has fallen.[206]

The recent information explosion in embryology, microbiology, genetics, and especially molecular biology has revealed in minute detail how plants and animals are constructed at the molecular level. If the Darwinian interpretation of homology is correct, then we would expect that the same homologies found at the macroscopic level also exist at

---

[205] Tautz, 1998, p. 17.
[206] Milton, 1997, p. 179.

the microscopic, biochemical, and genetic levels. What often is found by researchers in each of these fields, however, has greatly undermined the homology concept. So many exceptions now exist that molecular biologist Michael Denton concluded that the entire homology theory should be rejected.

> The validity of the evolutionary interpretation of homology would have been greatly strengthened if embryological and genetic research could have shown that homologous structures were specified by homologous genes and followed homologous patterns of embryological development. Such homology would indeed be strongly suggestive of "true relationship; of inheritance from a common ancestor." But it has become clear that the principle cannot be extended in this way. Homologous structures are often specified by non-homologous genetic systems and the concept of homology can seldom be extended back into embryology.[207]

In other words, in many cases, organs and structures which appear identical (or very similar) in different animals do *not* develop from the same structure or group of embryonic cells. It is not uncommon to find that fundamental structures, e.g., the alimentary canal, form from different embryological tissues in different animals. For example, in sharks the alimentary canal is formed from the roof of the embryonic gut cavity; in frogs, it is formed from the gut roof and floor; in birds and reptiles, it is formed from the lower layer of the embryonic disc or blastoderm.[208]

Even the idea of vertebrate forelimb homology, the classic example of homology referred to by Darwin, and cited in hundreds of textbooks as proof of evolution, now has turned out to be flawed. The reason

---

[207] Denton, 1986, p. 145.
[208] deBeer, 1971, p. 13.

is that the forelimbs often develop from *different* body segments in different species in a pattern that is unexplainable by evolution. The forelimbs in the newt develop from trunk segments 2 through 5; in the lizard, they develop from trunk segments 6 to 9; in humans, they develop from trunk segments 13 through 18.[209] This evidence shows the forelimbs usually are not developmentally homologous. As an example, Denton cited the development of the vertebrate kidney, which provides a challenge to the assumption that homologous organs are produced from

> homologous embryonic tissues. In fish and amphibia the kidney is derived directly from an embryonic organ known as the mesonephros, while in reptiles and mammals the mesonephros degenerates towards the end of embryonic life and plays no role in the formation of the adult kidney, which is formed instead from a discrete spherical mass of mesodermal tissue, the metanephros, which develops quite independently from the mesonephros.[210]

The last half-century of research has forced the arguments used by evolutionists to take on new meaning. For example, Dobzhansky argued that

> some die-hard anti-evolutionists still insist that homology means only that the Creator gratuitously chose to make homologous organs in quite unrelated organisms. This opinion may be said to be implicitly blasphemous: it actually accuses the Creator of arranging things so that they suggest evolution merely to mislead honest students of His works.[211]

---

[209] de Beer, 1971, pp. 8-9.

[210] Denton, 1986, p. 146.

[211] Dobzhansky, 1959, p. 228.

Of course, they are not only arranged in such a way that does *not* suggest evolution, but indeed they actually falsify evolution.

Genetics and Homology

According to evolutionary theory, homologous features are programmed by similar genes. Gene sequence similarity would indicate common ancestry since such similarities are unlikely to originate independently through random mutations.[212] If the bones of the human arm evolved from the same precursors as the wing of a bat and the hoof of a horse, as Darwinism teaches, then we should be able to trace these alleged homologies back to the DNA that codes for them. Some geneticists thought this knowledge would allow them to find the chemical formula required to produce an arm, leg, or other structure. But once biologists acquired a greater understanding of genetics, they found that what are labeled as homologous structures in different species often are produced by very different genes.

The concept of genetic homology is that features produced by similar genetic sequences will be phylogenetically homologous. However, there are so many exceptions to this that the idea cannot be said to be the rule, but rather the exception. The classic example of this is the dramatically differing effects that can be brought about from a single type of gene.

Mutations in certain homeotic genes in a fly can produce two pairs of wings instead of the normal one pair, or transform a fly's antenna into a leg, or even cause eyes to develop on a fly's leg. Genes similar to the homeotic genes used in fly's wings have been found in *most* other animal types, including mammals. Mice have a gene very similar to the gene that can transform a fly's antenna into a leg (Antennapedia), but in mice the corresponding gene

---

[212] Wells and Nelson, 1997.

affects the hindbrain; and although mice and flies share a similar gene which affects eye development (eyeless), the fly's multifaceted eye is profoundly different from a mouse's camera-like eye. In both cases (Antennapedia and eyeless), similar homeotic genes affect the development of structures which are non-homologous by either the classical morphological definition or the post-Darwinian phylogenetic definition. If similar genes can "determine" such radically different structures, then those genes aren't really determining structure at all. Instead, they appear to be functioning as binary switches between alternate developmental fates, with the information for the resulting structures residing elsewhere.[213]

In another example, the gene that controls the mouse's eye color also happens to control the mouse's physical size; but the gene that controls the fruit fly's eye color controls not the fly's size, but female sex organ morphology. So many genes in higher organisms have multiple effects that Ernst Mayr once suggested that genes which control only a single characteristic must be rare or nonexistent. The finding that a consistent one-gene/one-characteristic correspondence does not exist has been a major blow to homology. Because evolutionary biologists have failed to provide a biological basis for homology, Roth concluded "that the title of de Beer's 1971 essay – 'Homology, an unsolved problem' – remains an accurate description. . . . The relationships between processes at genetic, developmental, gross phenotypic and evolutionary levels remain a black box."[214] Biologists now recognize our efforts

> to correlate major phenotypic evolution with changes in gene frequencies ... have not been very successful. Detailed studies at the molecular level fail

---

[213] Wells and Nelson, 1997, p. 15.
[214] Roth, 1988, pp. 1, 16.

to demonstrate the expected correspondence between changes in gene products and the sorts of organismal changes which constitute the "stuff of evolution."[215]

Furthermore, evolution by DNA mutations "is largely uncoupled from morphological evolution."[216] The best example of this is the large morphological dissimilarity that exists between humans and chimpanzees despite an estimated 89% similarity in their DNA.[217] In short, we now know that in general

> the homology of structures such as organs or modules cannot be ascribed to inheritance of homologous genes or sets of genes. Consequently, organ homology cannot be reduced to gene homology ... to reduce homology to a continuity of [developmental] information. Information is not the same as genotypic nucleic acid. But what it is exactly, and how it is continuous, is still an unsolved problem.[218]

Blood Antigen-Antibody Test Once Used to Prove Evolution

Blood is critical for life; therefore blood homology once was used as an important "test" of evolutionary relationships.[219] Evolutionists claimed blood similarity was strong evidence that certain animals evolved from another animal, or that they both had a common ancestor. Professor Nuttall of Cambridge first developed a human blood test

---

[215] Wells and Nelson, 1997, p. 14.
[216] Raff and Kaufman, 1983, pp. 67, 78.
[217] Raff and Kaufman, 1983, pp. 67, 78.
[218] Sattler, 1984, p. 386.
[219] Brown, 1947.

that formed the basis for tests now used in several fields, including criminal investigation.[220]

To determine how close the animal is to human, the test evaluates the *amount* of precipitate produced by mixing human antibodies and animal blood antigens.[221] A precipitate does not form when the liquid is mixed with the blood of reptiles, and forms slightly with birds or other animals that are "low" on the theoretical evolutionary scale. When the blood of creatures *closer* to humans, such as monkeys, gorillas, and chimpanzees is added to human antibodies, a *larger* amount of precipitate forms.

As described by one biology text, this homology test was one of the most important evidences of evolutionary relationships because the more closely related "one animal is to another, the more nearly alike will be their blood proteins."[222] The *antigen-antibody test* uses antigens not normally existing in many animals, and when this antigen is injected into another animal, its white cells "respond by reproducing specific proteins called *antibodies*" and if

> a sample of human serum is mixed with a sample of rabbit serum, a settling out of material occurs because of the combining of the antigens and antibodies. The closer the relationship of the animals, the greater the amount of settling out that will occur when the antigens and antibodies combine. . . The more alike the blood of the test animals, the closer the [evolutionary] relationship. By injecting a series of rabbits with serum from different species, it has been possible to obtain a series of antibodies. Each of the antibodies is specific for the blood proteins of one kind of animal. Many thousands of tests have been performed. The results show that cats, dogs, and bears

[220] Davidheiser, 1969.

[221] Davidheiser, 1969.

[222] Frazier and Smith, 1974, p. 442.

are more closely related to one another than they are to other mammals. Sheep, deer, antelope, goats, and cows are closely related to one another, but not so closely related to bears, dogs, and cats.[223]

Sir Arthur Keith concluded that the test is "an exact method of determining the affinity of one species of animal to another."[224] Harvard's Ernest Hooton concluded that homology and blood tests alone provided sufficient proof to establish human evolution as fact:

> If there were no evidences of human evolution other than those proved by zoological classification and by blood tests, these alone would be sufficient to convince every impartial thinker that man and the anthropoid apes have evolved from some common ape-like ancestor... from a knowledge of the morphology and physiology of the anthropoid apes and of the lower primates, Huxley's scientific Saturnians would be driven to postulate the existence of man. For man is logically the next evolutionary step beyond the gorilla and the chimpanzee, or perhaps one should say the next *jump*.[225]

One early test rated Old World Monkeys "eight parts" away from humans, and New World Monkeys "twenty-two parts" away. This specific finding fit the evolution model, yet many findings did not, such as the discovery that sheep and horses were separated by only three parts. The gorilla test produces less precipitate than human blood, but chimpanzee blood produces *more* than human blood! Consequently, this blood test would indicate humans are a link *between* gorilla and chimpanzee!

---

[223] Frazier and Smith, 1974, pp. 442-443.
[224] Keith, 1928, p. 24.
[225] Hooton, 1931, pp. 46-47.

As the exceptions piled up, the test eventually was abandoned, relegating yet another "proof" for evolutionary naturalism to the scrap heap. Nuttall himself obtained enough negative results that he believed some common problem, such as the manner of death of the animal being tested, was causing incorrect results in a large number of cases.[226] However, the manner of death would not affect the test results - only blood type would.

Even the eminent Dr. Wassmann, who developed the blood test for syphilis, once published an effective critique of the blood precipitate idea. Similarity of blood, or any other body organ or part does not in itself "prove" evolution, only that a specific design has been reused by the Creator, often because it works perfectly well and therefore there is no need to modify it. A survey of older biology texts, those published before 1950, found this test often was mentioned, but biology and evolution texts published in the 1990s rarely, or never, mention this now totally discredited idea.

Vestigial Organ Homology

Another branch of comparative anatomy studies structures (in humans and other so-called "higher" forms of life) once believed by evolutionists to be the remains of structures required or useful in less-evolved, less-complex ancestral forms, but that now are no longer necessary. In this case, the homologous organ in the more- advanced animal is *less*-developed or even useless. Such homologous structures or organs are referred to as *vestigial*. Most examples are assumed remnants resulting from the loss of an earlier, more-developed structure.

Evolutionists used to proudly point to over a hundred such structures in humans, but the number has decreased consistently as anatomical knowledge increased. Today, only a couple of examples usually are mentioned, and there is no doubt that even the few examples

---

[226] Davidheiser, 1969, p. 273.

usually mentioned are useful and not vestigial. As Howitt[227] noted, the celebrated German anatomist Wiedersheim listed over 100 vestigial organs in the human body, but it has been found with increased knowledge that every one of them has an important function.

Most anatomists now hesitate to label *any* organ vestigial, especially since medical research has shown that *every* human body organ has at least some function, even though the full purpose of a few structures is not fully clear yet. The functions of a few organs once thought as vestigial are presently viewed as minor, or as serving in a back-up capacity.[228] Sir Arthur Keith[229] noted over a half-century ago that, as our knowledge of anatomy increased, the number of vestigial organs has decreased.

Moreover, even if some vestigial organs can be proven to exist, they provide support, not for evolution, but for *devolution* – i.e., evolution-in-reverse. What the evolutionists must demonstrate is that the development of *new and useful organs* is occurring today. Instead of trying to document that once-useful organs now are useless they also must prove that *a process* exists that can form new structures called **nascent organs**. Evidence for the development of new organs, or those in the process of evolving, would be a critical proof of evolution. As of now, no evidence of *any* nascent organ exists.

Summary

A recent summary of the evidence from homology concluded it "is an idealized principle that works under idealized conditions, but such conditions almost never apply."[230] Aboitiz even recommended evolutionary considerations should be considered as secondary.

---

[227] Howitt, 1970, p. 27.
[228] Scadding, 1981; Bergman and Howe, 1990.
[229] Keith, 1915.
[230] Tautz, 1998, p. 17.

What matters are the processes that create a body
plan, and not whether a shared plan implies the same
ancestry. *Under this perspective, perhaps a return to
the pre-Darwinian concept of homology* will be more
useful to biologists... [and the term homology] would
not be restricted to the discipline of morphology, and
should not be used in molecular biology.[231]

The current state of homology as evidence for evolution was
summed up by one biologist as follows:

The detection of homologies is the central endeavor
of comparative anatomy. They form the basis for
the reconstruction of phylogenetic history with
morphological methods. Homology is thus the central
concept of comparative anatomy, but its importance
for evolutionary biology is still in question. The
opinions range from a complete denial of its existence
to skepticism regarding its biological content and
to the view that homology is a fundamental and
interesting biological problem, which will find a
mechanistic explanation in developmental biology.
However, no satisfactory biological homology concept
has been proposed so far.[232]

Arguing that the complex came from the simple by comparative
morphology is not unlike ranking types and sizes of living abodes and
assuming that mansions evolved from doghouses via shacks, cottages,
and duplexes solely because of their gross superficial resemblance. The
argument from homology was answered almost three-quarters-of-a-
century ago by reasoning still fully valid today, concluding organ and
structure similarity

---

[231] Aboitiz, 1988, p. 28; emphasis added.
[232] Wagner, 1989, pp. 1157-1171; references in original not included in quote.

does not reveal origins. If we see houses of different sizes, built of exactly the same material, we do not say that the larger grew out of the smaller; we say that the same architect planned them all. Why deny to God the credit for originating species – at least, until one species can be traced to another?[233]

Our ability to reason, to determine right and wrong, to live according to a conscience, to exercise domination over plants and animals, to enjoy music and art, and to worship the Creator are only a small part of the enormous chasm that separates humans from *every other living creature*. Hypotheses used by evolutionists to support their naturalistic theory have been repeatedly proven wrong by advancing knowledge.

Unproved and unprovable, naturalistic evolution requires a belief in comparative anatomy that proves nothing, in embryological evidence now disproved, in nascent organs never discovered after two centuries of searching, and in scores of useless vestigial organs discovered to be quite useful. The history of the continual retreats of evolutionary arguments should force all persons to look critically at the current homology arguments, and other evidence, that in all likelihood soon will be relegated to the long history of erroneous ideas.

Why, then, do most scientists accept macroevolution theory? A major reason is because it is now the accepted worldview of scientists— an idea to which they are exposed from the earliest days of their education, and in which they are surrounded daily. Most scientists are influenced by social pressure, and many believers fear recriminations from their fellow scientists if they do not conform to what currently is viewed as correct. To prove their orthodoxy, many scientists have become unscientific and have embraced the religion of twentieth-century naturalism.[234] Belief in evolutionism requires a credulity induced partly by pressure to conform to a world of 'science' that is saturated with naturalism.

---

[233] Bryan, 1924, p. 130.
[234] See Johnson, 1993.

References

Aboitiz, Franscisco. 1988. "Homology: A Comparative or a Historical Concept?" *Acta Biotheoretica* 37(1):27-29.

Audesirk, Teresa, and Gerald Audesirk. 1999. *Biology: Life on Earth.* Upper Saddle River, NJ: Prentice Hall.

Barr, Stephen M. 1997. "Untangling Evolution." *First Things* 78, December, pp. 15-16.

Bergman, Jerry, and George Howe. 1990. *Vestigial Organs are Fully Functional.* Terre Haute, IN: Creation Research Books.

Berra, Tim. 1990. *Evolution and the Myth of Creationism.* Stanford, CA: Stanford University Press.

Berry, R.J., and A. Hallam. 1987. *The Encyclopedia of Animal Evolution.* New York, NY: Facts on File.

Boyden, Alan. 1947. "Homology and Analogy: A Critical Review of the Meaning and Implications of these Concepts in Biology." *The American Midland Naturalist* 37(3):648-669, May.

Brown, Arthur I. 1947. *Was Darwin Right?* Glendale CA: Glendale News.

Bryan, William J. 1924. *Seven Questions in Dispute.* New York, NY: Fleming H. Revell Co.

Cannatella, David. 1997. Review of *Homology* (1994), B.K. Hall, ed., and *Homoplasy* (1996), M.J., Sanderson and L. Hufford, eds. *Systematic Biology* 46(369):366-369.

Conklin, Edwin Grant. 1928. "Embryology and Evolution." In Mason, Frances. *Creation by Evolution.* New York, NY: Macmillan Publishers.

Darwin, Charles. 1872. *The Origin of Species, 6th Ed.* London, UK: John Murray.

Davidheiser, Bolton. 1969. *Evolution and the Christian Faith.* Nutley, NJ: The Presbyterian and Reformed Publishing Company.

Dawkins, Richard. 1996. *Climbing Mount Improbable.* New York, NY: W.W. Norton & Co.

Dobzhansky, Theodosius. 1959. *Evolution: Genetics and Man.* New York, NY: John Wiley & Sons.

de Beer, Sir Gavin. 1971. *Homology: An Unsolved Problem.* London, UK: Oxford University Press.

Denton, Michael. 1986. *Evolution: A Theory in Crisis.* Bethesda, MD: Adler and Adler.

Fisher, Helen E. 1982. *The Sex Contract.* New York, NY: William Morrow and Company.

Frazier, Ralph, and Herbert Smith. 1974. *The Biological Sciences: Investigating Man's Environment.* River Forrest, IL: Laidlaw Brothers.

Gould, Stephen J. 1988. "The Heart of Terminology." *Natural History* 97(2):24-31.

Hall, B.K. 1994. *Homology: The Hierarchical Basis of Comparative Biology.* New York, NY: Academic Press.

Hickman, Cleveland, Larry Roberts, and Allan Larson. 1996. *Integrated Principles of Zoology.* Dubuque, IA: William C. Brown.

Hoagland, Mahlon, and Bert Dodson. 1995. *The Way Life Works.* New York, NY: Random House.

Hooton, Earnest. 1931. *Up from the Ape.* New York, NY: Macmillan and Co.

Howitt, John. 1970. *Evolution: Science Falsely So-Called.* Toronto, Canada: Christian Crusade.

Johnson, Phillip. 1993. "Science Without God." *Wall Street Journal,* May 10, p. A10.

Jones, A.J. 1982. "A Creationist Critique of Homology." *CRSQ* 19(3):156-175.

Keith, Sir Arthur. 1915. *The Antiquity of Man.* London, UK: Williams and Norgate.

_____. 1928. *Concerning Man's Origin.* New York, NY: G.P. Putnam's Sons.

Kimball, John. 1965. *Biology.* Reading, MA: Addison-Wesley Publishing Company.

Kroeber, Elizabeth, Walter Wolff, and Richard Weaver. 1969. *Biology.* Lexington, MA: D.C. Heath Co.

McFadden, Carol, and William Keeton. 1995. *Biology: An Exploration of Life.* New York, NY: W.W. Norton & Company.

Milner, Richard. 1990. *The Encyclopedia of Evolution.* New York, NY: Facts on File.

Milton, Richard. 1997. *Shattering the Myths of Darwinism.* Rochester, VT: Park Street Press.

Moon, Truman, James Otto, and Albert Towle. 1963. *Modern Biology.* New York, NY: Holt, Rinehart and Winston.

Nye, Bill. 2014. *Undeniable: Evolution and the Science of Creation.* New York, NY: Saint Martin's Press

Prescott, Lansing, John Harley, and Donald Klein. 1990. *Microbiology.* Dubuque, IA:William C. Brown.

Raff, Rudolf A., and Thomas C. Kaufman. 1983. *Embryos, Genes, and Evolution*. New York, NY: Macmillan Publishers.

Roth, V. Louise. 1988. "The Biological Basis of Homology." In *Ontogeny and Systematics*, ed. by C.J. Humphrey. New York, NY: Columbia University Press, pp. 1-26.

Sattler, R. 1984. "Homology -- A continuing challenge." *Systematic Botany* 9(4): 382-394, December 1.

Scadding, S.R. 1981. "Do Vestigial Organs Provide Evidence for Evolution?" *Evolutionary Theory* 5:173-176.

Tautz, Diethard. 1998. "Debatable Homologies." *Nature* 395:17-19, September 3.

Wagner, G.P. 1989. "The Origin of Morphological Characters and the Biological Basis of Homology." *Evolution* 43(6):1,157-1,171.

Wellhouse, Walter, and George Hendrickson. 1928. *A Brief Course in Biology*. New York, NY: Macmillan Publishers.

Wells, Jonathan, and Paul Nelson. 1997. "Homology: A Concept in Crisis." *Origins and Design* 18(2):12-18, Fall.

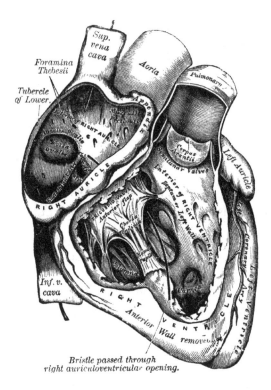

Foramina Thebesii

Tubercle of Lower.

Sup. vena cava

Aorta

Pulmonary

Left Auricle

RIGHT AURICLE

Appendix

Corpus Arantii

Semilunar Valve

Anterior of RIGHT VENTRICLE

Septum. Left Wall

Anterior Flap

Chordæ

Inf. v. cava

RIGHT VENTRICLE

Anterior Wall removed

Coronary left Ventricle

Bristle passed through right auriculoventricular opening.

THE HUMAN HEART FROM *GRAY'S ANATOMY* DEPICTING THE FOUR CHAMBERS AND THE VENTRICULAR SEPTUM. DRAWN BY HENRY GRAY (1825-1861). *ANATOMY OF THE HUMAN BODY*. FROM *GRAY'S ANATOMY* 1901 LEA BROTHERS & COMPANY PHILADELPHIA, PA P 552. THE HEART IS REQUIRED FOR VERTEBRATE LIFE, THUS IS AN EXAMPLE OF IRREDUCIBLE COMPLEXITY. ALTHOUGH AN ARTIFICIAL HEART CAN SUBSTITUTE FOR A SHORT TIME, THIS FACT DOES NOT MAKE A HEART UNNECESSARY.

CHAPTER 4

Irreducible Complexity:
A Major Problem for Darwinism

Introduction

The Irreducible Complexity concept has become central to the intelligent design-evolution controversy.[235] Irreducible complexity is defined as a functional system or entity that "contains a multipart subsystem (i.e., a set of two or more interrelated parts) that cannot be simplified without destroying the system's basic function."[236] This basic concept has been discussed using other terms long before Darwin.[237] Both intelligent design and irreducible complexity are not new ideas, but were used as far back as "Plato, Aquinas, and Paley" to argue for an intelligent creator of life.[238] Stanford biologist M. Trotter and his peers wrote that the "existence of complex (multiple-step) genetic adaptations that are 'irreducible' (i.e., all partial combinations are less fit than the original genotype) is one of the longest standing problems in evolutionary biology. In standard genetics parlance, these

---

[235] Boudry, et al., 2010; Braun, 2005; Behe, 1996; Miller, 1999; Miller, 2008.
[236] Dembski, 2004, p. 2; Ruse, 2003.
[237] Bartlett, 2010, p. 1.
[238] Ruse, 2007, p. 38.

adaptations require the crossing of a wide adaptive valley of deleterious intermediate stages.[239]

Efforts by Evolutionists to Refute it

Typical of efforts to refute the concept is the following:[240]

> This argument is basically a modern version of the long-since-debunked watchmaker argument, promoted two centuries ago by William Paley (1803). The idea is equivalent to saying that you can't have a watch without a watchmaker. But the argument as applied to biological systems has repeatedly been shown to be inapplicable. Yet irreducible complexity proponents maintain that the universe—and life itself—has this characteristic. They say that such wondrous and inexplicable things just could not have evolved over millions of years. Actually, for every biological example they adduce, biologists can explain how the system is not, in fact, irreducibly complex.

He concluded:

> In short, intelligent design takes the clearly antiscientific attitude that if we can't immediately explain something, we should give up trying to understand it and just attribute it to a "designer." Basically, all gaps in our knowledge would simply be filled by God. That approach would immediately put a stop to the scientific enterprise and the acquisition of new knowledge.

---

[239] Trotter, 2013, p. 2.
[240] Bobrowsky, 2006, pp.107-108.

As we will show, irreducible complexity has been carefully documented in the scientific literature. Furthermore, irreducible complexity is commonly described, or referred to, in the scientific literature on life, although often using terms other than 'irreducible complexity.' For example, one study, after noting some of the problems with evolution, discussed "genomics and the irreducible nature of eukaryote cells."[241] Another example is the common expression "the whole is greater than the sum of its parts."

The famous French naturalist Georges Cuvier discussed the requirement that just as a clock requires many parts that must be organized in a specific way to be functional, likewise certain biological structures must exist for life to be alive.[242] Darwin's major critic, George Mivart, also used a form of the irreducible complexity concept to argue against Darwinian evolution. Mivart discussed this concept in detail in a chapter titled "The Incompetence of Natural Selection" in his book, *On the Genesis of Species*. He argued in this chapter that body organs, such as the heart, could not function until the required set of parts first were constructed, and then properly assembled. Consequently, the heart is irreducibly complex.[243]

It was recognized centuries ago that damage to a single organ, such as the heart, could cause an animal's death. Thus, that organ was seen as required for life and was part of the irreducible complexity of that life-form. The military learned early that the reason certain body injuries are lethal is due to irreducible complexity. Sword wounds to certain body parts, such as the chest, are far more apt to be lethal than those to other parts, such as limbs.

The realization that certain organs were critical for life was reinforced as knowledge of anatomy increased. Early arguments for a creator, such as Paley's watchmaker theory, and later arguments against Darwinism, often focused on body anatomy's irreducible

---

[241] Kurland, et al., 2006, p. 1,011.
[242] Cuvier, 1834, p. 7.
[243] Mivart, 1871, pp. 19-85.

complexity. Even modern functional mechanical prosthetics are irreducibly complex.

Only recently have the cell, and even "simple" life-forms, been understood to possess a high level of complexity. Before this realization, scientists believed that some forms of life were quite simple in their composition. A famous example of this is a primitive "life-form" called *Bathybius haeckelii* that was discovered in the 1870s. The genus name of the new life-form came from its oceanic habitat and its species name after the leading champion of Darwinism, German biologist Ernst Haeckel.[244]

This putative non-cellular "organism" consisted of soft gelatinous matter discovered in North Atlantic Ocean sediment.[245] Although widely accepted by many leading scientists for several decades, this putative life-form was proven to be nothing more than rock formations or organic precipitates. The find was accepted as valid because it was widely believed simple life-forms were only slightly more complex than many common organic compounds, such as organic tar.

Darwin also believed that the cell was a simple structure and, consequently, its spontaneous generation was not viewed as a major impediment to his evolutionary theory. The recent cell biology and genetics revolution has forced the realization that all cells, including prokaryote cells, are among the most complex machines in the known universe. Scientist Mark Taylor noted that life is "endlessly complex" and, as a result, it is not "surprising that neo-Darwinism has provoked strong critical reactions from a variety of perspectives," and some "of the most thoughtful challenges to Darwinism have grown out of recent work done in complexity studies."[246]

The cell signaling system alone is "infinitely more complex" than believed just a few years ago, and "the more biologists look, the more complexity" they discover in life.[247] Quoting Cambridge structural

---

[244] Rehbock, 1975, p. 504.
[245] Rehbock, 1975, p. 504.
[246] Taylor, 2001, pp. 3, 182.
[247] Schnabel, 2010, pp. 664-665.

biologist Chris Dobson, Schnabel wrote: "Most modern proteins fold into globular structures. But their folding patterns are so complex that they couldn't have evolved by accident. ...If you had a machine that could generate protein sequences randomly, you would only rarely get one that can remain stable in the globular, soluble state."[248]

Complexity and Intelligent Design

Since a living cell is the most complex machine in the known universe, a more relevant mechanical example will here be used to explain irreducible complexity (IC), namely Philo Farnsworth's television invention. The history of the television's invention illustrates this system is useless until *every* central component has been invented and perfected to at least the minimum level required to function, which Farnsworth spent much of his life working toward achieving.[249]

The original first working television system *must* have a functional camera, a way of converting light variations into electrical signal variations, a method of broadcasting the signal into the atmosphere, a transmission-receiver system to pick up the signal, and a method to convert the broadcast signal into an electron gun signal in a cathode ray tube so as to paint the picture onto a fluorescent screen. Likewise, life requires a certain level of complexity before it can be alive—and until life is alive, the physiology required to live, including respiration and reproduction, cannot occur.

The enormous complexity of the cell, and the realization that a certain level of complexity is required for it to function, was a major impetus behind the growth of the modern intelligent design movement.[250] This realization has challenged what Darwin acknowledged was a critical problem with his theory: "If it could be demonstrated that any complex organ existed, which could not possibly

---

[248] Schnabel, 2010, p. 829.
[249] Stashower, 2002.
[250] Meyer, 2009.

have been formed by numerous, successive, slight modifications, my theory would absolutely break down."²⁵¹ Darwin's challenge, which he felt could eventually be solved, indicates that he believed irreducible complexity is falsifiable.

Oxford University Professor Richard Dawkins also argued that the irreducible complexity concept is falsifiable, and has been falsified because, he firmly believed, the origin of all life can be fully explained by evolution. Dawkins reasoned merely postulating a natural sequence of events that can produce an organ or structure falsifies the irreducible complexity claim for that structure. What has been called the "ancient 'Argument from Design,' also called the 'Argument from Paley's Watchmaker,' or the 'Argument from Irreducible Complexity,'" Dawkins called "the 'Argument from Personal Incredulity.'" But postulating some scenario to explain IC does not disprove irreducible complexity, only empirical evidence does. Likewise, even if Dawkins could "imagine a natural sequence of events whereby X could have come about," that does not prove it originated by natural means.²⁵² This is an example where one can accept a belief even if evidence for the belief does not exist! [Just ask Linus about the Great Pumpkin!]

To falsify the irreducible complexity concept itself requires falsification of *all possible examples* of irreducible complexity, an impossible task. Dawkins concluded that "the bacterial flagellar motor ... has recently ... been elevated to the status of icon," in support of the view that it could not have evolved. He responds dogmatically, because "it manifestly exists," it *must* have evolved because only materialist explanations are allowed in science.²⁵³ This is arrogant dogma, not empirical science.

However, he accepted the idea of "unevolvability as an explanation for why large animals like mammals don't grow wheels," and other impossible designs. In other words, Dawkins assumes *a priori* that naturalism accounts for all life, and for this reason irreducible

²⁵¹ Darwin, 1859, p. 189.
²⁵² Dawkins, 2004, p. 549.
²⁵³ Dawkins, 2004, p. 549.

complexity is an *invalid* argument to explain any structure that exists in the living world, but is a valid explanation for structures that do *not* exist. The reason, he concludes, is because he recognizes that irreducible complexity precludes Darwinism, and if a structure was irreducibly complex, it could not have evolved.

Why the Irreducible Complexity Concept is Important to Intelligent Design

Intelligent design theory is the conclusion that evidence for intelligence can be scientifically detected in life. To understand why the irreducible complexity concept is important in intelligent design theory, it is necessary to review scientists' current views of evolution. The standard evolution theory postulates that multi-molecular mechanisms, such as human legs, evolved by the

> progressive accretion of ancillary proteins onto some rudiment or foundation that is functionally useful but need not have been an organ of motility. This amplification took place, one gene at a time, under the guidance of natural selection: each modification conferred at least a small selective benefit.[254]

Although scientists can mentally "construct schemes that sound plausible" which could in principle account for the origins of "motility, mitosis or the secretory pathway," they "have no better alternative to offer ... and in the absence of time travel we may never discover what actually happened" in evolutionary history.[255] It is clear that design exists in the natural world, and evolution must account for this design in order to replace creationism.[256] The cell is a large collection of many

---

[254] Harold, 2001, p. 204.
[255] Harold, 2001, pp. 204-205.
[256] French, 1988, pp. 1-19.

hundreds of thousands of different complex protein machines, such as the RNA polymerase complex, ATP synthase, helicase, and the flagellar system, all of which must be accounted for by evolution from the small steps which evolution requires.[257]

Molecular biochemist Abigail Clements, et al., noted "Molecular machines drive essential biology processes, from protein synthesis and transport to genome maintenance, expression and inheritance."[258] Intelligent design supporters conclude that all molecular machines that must consist of two or more parts to function are irreducibly complex. All of these parts must be present as a matched and integrated set, and then properly assembled for the machine to function properly. By definition, if even only one of the required parts is missing, the machine will be non-functional.

Intelligent Design argues that evolution, which must occur in a stepwise fashion over a long period of time, cannot produce these complex machines for several reasons. One reason is that evolution is not goal-oriented, thus it cannot work towards a specific outcome. If a part of a machine happens to form as a result of mutations, all the parts the machine requires must also *concurrently* exist and be properly assembled in order for the machine to function.

Why a Set of Parts Must First Exist

Organisms containing parts that by themselves are non-functional, would result in many wasted resources. The organism would not only *not* have a selective advantage over other organisms, but in fact would be plagued with a handicap. A single part alone usually offers no advantage to an organism and even results in a lower level of efficiency due to making and recycling the part. For this reason, the part would tend to be lost from the population and evolution would be back to square one in forming the set of parts required for the new machine.

---

[257] Williams, 2007, pp. 109-115.
[258] Clements, et al., 2009, p. 15,791.

In other words, producing parts that are potentially useful, or could be useful, would not confer a selective advantage until the part was pragmatically beneficial as part of another whole functional system that conferred a selective advantage for the organism. There is no known way to store parts over time, such as an inventor might do, with the expectation that some part may come in handy someday. Functionless individual parts will not confer a survival advantage to the organism, and therefore will be recycled.

All required parts must be present *and properly assembled* for a machine to be functional. It must also convey a survival advantage for evolution to favor by selection (the co-option argument will be discussed in the next chapter). In all life, each part, as well as the entire machine, has the appearance of design.[259] This is the reason why the "origin of complex biological structures has always been a subject of interest and debate" in evolution.[260]

A number of researchers have concluded that irreducible complexity exists, but that some organizing principle other than 'intelligent design' causes "irreducible complexity" and current versions of complexity theory, such as that by Stuart Kauffman, do not provide the solution for its origin. What is needed is "insight and, more importantly, evidence."[261]

Furthermore, the "difference between life and non-life is a matter not of substance, but of *information*. Living things contain prodigious quantities of information. Most of the information is digitally coded in DNA, and there is also a substantial quantity [of information] coded in other ways."[262] The only known empirically documented source of information is intelligence.[263] Michael Polanyi, a Hungarian polymath who made major contributions to physical chemistry, also argued that both the mechanisms and information in DNA is irreducibly complex,

---

[259] Alberts, 1998, p. 291.
[260] Gregory, 2008, p. 338.
[261] DeRosa, 2004, p. 14.
[262] Dawkins, 2010, p. 405.
[263] Meyer, 2009; Collier, 2003.

and that this is a major problem for Darwinism.[264] The work of Polanyi, in turn, has influenced Michael Behe.

The Work of Michael Behe

Lehigh University biochemistry professor Michael Behe, in his best-selling 1996 book *Darwin's Black Box,* illustrated the enormous difficulties in explaining the evolution of the thousands of nanomachines and complex systems that living cells require by gradualistic mechanisms through the natural selection of phenotypic variations caused by mutations. Behe has documented that, in order for both living and non-living things to function, a certain minimum number of parts are always necessary. As Professor Bruce Weber opined, "Behe raises some interesting and important questions."[265]

Behe used the term *irreducible complexity* to describe his concept related to the biomolecules and other parts, such as minerals, necessary to produce the many thousands of complex machines required for life. Removal of one part beyond the minimum set or number required, and the machine (or organism) will no longer function properly—or will often not function at all.[266]

The example that Behe used to illustrate his irreducible complexity concept is the common household mousetrap, a machine that will not function unless it has a certain minimum number of properly assembled parts.[267] If it has fewer than this required minimum number of parts, it does not just catch mice less well, it does not catch *any* mice.[268] The independent parts function properly *only* within the entire functional unit, producing the reality Aristotle referred to as the "whole is greater than the sum of its parts."[269]

---

[264] Polanyi, 1968, pp. 1,308-1,312.
[265] Weber, 1999, p. 563.
[266] Behe, 2005, p. 33.
[267] Brosh, 2008, pp. 453-454.
[268] Behe, 2005, p. 34.
[269] Aristotle, p. 248.

Furthermore, the mousetrap cannot use just any part, but only specific parts that properly function within the machine to enable it to work as a unit. For example, a spring from a

> windup watch or toy car would be useless in a standard mousetrap. In fact, the spring in a mousetrap is essentially unique. Its length is critical to its role in the trap. If there were somewhat fewer or more coils, the ends of the spring would not be positioned correctly. The ends of the springs themselves are not coiled; rather, they're extended. One end presses against the wooden platform and the other oddly shaped end hooks over the hammer—the part of the trap that strikes the mouse. The positioning of both ends is crucial to the work of the spring. If either end was at a somewhat different angle coming off the main body of the spring, the trap would be ineffective. If either end was substantially longer or shorter, the system would again be compromised. It's clear that not only the whole trap, but also the spring and other pieces required multiple, coherent steps to produce.[270]

For this reason, Behe's definition of irreducible complexity included the requirement that all of the parts must be "well-matched, interacting parts that contribute to the basic function."[271] In other words, the entire machine must be well designed for a specific purpose.

Given this problem, it follows that the gradual evolution of living organisms is impossible. A life-form cannot exist unless—and until— it has a certain minimum number of parts to exist and reproduce. Reproduction is required in order for natural selection, thus evolution, to function. Therefore, it can be seen that the "minimum number of parts" found in the life-form must exist **before** evolution can begin to

---

[270] Behe, 2007, pp. 120-121.
[271] Behe, 2007, p. 120.

work! Examples Behe and others list of biological irreducible complexity include the blood clotting system, all enzymes and hormones, both the innate and adaptive immune system, the cell ubiquitin system, apoptosis, the cell signal transduction system, the cell telomere-telomerase system, DNA, RNA, transcription and translation, plus hundreds of others.[272]

The History of the Term

Before Behe, the term *irreducible complexity* was used by other researchers in a variety of academic disciplines. For example, Michael Katz, who is described on his book's back cover as having a "deep knowledge of biological processes" used the term to refer to structures in the natural world that cannot be "reduced to smaller or less intricate predecessor components" and still function. One example he provided is the human figure, which is "an example of a pattern-assembly system that is irreducibly complex."[273] He added a "creative act is characterized by its irreducible complexity."[274] Katz also used the term "intractably complex" to describe the same concept.[275]

After evaluating Behe's arguments, Neil DeRosa concluded that one of "Behe's strongest arguments in support of his thesis is that there are very few scientific papers published which explain how evolution works on a molecular level" to build complex irreducibly complex structures from simple irreducibly complex structures. Existing scientific papers that attempt to explain how evolution works at the molecular level are unconvincing. A survey of the papers published by the *Journal of Molecular Evolution* finds that not one paper has ever explained in detail how a complex biochemical system could have

[272] Behe, 1996, 2007.
[273] Katz, 1986, p. 27.
[274] Katz, 1986, p. 97.
[275] Katz, 1986, p. 87.

been produced by a gradual, step-by-step Darwinian fashion due to the natural selection of mutations.[276]

The "fact that none of these questions have been addressed, or solved, indicates the current lack of understanding of how biochemical systems evolved."[277] Nobel Laureate Francis Crick wrote that one reason for this state of affairs is

> it might be thought... that evolutionary arguments would play a large part in guiding biological research, but this is far from the case. It is difficult enough to study what is happening now. To try to figure out exactly what happened in evolution is even more difficult. Thus evolutionary arguments can usefully be used as *hints* to suggest possible lines of research, but it is highly dangerous to trust them too much.[278]

The New Research Problem

New discoveries in biochemical and cell biology research have compounded the irreducible complexity problem enormously. As a result, despite "imaginative but dubious efforts of Darwin fans over the past decade, it's extremely difficult to see how something like a mousetrap could actually evolve by something akin to a blind Darwinian search process."[279] A more accurate comparison of mousetraps to living cells is "an automated mousetrap factory that assembled the parts of the trap, set it, and reset the trap each time it went off. Clearly, the complexity of such a system is much greater than the complexity of the mousetrap alone."[280]

---

[276] Behe, 1996, p. 176.
[277] DeRosa, 2004, p. 14.
[278] Crick, 1988, pp. 138-139.
[279] Behe, 2007, p. 94.
[280] Behe, 2007, p. 94.

The odds against "winning the lottery" skyrocket as the number of parts required to fit into the system increases. Likewise, the difficulty of explaining how a mousetrap-making system could arise by Darwin's "numerous, successive, slight modifications" rises exponentially the more separate part types and numbers the system requires in order to function.[281]

Behe extended his irreducibly complex arguments in his 2007 book, noting that, as the number of parts increases, the probability of obtaining an irreducibly complex system exponentially decreases. One problem is that the "more pieces, and the more intricately they interact, the more opportunities there are to go wrong in building a system. Even with small systems, one can go wrong right off the bat, get trapped in a dead end, and never make it to the top of the castle."[282]

The Intraflagellar Transport System

One example of a highly and irreducibly complex system that is difficult to explain by neo-Darwinism is the intraflagellar transport system. This cellular system is essential for the formation and maintenance of both eukaryotic cilia and flagella. First discovered in 1993 by Keith Kozminski in the lab of Joel Rosenbaum at Yale University, this phylogenetically well-conserved complex system exists in the cilia and flagella of most known animal species, both extant and extinct.

The fact that the intraflagellar transport system is genetically very similar in both primitive and advanced eukaryotes is clear evidence of an irreducibly complex system that could not have evolved. If a significantly simpler functional system could have existed, it would exist in at least some life-forms, such as single cell life-forms, but it does not.

Careful "experimental work with all ciliated cells that have been examined… from algae to mice" has found that a "functioning cilium

---

[281] Behe,,, 2007, p. 94.

[282] Behe, 2007, p. 122.

requires a working intraflagellar transport. The problem of the origin of the cilium is ... intimately connected to the problem of the origin of intraflagellar transport. Before its discovery we could be forgiven for overlooking the problem of how a cilium was built."[283]

Biologists Acknowledge the Problem

Biologists can no longer vaguely dismiss the problem of irreducible complexity by claiming proteins effectively fold into the correct conformation alone and function properly in the cell without guidance. They must now acknowledge irreducible complexity presents a major problem for evolution.[284] The intraflagellar transport (IFT) problem is one example which has disproved the once common claim that abiogenesis is not problematic because the cell is a simple structure. The more we learn about life, the more complexity we see, and the level of irreducible complexity becomes more apparent. Only a century ago scientists thought that life could commonly originate spontaneously, and only a few decades ago many cell biologists believed that

> it was probably easy to put a cilium together; the pieces could probably just go together on their own. But now that the elegant complexity of IFT has been uncovered, we can ignore the question no longer ... Although Brown University biologist Kenneth Miller argued in response that the two-hundred component cilium is not really irreducibly complex, he offered no Darwinian explanation of the step-by-step origin of the cilium ... An updated search of the science journals ... shows no serious progress on a Darwinian explanation for the ultracomplex cilium.[285]

---

[283] Behe, 2007, pp. 120-121.
[284] Behe, 2007, pp. 120-121.
[285] Behe, 2007, pp. 94-95.

Behe concluded that, despite the enormous advances of "molecular biology as a whole, despite the sequencing of hundreds of entire genomes and other leaps in knowledge ... in the more than ten years since I pointed it out, the situation concerning missing Darwinian explanations for the evolution of the cilium is utterly unchanged."[286] The research progress of the last decade in cell biology has documented that the problem is even much worse than Behe claimed.

Irreducible Complexity Increases

Examples of such progress in cell biology research include the revolutions in epigenetics, protein folding, splicing variations that produce many gene transcripts from one gene, the ENCODE research project, revelations about the "guardian of the genome" (the p53 protein), the telomerase system, chaperone systems, histone regulation, and even recent discoveries about mitosis and meiosis functions.

Of note is that some cellular machines actually function like a mousetrap. Under the heading "Double Holliday junctions caught in the mousetrap," a gene called "BLM" produces a protein machine, the BLM complex, that "consists of several components, much like a mousetrap. With all the parts properly assembled the mousetrap will operate efficiently."[287] A DNA structure called a double Holliday junction is "caught" in the BLM complex, and a component of this complex, the RM12 structure, stabilizes and orchestrates the behavior of the BLM complex to ensure the double Holliday junction functions properly to promote chromosomal stability. [288]

---

[286] Behe, 2007, pp. 94-95.
[287] Brosh, 2008, p. 454.
[288] Brosh, 2008, p. 454.

Irreducible Complexity Levels

Irreducible Complexity (as a concept) can be divided into several levels. The most basic level is the *irreducible core*, the part of the system that, if one part were removed, the entire system could no longer function.[289] For example, in a clock, all of the parts necessary to keep time at the required accuracy level are the irreducible core. To be functional, a clock must tell the time within certain limits of accuracy—and beyond these limits it increasingly gives wrong information, which may make it worse than useless.

The non-core parts may include the crystal, the second hand, and the clock case. The core components required depend on the demands placed on the watch. If the watch is used to accurately time a foot race, the second hand would be part of the core required for the clock's specified function. If a watch was designed to be used in damp environments, the crystal and case design would become part of the core.

The basic function of any system consists of three elements: (1) what the system does in its natural setting or proper context, known as the system's *primary* or *main* function; (2) the minimum number of parts required for the system to perform adequately in its natural or proper setting; and (3) the manner in which the system performs its primary function, known as the system's *mode of function*. Because the basic function of a system includes its mode of function, its basic function is concerned not only with the system's *ends*, but also with its *means*.

For example, glue and nails can perform the same primary function of fastening together two parts, and do so equally well in many cases, but how they function is very different. In one situation glue may be superior, in another situation nails, and yet in other situations both may work equally well. In some structures nails may do more harm

---

[289] Dembski, 2004, p. 2.

than good, such as nailing two windowpanes together, which will often be inferior or damaging compared to using glue.[290]

Some entities, such as a city, involve *cumulative complexity*—one can remove a large number of houses and people without losing its "city-ness" but at some point, such as when only three or four families remain, it no longer has the traits we agree must exist to be labeled a city.

The Irreducible Complexity Concept in Research

The principle of Irreducible Complexity is used daily in molecular biology labs throughout the world. An example of a critically important technique that uses irreducible complexity is called *targeted gene replacements*, commonly referred to as *knockout genes*.[291] This research technique removes part of, or the entire gene, or disables a gene, and the results of its removal on the organism's functions are evaluated.[292]

This research technique is used to determine both the function of a gene and if the gene is required in order for a specific structure or system to function properly. The gene is viewed as required if its removal disables the function of one or more biological structures.

Another research technique involves removing select base pairs of a gene to determine which parts of the gene are critical, and what role each section plays in a specific gene. Yet another technique is to use mutant genes called "natural knock-out genes" to determine the function of a gene, or a gene section.

Critically important information has "been obtained from a vast number of studies of natural genetic mutations in both animals and humans, and on the targeted inactivation of a gene."[293] The results of these 'knockout' experiments are often completely unexpected,

---

[290] Dembski and Wells, 2007, p. 147.

[291] Hayden, 2010, p. 666.

[292] Old and Primrose, 1994.

[293] Morange, 2001, p. 4.

producing findings that sometimes contradict existing conclusions.[294] This fact negates Dawkin's argument that those who advocate irreducible complexity in biology

> always assume that biological adaptation is a question of the jackpot or nothing. Another name for the "jackpot or nothing" fallacy is "irreducible complexity" (ID) [here equated with Intelligent Design]. Either the eye sees or it doesn't. Either the wing flies or it doesn't. There are assumed to be no useful intermediates. But this is simply wrong. Such intermediates abound in practice—which is exactly what we should expect.[295]

As the preceding discussions document, the "jackpot or nothing" is a false analogy—the Irreducible complexity (IC) concept concludes only that a certain level of complexity is required to achieve a specific purpose, and a complexity below this level will cause the system to fail.

Minimum Requirements Necessary for Life

The simplest life-forms are single-celled animals, but many of the simplest life-forms are parasites that must live off other life-forms because they have *fewer* than the required minimum number of parts to function independently. Viruses are simpler than the simplest known cell, too simple to be classified by biologists as living. They are gene machines that transfer genes from a container (the virus protein body) into a cell, or from one cell into another cell. The viruses can reproduce *only* when their genes take over the host cell's reproduction machinery. Nonetheless, even viruses still require a minimum number of parts to function.

---

[294] Morange, 2001, p. 4.
[295] Dawkins, 2006, p. 122.

Research has determined that if a critical component of any one of the many systems required for life, such as the circulatory system, is absent or dysfunctional, the result is usually death—a fact that is a basic tenet of modern medicine.[296] Scientific articles about cell design documenting this fact now run into the millions and, to objective observers, this research renders the naturalistic evolution theory of the origin of the living cell improbable. A non-parasitic, non-viral life-form requires many billions of parts, all of which must be assembled correctly in order to function properly.

The set of parts required to construct a working cell is not unlike the parts of an automobile. The parts must as a set be functional when assembled, requiring them to fit properly with the other parts, including all necessary attachment points and functional coordination. Furthermore, all of the parts must be appropriately finished, maintained, and properly recycled or replaced when necessary. The tools that assemble the parts, such as jigs required to properly orient the parts to insure correct assembly, must all be compatible with the part set involved and its proper assembly and placement, as must the systems used to repair an automobile or a cell.

Irreducible Complexity All the Way Down

Bionanotechnology researchers have determined that irreducible complexity exists all the way down to at least the sub-molecular level. The enormity of biological complexity is gleaned when one considers the fact

> that individual living things are ordered aggregates of multiple macromolecules and supramolecular structures (potentially, billions and billions of them), belonging to distinct chemical classes (such as lipids, proteins, nucleic acids), with each individual

[296] Conn, 2006, p. 49.

macromolecule being at least as complex in structures and function [as a simple protein].[297]

Furthermore, the "irreducible complexity of biological systems is a central fact of practice in the biological sciences and drives the way biologists gather and disseminate information. It is the key informant of the culture of biologists."[298] According to chemist Susan Spitz, all atoms are irreducibly complex. She defines a chemical element as "a fundamental, essential, or irreducible constituent of a composite entity ... that cannot be reduced to simpler substances ... and that is composed of atoms having an identical number of protons in each nucleus."[299]

For example, a carbon-12 atom requires 6 protons, 6 neutrons, and 6 electrons. One less of any of these required particles and there is no longer a carbon-12 atom. Remove or add an electron, and an ion always results. Remove a proton, and a boron atom always results. Remove a neutron, and a carbon-11 isotope always results.

Some claim that this example is falsified when carbon is covalently bonded, such as in carbon dioxide. The example of irreducible complexity used was a carbon *atom*, not the *molecular compound* CO_2. Nonetheless, CO_2 itself is also an irreducibly complex structure because only one way exists to obtain CO_2 of a given isotope. A water molecule can use one of three types of hydrogen: protium (the most common type), deuterium (heavy water), or tritium (radioactive water). Each type of water is irreducibly complex.

It should be noted that ingestion of high levels of deuterium has been shown to contribute to disease, specifically cancer.[300] Evidence also exists that replacement of the daily fluid intake of cancer patients with deuterium depleted water exerts anticancer effects. Furthermore, chemical compounds can self-assemble only because of the inbuilt set

---

[297] Bhushan, 2007, p. 497.
[298] Bhushan, 2007, p. 497.
[299] Spitz, 2007, p. 172.
[300] Gyöngyi, et al., 2013; Kovács, et al., 2011.

of atomic forces, such as the charge pattern and three-dimensional structure and morphology of the individual elements.

Given the definition that *anything* requiring two or more parts to function properly is irreducibly complex, only units that require a *single quark* or lepton (the fundamental units of matter) are *not* irreducibly complex, but if quarks are confirmed to contain sub-quark particles, even this statement is not true.

Paley used this fact as evidence for an Intelligent Designer in the 1800s. Chemical elements can be produced naturally, given gravity, the electromagnetic force, and the strong and weak nuclear forces requirements. However, the question of whether irreducible complexity can evolve by natural means is a separate issue which must be evaluated once something is determined to be irreducibly complex. For this reason, given the above definition of irreducible complexity, the *only* way to refute the concept is to demonstrate, for example, that all of the properties of a fully functional eye or ear can be achieved by a single quark or lepton—or that all of the properties of an intelligent human, including the ability to reproduce with other humans, can be achieved by a single quark.

Objections to the Irreducible Complexity Concept

Critics have tried to refute the mousetrap example by noting that if one discards the base and fastens the remaining parts to the floor, the mousetrap will still function. Michael Ruse argues "Behe's example of a mousetrap is somewhat unfortunate, for it is simply not the case that the trap will work only with all five pieces in place. For a start, one could reduce the number to four by removing the base and fixing the trap to the floor."[301]

The problem with this claim is the floor now serves as the base, which is still required as a frame to which the parts must be fastened

---

[301] Ruse, 2003, p. 315.

for the system to function. Furthermore, even if the number of parts can be reduced by one part does not falsify the concept—it is falsified *only* if the machine can be reduced to a *single* part, such as a single quark or electron. If the minimum requirement is assumed to be five parts, and it is shown only four are actually required, then the five parts minimum conclusion is incorrect, not the irreducible complexity concept.

Often removing a part or two results in the unit not functioning as well, but even if it does work as well, this only means that the number of parts required to function at some level is one less than previously assumed. It is still irreducibly complex because a minimum number of parts is still required for it to function at some level. Weber concludes that simply because fewer parts can be shown to be required for a structure to function, such as the bacteria flagellum, this "does not obviate the problem of the emergence of the flagellum."[302]

Others argue that simple contrivances, such as holes in the ground, can also catch mice. Holes in the ground, though, cannot function as a conventional house mousetrap, nor are holes very effective in retaining mice—mice can often crawl, or dig, their way out of holes. Furthermore, to continue Behe's analogy, a hole in the ground is not an evolutionary path to a household mechanical mousetrap because holes require a very different design than a mousetrap. The hole would have to be filled in before starting over to build a better mousetrap, allowing the mice to temporarily flourish, ruling out this path.

Another example used to discredit the mousetrap illustration is a "splotch of glue can catch a mouse." Behe notes, however that it likewise "can't be turned into a mechanical trap. If the glue trap had to be discarded before starting over to make a mechanical trap, we'd be worse off than before."[303]

As noted, given the definition above, to falsify the concept it must be demonstrated that a fully functional machine or organism can

---

[302] Weber, 1999, p. 595.
[303] Behe, 2007, p. 122.

function, not with one fewer part—but with only a *single* part. Until then, the idea of irreducible complexity is valid, even if the number of parts for most factory-made machines or life systems can be reduced by one or a few parts and still function properly.

Other Criticisms of the Concept

Ever since Professor Behe popularized the term "irreducible complexity" in 1996, the concept has been extensively debated.[304] One problem is that irreducible complexity is not defined by its critics in the same way most intelligent design advocates define it. For example, Farmer and Habura define irreducible complexity as "some biochemical systems are too complex to have arisen through natural undirected process."[305] Complexity is involved, but it is not the focus. This fact is illustrated by Behe's mousetrap example, which, depending on the model selected, is a simple machine requiring only five or six parts.

Some critics acknowledge the Irreducible Complexity concept as valid, but argue some uses of it are illegitimate. The key element is a certain number of parts are required before a system will function, five parts in the case of the portable house mousetrap. Dawkins argues that Darwinists believe life has evolved by evidence such as homology or the fossil record, therefore Irreducible Complexity could not be true, but it is

> perfectly legitimate to propose the argument from irreducible complexity as a possible explanation for the lack of something that doesn't exist, as I did for the absence of wheeled mammals. That is very different from evading the scientist's responsibility to explain something that *does* exist, such as wheeled bacteria. Nevertheless, to be fair, it is possible to imagine validly

---

[304] Weber, 1999, pp. 593-605.
[305] Farmer and Habura, 2010, p. 3.

using some version of the argument from design, or the argument from irreducible complexity.[306]

Dawkins provides what he considers an example of a "legitimate" use of Intelligent Design (ID) Theory: Future visitors from outer space, who mount archaeological digs of our planet, will surely find ways to distinguish designed machines such as planes and microphones, from evolved machines such as bat wings and ears. It is an interesting exercise to think about how they will make the distinction. They may face some tricky judgments in the messy overlap between natural evolution and human design.[307]

The late Stephen Gould also has provided an example of what he considered a legitimate use of Irreducible Complexity, namely that history "has built irreducible complexity and variety into the bounteous world of organisms. Diversity reigns at the superficial level of overt phenomena—animal colors serve many different functions. The unifying principles are deeper and more abstract."[308] In other words, irreducible complexity laws exist only at the foundation of life, allowing the entire history of life to unfold.

Gould expanded this view further, concluding that at the foundation of the enormous complexity of life, "lies nature's irreducible complexity. Organisms are not billiard balls, propelled by simple and measurable external forces to predictable new positions on life's pool table. Sufficiently complex systems [such as life] have greater richness."[309]

Both Gould and Dawkins argue that illegitimate uses of irreducible complexity include attempts to disprove Darwinism, but never clearly delineate illegitimate from legitimate uses of the concept. As noted, although critics have been able to propose systems which still function

---

[306] Dawkins, 2004, p. 549.
[307] Dawkins, 2004, p. 549.
[308] Gould, 1991, p. 226.
[309] Gould, 1980, p. 16.

somewhat satisfactorily with one or more fewer parts than were originally assumed necessary, this does not negate the concept.

The Junk-Gene Claim Criticism

One critique of Behe and *Darwin's Black Box* by biologist Keith Robison attacks the analogies Behe uses to illustrate his irreducible complexity theory, such as the mousetrap example. Robison claims that the human genome contains mostly "junk," "pseudogenes," and other useless sequences with no apparent purpose, that a "designer" would *not* have utilized. However, DeRosa notes that this "argument is weak because it tries to second- guess what the hypothetical 'designer' might do, and also because it presumes to know, at this early stage of genetic science, what is, and what is not, 'junk' in the genome."[310]

Biologists now know that most of the genome once widely labeled as "junk" is used for genetic regulation, such as to produce micro RNA (miRNA) and interference RNA (iRNA), and also functions as "silent genes" in addition to other uses.[311] The ENCODE project has found evidence that 80 percent or more of the DNA once classified as "junk" has critical functions, mostly regulatory.

Another criticism centers on the "cascade" idea in which a gene or chemical reaction triggers another reaction in a chain reaction. Robison argues that cascades, such as the blood-clotting example used by Behe, are not irreducibly complex; neither each individual step of the cascade, nor as a whole. He reasons that cascades are not irreducibly complex because some species, such as sharks, use modified versions of these cascade chains. He also notes that humans can sometimes survive with certain modified or missing structures.

Robison claims that the Krebs cycle, which is a critical part of the glucose metabolism system necessary for life, is another complex biological system that is not irreducibly complex because there exist

---

[310] DeRosa, 2004, p. 17.
[311] Makalowski, 2003; Kondrashov, 2005.

numerous "shortcut pathways" that bypass parts of the cycle. He then asks, if the Krebs cycle is not irreducibly complex, how can we have any confidence in our ability to recognize any such a system in life?[312] The solution is to do the research required to answer this question, which is no frivolous exercise, but critical in medicine.

Furthermore, the fact that several pathways exist and some require fewer parts than others, does not negate the fact that both the parts and the system as a whole are irreducibly complex. A functional cycle less complex than another one is still irreducibly complex. Reducing the cycle by one step does not negate the fact that it still requires the remaining parts of the cycle. It would not be irreducibly complex only if a single quark were responsible for the biochemical results that the Krebs cycle achieves.

Conclusions

The "origin of complex biological structures has long been a subject of interest and debate."[313] To conceptualize and better understand the debate, the concept of irreducible complexity has been used by both supporters and opponents of Intelligent Design. The main issue is that natural selection can only select for a biological system that is functioning. In a system where several parts, properly assembled, are necessary for function, irreducible complexity, natural selection cannot work to accumulate and assemble any individual part(s) prior to full assembly and function.

The evidence reviewed in this chapter also effectively falsifies Judge Jones's conclusion that "Professor Behe's claim for irreducible complexity has been refuted in peer-reviewed research papers and has been rejected by the scientific community at large."[314] The judge also irresponsibly ruled that irreducible complexity is a "religious"

---

[312] DeRosa, 2004, p. 17.

[313] Gregory, 2008, p. 358.

[314] *Kitzmiller v. Dover*, 2005, p. 79.

concept.[315] Given the definition outlined in this paper, every part of the material universe is irreducibly complex except possibly the fundamental particles, such as bosons (force carrying particles) and fermions (the fundamental matter particles divided into quarks and leptons, such as electrons and neutrinos). Thus, according to Judge Jones's decision, everything is religious.

This Irreducible Complexity fact also effectively responds to Darwin's challenge to demonstrate that if "any complex organ existed, which could not possibly have been formed by numerous, successive, slight modifications, my theory would absolutely break down."[316]

To adequately cover the challenge irreducible complexity creates for Darwinism would require a full-length book. This review briefly covers only some of the major issues, primarily the evidence required to document that Irreducible Complexity is a valid concept supported by massive empirical research. The implications beyond the Irreducible Complexity concept include the fact that the appearance of design in life is a central reason why people believe in God.[317]

Nonetheless, "No serious scientific theory can ignore Darwinism. It is much too logical and it explains too many facts" —but not all facts. It does not solve the Irreducible Complexity problem. It does not "explain how life began on Earth in the first place. It doesn't explain the sudden appearance of myriad species at different periods [in the geological record], or the gradual progression from simple to more complex life forms."[318]

The main issue for evolution is, according to a leading scientist dealing with complexity in applied biology, Professor Stuart Kauffman, "all living things seem to have a minimal complexity below which it is impossible to go" to be alive, a state called Irreducible Complexity.[319] An example he gives is the fact that "all free living cells must have at

---

[315] Calvert, 2009.
[316] Darwin, 1859, p. 189.
[317] D'Souza, 2007, p. 140.
[318] DeRosa, 2004, p. 117.
[319] Kauffman, 1995, p. 42.

least the minimum molecular diversity of pleuromona." The simplest free-living cells possible must have a few hundred genes plus all of the complex molecular machinery to translate those genes into proteins.[320]

This has always been the major stumbling block for abiogenesis and for the existence of all macroevolution. Furthermore, due to the recent explosion in the biochemical knowledge of the cell, the problem of Irreducible Complexity for Darwinism is more important today than ever before.

---

[320] Kauffman, 1995, p. 42.

References

Alberts, Bruce. 1989. The Cell as a Collection of Protein Machines: Preparing the Next Generation of Molecular Biologists. *Cell.* 92:291.

Aristotle. *Metaphysica: Book VIII* (Eta, Part 6). Harmondsworth, England: Penguin Books.

Bartlett, Jonathan. 2010. "Irreducible Complexity and Relative Irreducible Complexity: Foundations and Applications." *Occasional Papers of the BSG,* no. 15:1-10.

Behe, Michael. 1996. *Darwin's Black Box.* New York, NY: The Free Press.

_____. 2005. "Molecules Were Designed by a Creator," in Eric Braun (editor). *Creationism Versus Evolution.* New York, NY: Greenhaven Press.

_____. 2007. *The Edge of Evolution: The Search for the Limits of Darwinism.* New York, NY: Free Press.

Bhushan, Bharat. 2007. *Springer Handbook of Nanotechnology.* Second revised edition. New York, NY: Springer Publishing.

Bobrowsky, Matthew. 2006. "Dealing with Disbelieving Students on Issues of Evolutionary Processes." *Astronomy Educational Review* 1(40):95-118.

Boudry, M., S. Blancke, and J. Braeckman. 2010. "Irreducible incoherence and intelligent design: A look into the conceptual toolbox of a pseudoscience." *Quarterly Review of Biology* 85(4):473-482.

Braun, Eric. 2005. *Creationism versus Evolution.* New York, NY: Greenhaven Press.

Brosh, Jr., Robert M. 2008. "The Bloom's Complex Mousetrap." *Nature* 456:453-454, November 27.

Calvert, John H. 2009. "Kitzmiller's Error: Defining "Religion" Exclusively Rather

Than Inclusively." *Liberty University Law Review* 3(2):213-328, Spring.

Clements, Abigail, Dejan Bursac, Xenia Gatsos, Andrew J. Perry, Srgjan Civciristov, Nermin Celik, Vladimir A. Likic, Sebastian Poggio, Christine Jacobs-Wagner, Richard A. Strugnell, and Trevor Lithgow. 2009. "The Reducible Complexity of a Mitochondrial Molecular Machine." *PNAS* 106(37):15,791-15,795, July 24.

Collier, John. 2003. "Hierarchical Dynamical Information Systems With a Focus on Biology." *Entropy,*5(2):100-124.

Conn, Michael. 2006. *Handbook of Models for Human Aging.* New York, NY: Academic Press.

Crick, Francis. 1988. *What Mad Pursuit: A Personal View of Scientific Discovery.* New York, NY: Basic Books.

Cuvier, Georges. 1834. *Cuvier's Animal Kingdom: Arranged According to Its Organization, Translated from the French, and Abridged for the Use of Students.* London, UK: Orr and Smith.

Darwin, Charles. 1859. *Origin of Species,* London, UK: John Murray.

Dawkins, Richard. 2004. *The Ancestor's Tail: A Pilgrimage to the Dawn of Evolution.* Boston, MA: Haughton Mifflin.

_____. 2006. *The God Delusion.* Boston, MA: Houghton Mifflin Company.

_____. 2010. *The Greatest Show on Earth: The Evidence for Evolution.* New York, NY: Free Press.

Dembski, William. 2002. *No Free Lunch.* Oxford, England: Rowman & Littlefield Publishers.

_____. 2004. "Irreducible Complexity Revisited." *PCID* 3(1):1-47, November.

_____ and Jonathan Wells. 2007. *The Design of Life*. Dallas, TX: The Foundation for Thought and Ethics.

DeRosa, Neil. 2004. *Apocryphal Science: Creative Genius and Modern Heresies*. Dallas, TX: Hamilton Books.

D'Souza, Dinesh. 2007. *What's So Great About Christianity?* Washington, D.C.: Regnery Publishing.

Farmer, Mark A., and Andrea Habura. 2010. "Using Protistan Examples to Dispel the Myths of Intelligent Design." *Journal of Eukaryotic Microbiology* 57(1):3-10.

French, Michael J. 1988. *Invention and Evolution: Design in Nature and Engineering*. New York, NY: Cambridge University Press.

Gould, Stephen Jay. 1980. *The Panda's Thumb: More Reflections in Natural History*. New York, NY: W.W. Norton & Company.

_____. 1991. *Bully for Brontosaurus: Reflections in Natural History*. New York, NY: W.W. Norton & Company.

Gregory, T. Ryan. 2008. "The Evolution of Complex Organs." *Evolution Education Outreach*. 1(4):358-389, October 10.

Gyöngyi, Zoltán, Ferenc Budán, István Szabó, István Ember, István Kiss, Krisztina

Krempels, Ildikó Somlyai, and Gábor Somlyai. 2013. "Deuterium Depleted Water Effects on Survival of Lung Cancer Patients and Expression of Kras, Bcl2, and Myc Genes in Mouse Lung." *Nutrition and Cancer* 65(2):240–246.

Harold, Franklin M. 2001. *The Way of the Cell: Molecules, Organisms, and the Order of Life*. New York, NY: Oxford University Press.

Hayden, Erika. 2010. "Life is Complicated." *Nature* 464(7289):664-667, April 1.

Katz, Michael J. 1986. *Templates and the Explanation of Complex Patterns*. Cambridge, MA: Cambridge University Press.

Kauffman, Stuart. 1995. *At Home in the Universe: The Search for the Laws of Self-Organization and Complexity*. New York, NY: Oxford University Press.

Kitzmiller vs. Dover Area School District, et al. 2005. In the United States District Court for the Middle District of Pennsylvania. Case No. 04cv2688, Judge Jones.

Kondrashov, Alexey S. 2005. "Evolutionary biology: Fruit fly genome is not junk." *Nature* 437(7062):1106a, October 20.

Kovács, A., I. Guller, K. Krempels, et al. 2011. "Deuterium depletion may delay the progression of prostate cancer." *Journal of Cancer Therapy* 2(4):548-556.

Kurland, Charles, Lesley Collins, and David Penny. 2006. "Genomics and the Irreducible Nature of Eukaryote Cells." *Science* 312(5776):1011-1014, May 19.

Makalowski, Wojciech. 2003. "Perspectives Genomics: Not Junk After All." *Science* 300(5623):1246–1247, May 23.

Meyer, Stephen C. 2009. *Signature in the Cell: DNA and the Evidence for Intelligent Design*. New York, NY: HarperOne.

Miller, Kenneth R. 1999. *Finding Darwin's God: A Scientist's Search for Common Ground Between God and Evolution*. New York, NY: Harper Collins.

_____. 2008. *Only a Theory: Evolution and the Battle for America's Soul*. New York, NY: Viking Press.

Mivart, George. 1871. *On the Genesis of Species*. Chapter 2: "The Incompetency of Natural Selection," pp. 19-85. New York, NY: D. Appleton & Co.

Monod, Jacques. 1971. *Chance and Necessity.* New York, NY: Alfred A. Knopf Publishing.

Morange, Michel. 2001. *The Misunderstood Gene.* Cambridge, MA: Harvard University Press.

Old, Robert W., and Sandy B. Primrose. 1994. *Principles of Gene Manipulation: An Introduction to Genetic Engineering,* 5th Edition. Cambridge, MA: Blackwell Science.

Polanyi, Michael. 1968. "Life's Irreducible Structure." *Science* 160(3834):1308-1312, June 21.

Polis, Dennis F. 2010. "Evolution: Mind or Randomness?" *Journal of Interdisciplinary Studies* 22(1/2):32-66.

Rehbock, Philip F. 1975. "Huxley, Haeckel, and the Oceanographers: The Case of *Bathybius haeckelii.*" *Isis* 66(4):504-533.

Ruse, Michael. 2003. "Modern Biologists and the Argument from Design." Chapter 17 in *God and Design: The Teleological Argument and Modern Science,* ed. by Neil Manson. New York, NY: Routledge, pp. 308-325.

_____. 2007. "The Argument from Design." In *The Panda's Black Box.* Edited by Nathaniel Comfort. Baltimore, MD: Johns Hopkins University Press, pp. 18-39.

Schnabel, Jim. 2010. "The Dark Side of Proteins." *Nature* 464(8):828-829, April 7.

Spitz, Susan (ed). 2007. *The American Heritage Medical Dictionary.* Boston, MA: Houghton Mifflin.

Stashower, Daniel. 2002. *The Boy Genius and the Mogul: The Untold Story of Television.* New York, NY: Broadway Books.

Taylor, Mark. 2001. *The Moment of Complexity.* Chicago, IL: University of Chicago Press.

Trotter, M.V., D.B. Weissman, G.I. Peterson, K.M. Peck, and J. Masel. 2013. "Cryptic Genetic Variation Can Make Irreducible Complexity a Common Mode of Adaptation." Ithaca, NY: Cornell University, arXiv:1310.6077v1, https://arxiv.org/abs/1310.6077.

Weber, Bruce H. 1999. "Irreducible Complexity and the Problem of Biochemical Emergence." *Biology and Philosophy* 14:593-605, October.

Williams, Alex. 2007. "Life's Irreducible Structure—Part 1: Autopoiesis." *Journal of Creation* 21(2):109-115.

CHAPTER 5

Co-option Fails to Explain the
Evolution of Complex Features

Introduction

The process of using existing cell or body parts, such as genes, organs, proteins, glycolipids, or glycoproteins in a unique way to produce a new structure is called **co-option**.[321] A similar concept, called **pre-adaptation**, hypothesizes that new molecular machines formed from pre-existing parts to perform functions other than those for which they were originally designed.[322]

One proposed example is the bacterial flagellum, which utilizes ten proteins that are also employed in the type III bacteria secretory system used by bacteria for pumping substances into other organisms.[323] Professor Kenneth R. Miller concludes from this observation that "irreducible complexity is nonsense" because a set of proteins in one system simply can be rearranged to produce new structures.[324]

Dawkins argues that the "key to demonstrating Irreducible Complexity is to show that none of the parts could have been useful

---

[321] True and Carroll, 2002, p. 53; Barve, et al., 2013.
[322] Miller, 2008.
[323] Dawkins, 2006, p. 131.
[324] Miller, 1999, p. 150.

on its own … In fact, molecular biologists have no difficulty in finding parts functioning outside the whole, both for the flagellar motor and for Behe's other alleged examples of irreducible complexity."[325] Numerous examples are claimed in the literature, such as genomic evolution of the placenta by co-option, duplication, and divergence.[326] In short, the concept of co-option appears to explain those structures claimed to be IC.[327]

Lethal Problems with the Co-Option Argument

Although many, or even most, of the parts of an irreducibly complex system may have functions in other irreducibly complex systems, this claim misses the central point of the Irreducible Complexity concept. A major component of the bacterial flagellum is carbon, and carbon plays many roles in many different molecules. Carbon atoms can function not only in pencil lead, but also in diamonds and graphite lubricants, to name a few examples.

The existence of carbon atoms does not explain how ATP synthase, or any other biological structure using carbon, evolved. What must be explained is both the existence of the required parts *and* the specific assembly of these parts required to function as a unit. Even the examples of carbon allotropes are irreducibly complex because a single carbon atom will not produce a diamond, a graphite lubricant, or a pencil lead. A *properly assembled* set of carbon atoms is required in all three of these cases, and this is the central issue of IC.

All of these materials consist of pure carbon atoms that must be assembled differently to produce diamonds, graphite, and carbon pencil lead. The key to the differences in these examples is the proper assembly of the required set of parts, in this case the atoms that make the specific carbon allotrope. Diamonds, graphite lubricants, or pencil

---

[325] Dawkins, 2006, p. 131.
[326] Knox, et al., 2008, pp. 695-705.
[327] McLennan, 2008, pp. 247-258.

lead are all examples of the cumulative complexity noted above, and must be assembled properly in order to function in these three distinct ways.

In reality, the co-option claim only demonstrates the fact of irreducible complexity because even if co-option could occur, the cell in which the co-option occurred must itself have originally been irreducibly complex to be a living cell. This fact has so far proven to be an insurmountable obstacle for all abiogenesis theories.

The co-option argument does not refute the Irreducible Complexity concept, but only ignores the problem of both the part's and the structure's origins. The existence of the parts used in one system found in another system does not explain the *origin* of the functioning system itself because the proper design, selection, and *assembly* of the parts in the correct location and special orientation required are all critical to produce a functional system.[328] This requires the existence of an assembly machinery system. In cells, the necessary scaffold proteins are required to place the correct parts in the proper location at the correct time in the assembly process.[329]

In the television system example, even if the parts used to produce a working television were co-opted—which many of them were—the system is still irreducibly complex. The fact that most of the parts in a television transmission-receiver system are used in other electronic devices does not negate the fact that a certain minimum number of parts are required in order for the entire television system to function.

Furthermore, in Behe's words, the correct number of each part must exist and they must be well matched, meaning that they are manufactured to the required specifications and tolerances at the correct time.[330] The parts must then be moved to the proper assembly location in the *order* needed and at the *time* needed. The many complex enzymes required to assemble the parts must also be transported to the correct location and positioned in the correct order so as to

---

[328] Dembski and Wells, 2007.

[329] Alberts, 1989; Behe, 1996.

[330] Behe, 2005.

construct a functional unit. The parts transportation system is also irreducibly complex, as are the enzymes used to manufacture and properly assemble the required parts.

Likewise, to produce a television, once the necessary parts are manufactured to the required specifications, and made available, the following steps are necessary to assemble the working system: selection of the correct parts, transporting them to the work-site, then assembling the pieces together in the correct orientation. This final assembly may require rivets, screws, solder, glue, or some type of clamp.

To deal with this problem, Behe introduced the "step concept," which resembles the Irreducible Complexity concept. Both concepts require the design and implementation of multiple factors to produce a functional system or part. "But 'steps' goes further, asking how many separate *actions*—not just separate *parts*—are required to produce a workable system. The concept of 'steps' is especially useful [to] locate the edge of evolution with greater precision."[331]

Cornell University geneticist John Sanford noted that "each *part* has no value except within the context of the *whole* functional unit, and so irreducible systems have to come together all at once, and cannot arise one piece at a time."[332] In the case of a mousetrap, even if all the pieces are sitting neatly next to each other on the inventor's workbench, they cannot properly self-assemble together into a functional unit by chance—or by any realistic evolutionary mechanism. A human must assemble the properly designed parts.

The parts must first simultaneously come together as a functioning system in the mind of a designer. It is in the realm of *mind* that complexity first exists and becomes integrated.[333] The creation of this mental design must then be translated into the steps required to manufacture the proper parts to the specifications that can be assembled to produce a workable machine, for example in the case of a television.

---

[331] Behe, 2007, pp. 121-122.
[332] Sanford, 2005, p. 133.
[333] Sanford, 2005, p. 133.

An evaluation of machines that are designed by humans reveals that co-option is close to universal—many mass produced standard parts are used in a wide variety of electrical and mechanical contrivances. When designing a new product, to achieve the required function of the new assembled unit, engineers often select parts from the millions that already exist. Common examples of standard generic parts manufactured for a wide variety of uses include various fasteners (screws, bolts, cotter pins, and rivets) and the family of electronic parts, such as capacitors, transistors, and micro-switches.

Many reasons exist for the common practice of using existing parts, including lower cost, design efficiency, and reliability. Producing fifty-million of one micro-switch type, instead of one million of each of fifty different types, lowers enormously the cost for each unit. Also, utilization of a part with proven design and a documented reliability record is preferred over a new design that may potentially be superior, but lacks a proven reliability history.

It also is far easier, and much more practical, to design new equipment by utilizing existing parts, which is how many electrical and mechanical devices first appeared on the market. The early VCRs were a conglomeration of a wide variety of standard parts obtained from numerous sources. Design improvements have resulted in combining different parts to require fewer total parts until, today, a modern VCR (now DVD) uses a fraction of the parts employed in the original, and also weighs a fraction of the weight of the original. Other examples include automobiles, all of which use similar tires, batteries, filters, light bulbs, and fasteners.

Co-option in the mechanical and electrical worlds clearly requires intelligent design. Because the parts employed are also used in other inventions does not negate the fact that an invention is irreducibly complex. Selection of the optimal components for a new application typically requires highly trained individuals, such as manufacturing representatives, to help determine the appropriate parts required for a specific application, according to the customer's requirements, from the large number of parts available. These parts are then modified by intelligence, often by highly trained engineers or specialists, to function with other parts as a functional unit.

The fact that many of the parts which were co-opted are similar to existing parts raises a problem for evolutionary explanations of such co-option. In the evolutionary view, there would be intermediate parts evolved along the way from the old useful parts to the new useful parts. The intermediate parts, if not used in a functional structure, would normally be labeled by the protein ubiquitin and recycled, thereby wasting resources. The intermediate parts also could result in a selective disadvantage to the cell, or could even prove to be toxic, thus damaging it.

Evolution *In Situ* Is Often Less Problematic

Just as constructing a new building often costs less than repairing and refitting an old one, likewise, the evolution of parts *in situ* would often seem to require fewer steps to produce a new structure compared to co-opting a wide variety of existing parts from different locations in the cell. Science often requires starting with a creative imagination to produce a hypothesis.[334] Selecting existing parts to construct a new structure is not only evidence of intelligence, but it is even difficult to imagine a scenario or mechanism in which Darwinian evolution could pick and choose a wide variety of specific parts to achieve a new functional structure that aids survival.

Mutations as the Designer

The mechanisms that produce most mutations are well understood but, conversely, no evidence exists of mechanisms that can systematically rearrange structural parts in order to produce new functional structures, or even just rearrange parts to produce a new type of

---

[334] Dawkins, 2010.

structure. While it is conceivable that many mutations could produce beneficial effects, it is difficult to even imagine a "just-so story" that explains how a naturalistic mechanism could cobble different existing parts together by co-option to produce new functional structures that aid survival — as evolutionists claim.[335] Conversely, although still a "just-so story", one *can* visualize the gradual *perfection* of the parts of a structure *in situ* that results in improving both its function and its performance.

From what is currently understood about assembly instruction systems that direct the building of living cells, no known way exists to cause, or even allow, individual parts to be reshuffled around during evolution so that a new functional arrangement is produced that aids in the cell's survival. Even if one existed, cobbling parts together almost invariably would produce a harmful or non-functional structure, not a workable system that aids survival, because very few of the many possible arrangements are functional.[336] Abnormal development in life most always produces abnormal, often deformed, bodies, not better bodies.

The only plausible known mechanism that could select existing parts to construct a new structure is transposition (commonly called "jumping genes"). However, transposition only shuffles *existing* genetic information around; it does not shuffle the complex guidance system that is required for properly assembling a completely new functional structure from many existing different parts.

Furthermore, transposition of genes to specific locations would be required for recombination of existing parts to produce a new system. Transposition could also rapidly cause genetic meltdown by splicing genes into the middle of an existing gene or disrupt the genetic regularity controls, thereby destroying that gene's function. Conceptualizing how co-option could function in living organisms requires an understanding of how the assembly instruction systems of life function.

[335] Sanford, 2005.
[336] Schnabel, 2010, p. 829.

The Pleiotropy Problem

The co-option theory is also very problematic because a cell is a highly harmonious and interconnected complex system consisting of many billions of parts that all must function together as a unit. For this reason, a single change in a gene often affects many other genes, and could even affect the entire biological system. The high level of inter-relatedness existing in all life works against evolutionary change because even if a mutation improves the function of one part in a cell unit, it often will cause dysfunction, or less-effective function, in other cell proteins or systems.

This concept, called pleiotropy, is a major reason why an alteration in a single gene can result in so many different body alterations, many of which are dysfunctional. Mutations often result in a wide variety of different health problems, many of which seemingly have little or nothing to do with each other. An often-cited example is sickle cell anemia, which causes numerous adverse effects in the body from mini-strokes to spleen damage.

Pleiotropy is also a major reason why almost all drugs produce side effects. When developing new drugs, many otherwise very effective drugs do not make it to the open market because the side effects are considered far too serious, too common, or otherwise unacceptable. In other words, life is irreducibly complex at numerous levels, and alteration of one part of an irreducibly complex system at one level, such as the protein or organelle level, often affects all other levels—from the cellular level, to the organ level, to the organ-system level (such as the respiratory system), and finally to the organism level (for example, the individual human).

Due to redundancy, many changes are lethal only beyond a certain threshold.[337] The co-option claim does not alter the fact that "there are presently no detailed Darwinian accounts of the evolution of *any* biochemical or cellular system, only a variety of wishful

---

[337] Conn, 2006.

speculations."[338] Even if a system existed that could produce new organs or structures by selecting from existing parts as the co-option theory postulates, in almost all cases it would produce some damaging or lethal arrangements, and could cause an enormous level of damage to life.

Gene Duplication Solution

Professor Susumu Ohno proposed that the problems with the co-option claim could be partially salvaged by the idea of gene duplication. The theory postulates that if two complete sets of genes existed that produced the same protein or structure due to gene duplication, one gene set could be modified by evolution to produce a new specific structure that allowed the other gene to maintain its previous function.[339] However, if this condition occurred, the excess protein or structures produced when gene duplication first occurred would likely be problematic for several reasons, and thus gene duplication would virtually always be selected against.

Furthermore, both genes would be almost equally susceptible to mutations. Also, while one set is accumulating mutations, it is likely to be transitioning from a functional state to a less- or non-functional state, producing non-functional or even harmful proteins before acquiring some putative alternative new gene. As a result, animals with the extra set of genes would be at a disadvantage, and may even be more likely to be selected out from the population before acquiring a new function. This illustrates the major problem we have identified, viz., the original design arrangement could not have been produced without intelligent design.

[338] Harold, 2001, p. 205.
[339] Ohno, 1970.

Co-Option Involved in Part Modifications

A variation of co-option is to locate similar proteins or other organic molecules in a cell type and argue that one set evolved into another set. For example, Professor Abigail Clements, et al., identified a set of proteins in alpha-proteobacteria similar to those in eukaryote mitochondria.[340] Similarity of proteins, though, does not prove one life-form evolved from a different life-form. Proof requires more than just sequencing the gene that produces a protein, evaluating the protein conformation, and then hypothesizing how one gene evolved from another gene.

Protein similarity often exists due to similar functional requirements, not evolution. Proteins involved in protein transport would be expected to be very similar, as is true of a large number of all proteins involved in all life. Protein transport machines located in the mitochondria that move proteins across the mitochondrial membrane perform the critical functions involved in transferring energy. These structures are all well-designed examples of nanotechnology.[341]

Cell biology research has documented that basic prokaryotic and eukaryotic cell designs are essentially the same in all life-forms. The function of DNA, mRNA, and protein in the cell are also so similar that human genes can be spliced into bacteria to produce human proteins, such as insulin, human growth hormone (HGH or hGH, aka somatotropin), and tissue plasminogen activator (tPA).[342] Aside from a few minor exceptions in bacteria, the genetic code also is identical in all cells as well as being universal in the sense that similar codons are assigned to identical amino acids.

The protein synthesis machinery design is also practically identical in all cells. Therefore, in terms of basic biochemical design, "no living system can be thought of as being primitive or ancestral with respect to any other system, nor is there the slightest empirical hint

---

[340] Clements, 2009, p. 15,791.

[341] Bhushan, 2007; Myer, 2009.

[342] Houdebine, 2009.

of an evolutionary sequence among all the incredibly diverse cells on earth."[343] Nobel Laureate biochemist Jacques Monod added, for these and other reasons, scientists

> have no idea what the structure of a primitive cell might have been. The simplest living system known to us, the bacterial cell, [is] a tiny piece of extremely complex and efficient machinery... Its overall chemical plan is the same as that of all other living beings. It employs the same genetic code and the same mechanism of translation as do ... human cells. Thus the simplest cells ... have nothing "primitive" about them...no vestiges of truly primitive structures are discernible.[344]

These insights have been confirmed by molecular biological research in the decades since these statements were published.[345]

The Origin of the Parts Problem

The co-option explanation attempts to account for irreducible complexity by the cell selecting existing cell and protein parts to form new structures. This view is problematic, both because of the difficulty in explaining the origin of the existing parts, and the difficulty in explaining the origin of the assembly mechanisms involved in assuring their proper function. "Co-option" explanations address neither problem. Co-option simply assumes the parts already exist and speculates on their past diverse assembly possibilities.

Gradualistic and co-option models of evolution are accepted partly because of philosophical constraints, not empirical evidence.

---

[343] Denton, 1986, p. 250.
[344] Monod, 1971, p. 142.
[345] For example, see Weber, 1999; Kurland, et al., 2006; and Brosh, 2008.

As Harold admits, evolutionists "reject, as a matter of principle," not because of evidence, "the substitution of intelligent design for the dialogue of chance and necessity."[346] This philosophical constraint prevents scientists from considering all possible avenues, including intelligent design, to explain the origin of life. To fully understand reality, science must be free to explore all viable research avenues.

Evolution of Protein, Lipid, and Carbohydrate Parts

The lack of evidence for the evolution of any of the basic original parts supposedly co-opted into new structures was detailed by Professor French:

> Among these great innovations in design, the crucial inventions of nature, the earliest have left no trace of their development in the fossil record. The organization of living material in a cell with a cell wall and a nucleus, the transmission of the blueprint of its design and its means of self-construction and the very important device of sexual reproduction, all developed in minute organisms which have left little evidence.[347]

The basic parts thus must first exist in order for co-option to occur, and until their creation is explained, it is premature to claim that co-option of existing parts, or the moving around of existing parts, explains the systems that employ those parts.

---

[346] Harold, 2001, p. 205.
[347] French, 1988, p. 19.

JERRY BERGMAN, PH.D.

The Scaffolding/Roman Arch Theory

Related to the co-option theory is the "scaffolding/Roman arch" theory. The example usually cited to illustrate this concept is that the construction of a Roman arch requires a scaffold, and when the core arch parts, including the keystone, are properly in place, the scaffold can be removed, allowing the arch to stand on its own. This example is used in an attempt to support the claim that one can achieve functional complexity by *removing* unnecessary components.

Scaffolding systems are common in human construction projects requiring temporary structures, such as forms to shape concrete until it dries. When the concrete has solidified the forms are removed. Thus, the forms are a necessary part of the design used to produce an irreducibly complex end-goal. However, this requires a higher level of irreducible complexity to produce an end-goal that has a lower level of irreducible complexity. The scaffolding itself is also irreducibly complex, adding another level of complexity to the structure's manufacturing process.

Those who use this example have yet to provide a comparable example in the evolution of life. Furthermore, the theory does not change the fact that the basic function of an irreducibly complex system can exist *only* when all of the core components are in place.[348] If the keystone is not in place, the arch will collapse when the scaffold is removed. Lastly, a review of the literature fails to reveal a detailed model of a system that employs scaffoldings to generate irreducibly complex systems from non-irreducibly complex systems.[349]

While "scaffold" systems are commonly used in cells for constructing cellular machinery, when construction is complete, the scaffold system is removed and the parts recycled. Instead of solving the problem of explaining Irreducible Complexity, scaffolding theory makes the system *more* irreducibly complex because the level of irreducible complexity required to produce the structure by the

[348] Dembski, 2004, p. 19.
[349] Dembski, 2002; Dembski and Wells, 2007.

scaffolding technique is greater than the irreducible complexity that exists in the structure itself when completed.

Conclusions

Major problems exist with the claim that complex structures can be produced via *exaptation,* a concept that includes co-option and preadaptation. *Preadaptation* is the theory that a protein which evolved to serve one function can subsequently be co-opted to serve another role in the cell. The conditions that would *all* have to be met to accept the co-opted based explanation for the origins of Irreducible Complexity include the following:

1. **Availability**: the parts must first exist for recruitment to produce the new structure. The parts capable of performing the highly specialized tasks for a flagellum include those required to produce the paddle, rotor, and motor. Even though they all serve some other function, or no function, they all *as a set* must first exist before they can be co-opted.

2. **Synchronization**: the availability of these parts would have to be synchronized so that, at some point, either individually or in combination, they are all concurrently available to produce a functional structure, or at least one that has some beneficial function.

3. **Localization**: every one of the selected parts must be manufactured, and then transported so that they are available at the same "construction site," at the time they are required to assemble the new structures to produce a functional system.

4. **Coordination**: the parts must be correctly and properly positioned in 3-D space so they can be properly assembled. The enzymes that produce the bonds required for proper assembly must also concurrently exist. Even if all of the parts are available at the proper time, the vast majority of

assembly variations will be non-functional or dysfunctional. This coordination usually requires a complex machine such as a spliceosome, plus ATP synthase, DNA polymerase, or an assembly jig system such as a ribosome, to properly assemble the required parts.

5. **Interface compatibility:** the parts must be mutually compatible, well-matched and capable of properly interacting as a functional unit. In the case of the flagellum, even if a paddle, rotor, and motor are assembled in the correct order and correct position, they also must properly interface during their mechanical operation.[350]

In addition, in many cases a regulation system also must exist, such as miRNA and iRNA.

Structures such as a bacterial flagellum contain thousands of proteins, and each protein contains hundreds or even thousands of parts, including amino acids, glucose, and lipids. Furthermore, each gene that produces these parts has about 50,000 component parts.[351]

A "simple" *E. coli* bacterial cell is not simple, but has a whopping 4,288 genes, made up of 255,000 nucleic acid molecules consisting of 660 different nucleic acid types. In addition, a single *E. coli* cell contains about 1,900 different kinds of proteins and 2.4 million total protein molecules, plus 1.4 million polysaccharide molecules and up to 22 million lipid molecules. It also requires millions of mineral molecules made up of 10 to 30 different mineral types and about 24 billion water molecules.[352]

Specifically, the Irreducible Complexity concept successfully challenges naturalistic evolution. These multi-millions of components cannot be produced and properly assembled by natural selection alone acting on mutations or any other sources of genetic variation. For this reason the creation of life requires intelligent direction.[353]

---

[350] Menuge, 2004, pp.104-105.

[351] Sanford, 2005, p. 135.

[352] Ashton, 2012, pp. 40-41.

[353] Behe, 2005.

References

Ashton, John. 2012. *Evolution Impossible*. Green Forest, AR: Master Books.

Alberts, Bruce. 1998. "The Cell as a Collection of Protein Machines: Preparing the Next Generation of Molecular Biologists." *Cell* 92(3):291-294, February 6.

Barve, Aditya, and Andreas Wagner. 2013. "A Latent Capacity for Evolutionary Innovation through Exaptation in Metabolic Systems." *Nature* 500:203-206, July 14.

Behe, Michael. 1996. *Darwin's Black Box*. New York, NY: The Free Press.

_____. 2005. "Molecules Were Designed by a Creator." In Eric Braun (editor), *Creationism Versus Evolution*. New York, NY: Greenhaven Press.

_____. 2007. *The Edge of Evolution: The Search for the Limits of Darwinism*. New York, NY: Free Press.

Bhushan, Bharat. 2007. *Springer Handbook of Nanotechnology*, Second revised edition. New York, NY: Springer Publishing.

Brosh, Jr., Robert M. 2008. "The Bloom's Complex Mousetrap." *Nature* 456(7221):453-454, November 27.

Clements, Abigail, Dejan Bursac, Xenia Gatsos, Andrew J. Perry, Srgjan Civciristov, Nermin Celik, Vladimir A. Likic, Sebastian Poggio, Christine Jacobs-Wagner, Richard A. Strugnell, and Trevor Lithgow. 2009. "The Reducible Complexity of a Mitochondrial Molecular Machine." *PNAS* 106(37):15,791-15,795, July 24.

Conn, Michael. 2006. *Handbook of Models for Human Aging*. New York, NY: Academic Press.

Dawkins, Richard. 2006. *The God Delusion.* Boston, MA: Houghton Mifflin Company.

_____. 2010. *The Greatest Show on Earth: The Evidence for Evolution.* New York, NY: Free Press.

Dembski, William. 2002. *No Free Lunch.* Oxford, England: Rowman & Littlefield Publishers.

_____. 2004. "Irreducible Complexity Revisited." *PCID* 3(1):1-47, November.

_____, and Jonathan Wells. 2007. *The Design of Life.* Dallas, TX: The Foundation for Thought and Ethics.

Denton, Michael. 1986. *Evolution: A Theory in Crisis.* Bethesda, MD: Adler and Adler.

French, Michael J. 1988. *Invention and Evolution: Design in Nature and Engineering.* New York, NY: Cambridge University Press.

Gould, Stephen Jay, and Elisabeth S. Vrba. 1982. "Exaptation—A Missing Term in the Science of Form." *Paleobiology* 8(1):4-15, Winter.

Harold, Franklin M. 2001. *The Way of the Cell: Molecules, Organisms and the Order of Life.* New York, NY: Oxford University Press.

Houdebine, Louis-Marie. 2009. "Production of Pharmaceutical Proteins by Transgenic Animals." *Comparative Immunology, Microbiology and Infectious Diseases* 32(2):107–121, March.

Knox, Kirstin, and Julie Baker. 2008. "Genomic Evolution of the Placenta Using Co-option and Duplication and Divergence." *Genomic Research* 18(5):695-705, May.

Kurland, Charles, Lesley Collins, and David Penny. 2006. "Genomics and the Irreducible Nature of Eukaryote Cells." *Science* 321(5776):1011-1014, May 19.

McLennan, Deborah. 2008. "The Concept of Co-option: Why Evolution Often Looks Miraculous." *Evolution Education Outreach* 1(3):247-258.

Menuge, Angus. 2004. *Agents under Fire: Materialism and the Rationality of Science.* New York, NY: Rowman & Littlefield.

Meyer, Stephen C. 2009. *Signature in the Cell: DNA and the Evidence for Intelligent Design.* New York, NY: HarperOne.

Miller, Kenneth R. 1999. *Finding Darwin's God: A Scientist's Search for Common Ground Between God and Evolution.* New York, NY: Harper Collins.

_____. 2008. *Only a Theory: Evolution and the Battle for America's Soul.* New York, NY: Viking Press.

Monod, Jacques. 1971. *Chance and Necessity.* New York, NY: Alfred A. Knopf Publishing

Ohno, Susumu. 1970. *Evolution by Gene Duplication.* New York, NY: Springer-Verlag.

Sanford, John. 2005. *Genetic Entropy & The Mystery of the Genome.* Lima, NY: Ivan Press.

Schnabel, Jim. 2010. "The Dark Side of Proteins." *Nature.* 464(8):828-829, April 7.

True, John, and Sean Carroll. 2002. "Gene Co-Option in Physiological and Morphological Evolution." *Annual Review of Cell Developmental Biology* 18(1):53-80.

Weber, Bruce H. 1999. "Irreducible Complexity and the Problem of Biochemical Emergence." *Biology and Philosophy* 14:593-605.

GREGOR MENDEL, THE FOUNDER OF MODERN GENETICS. THE FRONTISPIECE IS FROM WILLIAM BATESON. 1902. P. 4 OF *MENDEL'S PRINCIPLES OF HEREDITY: A DEFENSE*. CAMBRIDGE, ENGLAND: CAMBRIDGE UNIVERSITY PRESS.

CHAPTER 6

Pseudogenes —
Junk DNA or Intelligent Design?

Introduction

Human genome mapping has identified enormous sections of DNA that do not code for proteins. This observation was soon heralded as support for evolutionary naturalism.[354] Called "junk" DNA, or "non-informational" DNA, it includes DNA sequences such as repeated sequences, introns, and pseudogenes.[355] Pseudogenes are a specific DNA type that, although very similar to protein coding genes, are believed by evolutionists to be damaged genes and, as a result, no longer able to code for protein.[356]

Mutations theorized to have damaged the original genes include frame shifts, insertions, and deletion mutations. These can result in gene non-functionality and also cause modifications that damage regulatory elements, especially the initiation and termination sequences. As a result, the gene no longer produces functional proteins. Although pseudogenes lack promoters and/or enhancers and appear to contain

---

[354] Holmes, 1995.
[355] Doolittle, 1993; Bergman, 1994, 2001.
[356] Chen, et al., 2002.

crippling mutations, such as frame shift mutations or premature stop codons, they "do tend to retain their characteristic intron-exon structure" which provides a hint of their function.[357]

Pseudogenes are an important topic in the creation-evolution controversy because neo-Darwinists commonly argue that an Intelligent Creator would not have created large amounts of useless, or even harmful, genes such as pseudogenes. Rather, neo-Darwinists argue that they are the result of a blind, purposeless mechanism such as evolution. Because pseudogenes have sequences that are very similar to functional genes, they are often labeled as "dead" or "disabled" genes.[358] Specifically, neo-Darwinists postulate that pseudogenes are evolutionary relics, molecular fossils that have accumulated during 'deep time,' and, therefore, can be used to help determine evolutionary history or phylogeny.[359] This view interprets pseudogenes as "long-dead genes ... that litter our chromosomes ... vestiges of old code associated with defunct [genetic] routines."[360]

For example, Richard Dawkins concludes that pseudogenes "are genes that once did something useful but have now been sidelined and are never transcribed or translated" into protein.[361] In addition, he concluded, "What pseudogenes are useful for is embarrassing creationists. It stretches even their creative ingenuity to make up a convincing reason why an intelligent designer should have created a pseudogene—a gene that does absolutely nothing and gives every appearance of being a superannuated version of a gene that used to do something."[362]

---

[357] Pink, et al., 2011, p. 792.
[358] Hernandez, et al., 1998.
[359] Lee, 2003.
[360] Gerstein and Zheng, 2006, p. 49.
[361] Dawkins, 2009, p. 332.
[362] Dawkins, 2009, p. 332.

History of Pseudogene Research

Pseudogenes were first reported in the literature in 1977 by professors Jacq, Miller, and Brownlee.[363] In the years since, large numbers of putative pseudogenes have been identified in humans and a wide variety of other species. All animals, especially mammals, contain a large number of pseudogenes, and a few putative pseudogenes have even been identified in bacterial genomes.[364] A decade ago the estimate was that about 20,000 pseudogenes exist in humans alone, close to the number of functional genes.[365]

Some genes contain DNA sequences that help to regulate or control the timing of various gene activities. Pseudogenes lack some or all of these controlling elements, such as a promoter site (RNA polymerase binding site for start transcription units), various regulators that control the level of protein produced, the specific code for the amino acid sequence of the protein produced during translation, and the start and stop codons to regulate translation into proteins.[366] Many pseudogenes also appear to contain extra stop codons, premature stop signals, or have abnormal or missing flanking regulatory elements.[367] Ironically, one reason why they have been extensively researched is that their similarity to functional genes has resulted in Darwinists considering many of them evolutionary relatives of normally functioning genes.[368]

However, new research shows that the required regulatory DNA sequences are not always in the normal location close to the gene, nor can they always be readily identified. The fact that some of these signals are located at a great distance from the gene presents a major difficulty in determining if a gene is a pseudogene. When these regulatory sequences are identified, technically the gene is no longer considered a

---

[363] Jacq, et al., 1977.
[364] Andersson and Andersson, 2001, p. 829.
[365] Hirotsune, et al., 2003; Svensson, et al., 2006.
[366] Gibson, 1994; Balakirev and Ayala, 2003.
[367] Gibson, 1994.
[368] Dawkins, 2009, p. 332.

pseudogene, even though it may still be labeled as such. Consequently, we now recognize that there is often no clear distinction between genes and pseudogenes.[369]

Origin of Pseudogenes

Contrary to Dawkins' assumptions, pseudogenes are not contradictory to creation. The creation model accounts for genome degradation caused by mutations by anticipating the existence of genes that have subsequently lost function since their original creation.[370] This includes pseudogenes categorized as disabled genes. These pseudogenes are complete genes that appear to be damaged by mutations which prevent transcription or translation. A classic example is the L-gulono-Y-lactone oxidase (GLO) gene in primates and humans that is missing several of the exons to code for a functional enzyme necessary for the manufacture of vitamin C.[371]

However, not all pseudogenes can be accounted for by genomic degradation. One popular theory proposes that many pseudogenes arose from genetic mistakes during gene duplication, such as an unequal cross-over. This could result in an extra copy of a functional gene, which is not immediately eliminated from the genome.[372] If the gene copy did not cause a detrimental effect on the organism, the duplicated gene could subsequently accumulate mutations. Mutations that occur in pseudogenes are assumed to be neutral, or near neutral. Thus, the organism would survive even though the mutation load in these genes was assumed to have slowly increased over time.

For this reason, mutations would be expected to accumulate in genes to produce pseudogenes. The older the pseudogene, the more mutations it would contain. The gene duplication possibility for

---

[369] Zheng and Gerstein, 2007.
[370] Sanford, 2005.
[371] Nishikimi, et al., 1994; Cooper, 1999.
[372] See Bergman, 2006.

pseudogene origin has been suggested because, until recently, most pseudogenes were not known to have a function. Because pseudogenes are often similar to known functional genes, gene duplication that results in useful genetic changes may have occurred, but this does not explain the origin of the original gene.

Unprocessed and Processed Pseudogenes

Two basic classes of pseudogenes have so far been identified, **unprocessed** and **processed pseudogenes**. [373]

Unprocessed pseudogenes appear to be copies of active genes. The most common examples are the alpha-globin and beta-globin pseudogenes. These unprocessed or duplicated pseudogenes are often found in clusters near similar, but functional, genes on the same chromosome. [374] This pseudogene type usually contains the same introns and flanking regulatory sequences as do functional genes. [375] Expression of these pseudogenes is assumed to be prevented by the lack of transcription initiation sequences or premature stop codons that result in truncated proteins during translation. Another difference that may also exist between unprocessed pseudogenes and functional genes is that the former contains what appear to be many point mutations, deletions, and insertions. [376]

Processed or retro-transposed pseudogenes may be another source of pseudogenes. [377] These genes are believed to result from the reverse transcription of processed mRNA, which results from retro-transposition followed by an insertion of the copy DNA somewhere into the genome. [378] Retro-transposons are products of transcription (i.e., RNA), which then serve as the template for the production of DNA.

---

[373] Wen, et al., 2012.
[374] Brown, et al., 1996.
[375] Doolittle, 1993.
[376] Thiele, et al., 2003.
[377] Jackers, et al., 1996.
[378] Fairbanks and Maughan, 2006.

These DNA sequences are then reintegrated into genomic DNA, thus resulting in a duplicated gene. These so-called processed pseudogenes are commonly found on chromosome locations different from their functional counterparts.

DNA transcripts called messenger RNA (mRNA) carry the instructions for protein synthesis from the nucleus to the cell cytoplasm. The mRNA sequence consists of exons, which code for specific proteins. These exons are separated on the RNA strand by certain non-coding spacer sequences called introns. Processing of mRNA involves removing the intron sequences and splicing the exons together to form an edited mRNA copy.[379] This processed copy is then used for the production of proteins called translation. Some pseudogenes have introns removed after transcription, suggesting to some that they once were functional genes. It also suggests that they are still functional, even if their function is currently unknown.

Processed pseudogenes are believed to be produced after mRNA is edited to remove introns. The mRNA is then copied back into DNA by a reverse transcription process. The copy of mRNA, called copy DNA or cDNA, is then integrated back into the chromosome. A specific non-pseudogene example of this process is the L-1 family of repetitive DNA sequences.[380] Why this processing occurs is still unknown, but if past experience is any guide, the existence of this complex process indicates these pseudogenes have an important function in the cell.

Processed pseudogenes can produce complete copies of a specific coding sequence, and may also contain additional inserted sequences. However, these pseudogenes lack certain other sequences required for protein translation. Because processed pseudogenes are produced from processed mRNA, they lack introns and the necessary upstream regulatory sequences, (those existing in front of the gene), required for genes to direct and control protein assembly. Conversely, exceptions exist, but these altered pseudogenes often terminate in a series of

---

[379] Kandul and Noor, 2009.
[380] Jurka, 1989.

adenines called a poly-A-tail, as do functional genes. Most of these pseudogenes are also flanked by **direct repeats**; structures associated with movable genetic elements that may play a role in assisting the process of splicing pseudogenes into chromosomes.[381]

Pseudogenes and the Origins Debate

Pseudogenes are of major interest in the origins debate. Darwinists have assumed that the fact they closely resemble functional genes and have no known function is evidence for evolution and against intelligent design. Miller argues that "Intelligent design cannot explain the presence of non-functional pseudogenes unless it is willing to allow that the designer made serious errors, wasting millions of bases of DNA on a blueprint full of junk and scribbles. Evolution, in contrast, can easily explain them as nothing more than failed experiments in a random process of gene duplication in a genome of evolutionary remnants."[382]

In other words, an intelligent designer would not create an organism with a large number of useless parts, and these worthless genes are evidence that the genome was not designed. Hence, a creator did not play a role in the origin of the genome. However, as noted above, the claim that these genes are degraded functional genes is exactly what creationism predicts would occur due to the Fall of Man and Curse on Creation recorded in Genesis, Chapter 3.

Evolutionists also argue that the origin of pseudogenes is largely a result of chance, the outworking of natural law, the contingencies of history, and deficiencies in the entire genetic system. This view, however, has been forced to change due to the results of continuing discoveries in molecular biology and genetics. Some commentators conclude that the molecular revolution has produced more scientific knowledge in the past three decades than has accumulated in Science's

---

[381] Gibson, 1994.

[382] Miller, 1994, p. 25.

entire history and, if this trend continues, our view of the genome will no doubt continue to be revolutionized.[383]

In addition, some Darwinists argue, besides duplicated genes, pseudogenes also provide an additional mechanism for evolutionary change. They reason if pseudogenes serve no role in the organism, this permits an accumulation of non-lethal mutations. This allows the evolution of genes to become functional when enough mutations occur to produce a gene that confers a survival advantage to the organism. In other words, these Darwinists argue that many mutated pseudogenes would *not* be lethal because they are not necessary for life, but selection would favor them if enough mutations occurred so the gene *could* become beneficial in the future. In this way, they argue, pseudogenes could evolve to become useful genes.

A major problem with this evolutionary claim is that genes which are in fact pseudogenes cannot be selected for by natural selection because, by definition, they lack the sequences for transcription, thus would not help the organism. Instead, as non-functional, they would waste enormous energy and resources when they are copied, producing many hundreds of trillion of useless genes during the cell division of the 50 to 100 trillion adult human cells. This evolutionary idea is far-fetched and seriously problematic on a number of other grounds.

For the pseudogene to be selected, other mutations must also occur to enable the former pseudogene to be translated, and it will be selected for only if it has a beneficial function. If a gene can be translated, it is by definition not a pseudogene, and is assumed to have a function. A gene that cannot be transcribed will not undergo positive selection. If a pseudogene evolved that was useful in the organism, it must also evolve the many appropriate control sequences required for its regulation and proper function. Positive selection could not occur until all of the required control sequences *as a set* first existed. If a new beneficial gene was able to acquire the control mechanisms required to restore

---

[383] Willingham and Gingeras, 2006.

function, as evolutionists assume, so would a myriad of other currently harmful genes.

Another problem with the evolutionary interpretation of pseudogenes is that many or even most genes are pleiotropic, meaning that the gene produces proteins affecting more than one cell function.[384] Consequently, changing one gene will affect other proteins and cell functions. In addition, most biological structures and biochemical systems, such as blood clotting, require many genes—thus are polytrophic. All of the necessary parts must exist as part of a highly integrated functional set in order for the system to work.[385]

Similarity Indicates Function

Researchers have found that unprocessed pseudogenes exist in a wide variety of organisms. When genes for equivalent proteins in different species are compared, the coding sequences often differ in both expected and unexpected ways. Likewise, the more taxonomically similar the two species are, often the more similar their pseudogene DNA sequences. This is true in general, especially for specific enzymes, although some major exceptions exist to this overall pattern.

The fact that many pseudogenes are highly conserved, similar in both so-called primitive and advanced life-forms, and many are very similar in humans and other organisms, supports the conclusion that most of them have a function. It also supports the conclusion that the genome is a complex, very organized, well-designed system, and not a haphazard accumulation of genes originally formed as a result of mutations in an ancestral form and then inherited largely unchanged for eons down to our generation.

Similar pseudogene sequences in two related animals that supposedly originated from a common ancestor are called orthologous.[386] This

---

[384] Bergman, 2010.
[385] Behe, 1996.
[386] Gibson, 1994, p. 91; Woodmorappe, 2000.

similarity in different animals is used by both Darwinists and creationists to argue most pseudogenes have a function. The fact that pseudogenes "exhibit evolutionary conservation of gene sequence, reduced nucleotide variability, excess synonymous over non-synonymous nucleotide polymorphism, and other features that are expected in genes or DNA sequences that have functional roles" is evidence that they have one or more functional roles in the organism.[387]

Gene conservation is one of the strongest arguments for pseudogene function. If they were non-functional, mutations would accumulate and would not be conserved in the genome. Comparisons of DNA sequences from primates, including humans and chimps, reveal a considerable number of very similar pseudogenes, both in their sequence and positional relationship. One of the best-known examples is the *eta-globin* gene, which is part of the β-like globin gene family. Eta-globin is classified as a pseudogene only because it has no known start codon and several stop codons.

Evolutionists attempt to explain the sequence similarities of both genes and pseudogenes as a result of their inheritance from a common ancestor. Their often minor differences are attributed to the accumulation of mutations that have occurred since the species diverged from their hypothetical common ancestor. Conversely, creation explains the existing sequence similarities due to common designs because they serve similar functions. Chimps, gorillas, and humans all have the exact same number of beta-globin genes, that are arranged on the chromosome in the same order, a similarity that is strongly an indicator of functionality.[388] Another argument for the function of many or most pseudogenes is the fact that pseudogenes "are pervasive, and usually abundant, in all eukaryotic organisms."[389] Humans have about 12,000 DNA sequences that are evidence of pseudogenes and

---

[387] Balakirev and Ayala, 2003, p. 123.

[388] Lalley, et al., 1989.

[389] Wen, et al., 2012, p. 27.

comparative analysis of processed pseudogenes in the mouse and human genomes has surprisingly demonstrated that 60% of the processed pseudogenes are conserved in both mammalian species. The high abundance and conservation of the pseudogenes in a variety of species indicate that selective pressures preserve these genetic elements, and suggest that they may indeed perform important biological functions.[390]

Evolutionists also overlook the fact that the function of only a small number of the 200,000 kinds of proteins are fully understood. Sequence differences in many cases could reflect primarily differences required for the proteins to function properly in the various biological environments existing in different life-forms. The differences could also be the result of regulatory requirements of different animals. Likewise, pseudogenes would logically be similar if they have functions that constrain variation. The similarity of life is especially strong at the cellular level—the basic, undifferentiated eukaryotic cell structure existing in all animal life is almost identical. Too much variation from the required design could cause malfunction, resulting in disease or even death.

Useless Gene Hypothesis is Critical for Evolution

The useless gene hypothesis is a critical support for evolutionary assumptions about pseudogenes, but the theory breaks down when the earlier putatively "less-evolved" organism stage is evaluated. For example, *Escherichia coli* sequence evaluations reveal wall-to-wall genes (4,253 genes in its only 4.5 million DNA base pairs). Humans have just over three billion base pairs and only about 23,000 genes.[391] In

---

[390] Wen, et al., 2012, p. 27.
[391] Mishra, 2010, p. 16.

bacteria, the ratio of genes to DNA base pairs is 1 to 1,050; in humans, it is 1 to 100,000, a 95-times greater level.[392]

The pseudogene function issue is inextricably linked with the role of all non-coding DNA, including introns, satellite DNA (highly repetitive short DNA sequences), and other repetitive sequences.[393] Estimates of the number of non-gene coding DNA range from close to 5% for some bacteria, to 70% for some roundworms, to about 95% for humans.[394] Bacteria and viruses are said to contain wall-to-wall genes. It is significant that, in general, the "higher" the life-form, the *greater* the percent of non-coding DNA is contained in its genome. The fact that more complex life-forms tend to have proportionally more non-coding DNA also indicates that it has a function.[395] Another evidence for their function is the ENCODE project findings that many pseudogenes *are* transcribed, contradicting the once-common conclusion that

> most pseudogenes lost transcribed activity either due to their integration into the silent region of the genome or due to mutation of the promoter or auxiliary regulatory elements. However, recent increasing evidence has demonstrated that pseudogenes represent a significant proportion of the "transcriptome" in various organisms ... Evidence of expression of pseudogenes has been demonstrated not only in animals but also in plants.[396]

The ENCODE research project has found that most of the non-gene coding DNA has a critical role in the cell, mostly a regulatory function.

[392] Zheng and Gerstein, 2007, p. 220.
[393] Elder and Turner, 1995.
[394] Gibson, 1994, p. 104.
[395] Zheng and Gerstein, 2007.
[396] Wen, et al., 2012, pp. 28-29.

Gene Duplication Theory Problem

If most pseudogenes are indeed functionless, we would not expect that they would arise by the process of gene duplication gone awry. One reason is such gene duplication is evidence of deterioration, not evolutionary progress. Repetitive DNA, such as triplet repeat expansion disorders, are often associated with disease, such as Huntington's disease.

The function of many of the repetitive classes of non-protein coding DNA is now understood. For example, one set of moderately repeated DNA codes is now known to code for transfer RNA and ribosome RNA.[397] The genes that code for the five different histone types are usually clustered together on the genome, and this cluster forms a tandemly repeated array containing up to one hundred copies. Similarly, even globin and immunoglobulin genes are arranged as tandemly repeated arrays. These discoveries have significantly reduced the amount of alleged junk DNA. In short, if

> Pseudogenes are dysfunctional, why are they so highly expressed? Two possibilities may explain it. One possible explanation is that these pseudogenes are only incidental byproducts in the transcription events of other genes, because they are under the effect of the same promoters. An alternative explanation, which we are more inclined to accept, is that the pseudogene transcripts are in fact functional but not random products. More and more accumulating examples support this alternative explanation.[398]

---

[397] Zubay, 1995, p. 641.
[398] Wen, et al., 2012, p. 29.

Some Known Functions of Pseudogenes

As DNA research has progressed, functions for non-coding DNA have gradually been determined, and evidence that some, or even most, pseudogenes are functional has steadily accumulated.[399] Unprocessed pseudogenes are usually found on the same chromosome in clusters near similar, but functional sequences, indicating both order and function. A major factor that has influenced this view is the discovery that, although the gene control system is generally located a few bases upstream of the coding exons, more and more exceptions to this system have been discovered.[400]

Sometimes a functional mRNA is found to be produced from what was assumed to be a pseudogene. This assumption was disproved due to locating start codons that are either cryptic or located at a considerable distance from the gene's open reading frame (i.e., the DNA-sequence span between a start codon, ATG, and the nearest stop codon). In addition, the extra stop codons in many pseudogenes were found to be regulation elements that were selectively removed to allow for variation in the gene's products. One study of a pseudogene found that transcription began after a stop codon and produced a functional protein receptor. This pseudogene was previously assumed to be created by a frame-shift mutation.[401]

Gene regulation is now recognized as enormously complex, and the distribution of regulation factors in the genome is so widespread that the gene concept, as a *discrete* DNA region, has now been rejected.[402] As Balakirev and Ayala conclude, "pseudogenes that have been suitably investigated often exhibit functional roles, such as gene expression, gene regulation, and generation of genetic (antibody, antigenic, and other) diversity."[403]

---

[399] Wen, et al., 2012, pp. 28-29.
[400] Willingham and Gingeras, 2006, p. 1215.
[401] Balakirev and Ayala, 2003, p. 137.
[402] Pearson, 2006.
[403] Balakirev and Ayala, 2003, p. 123.

The observation that some genes once classified as pseudogenes have now been determined to have a function indicates that many more may be functional. For example, the chicken calmodulin gene, once considered nonfunctional, is now known to have an important function.[404] The pseudogenes that are transcribed but not translated, indicates a function for the transcript other than making protein. Studies of mouse pseudogenes indicate that as many as 50 percent can be transcribed.[405] Tam, et al., found a subset of pseudogenes that generate endogenous small interfering RNAs (endo-siRNAs) which

> are often processed from double-stranded RNAs formed by hybridization of spliced transcripts from protein-coding genes to anti-sense transcripts from homologous pseudogenes. An inverted repeat pseudogene can also generate abundant small RNAs directly. A second class of endo-siRNAs may enforce repression of mobile genetic elements, acting together with Piwi-interacting RNAs.[406]

Some classes of small RNAs that regulate transcription by blocking the translation of mRNA originate from what were once thought to be pseudogenes.[407]

Another function of pseudogenes is to bond to active genes during DNA replication to help stabilize the DNA. Some pseudogenes are involved in gene conversions or in recombination with functional genes to produce mRNA transcript variations; a design used in order to create protein variations.[408] Willingham and Gingeras concluded that the "widespread occurrence of non-coding RNAs—unannotated eukaryotic transcripts with reduced protein coding potential—suggests

---

[404] Yoshikazu and Yasuhiro, 1989; Adams, Knowler, and Leader, 1992, p. 307.
[405] Zheng and Gerstein, 2007.
[406] Tam, et al., 2008, p. 534.
[407] Guo et al., 2009.
[408] Balakirev and Ayala, 2003, p. 123.

that they are functionally important."[409] Some pseudogenes serve as "reservoirs of genetic variability" and this discovery has opened up a whole new area of research that has helped to explain the enormous variety of life existing in the living world.

Pseudogenes are also postulated to have many other functions, including assisting active genes, gene silencing, and regulating development.[410] Much of this research is ongoing and the results are still tentative. For example, evidence that pseudogenes may have a specific and important gene regulatory role has been derived from several studies. Further research, though, has questioned the findings of at least one study, that by Hirotsune et al. (2003), discussed below.

The Hirotsune Study

In 2003, Hirotsune et al.[411] reported that a mouse pseudogene served a regulatory role in development. They obtained a line of transgenic mice that died soon after birth due to multiple organ failure. Subsequent investigations concluded transcription of the *Mkrn1-ps1* pseudogene was disrupted in these mice by an insertion of the *Sex lethal* gene. In wild-type mice, *Mkrn1-ps1* pseudo-RNA was believed to be essential for mRNA isoform stability produced from the parental gene makorin 1. The proposed function of *Mkrn1-ps1* was also supported by finding abnormal development of the transgenic mice could be reduced by *Mkrn1-ps1* or *Mkrn1* by over-expression.

The evidence appeared so compelling that the researchers concluded they had identified a functional mammalian pseudogene. However, in a follow-up study, Gray et al. found evidence that *Mkrn1-ps1* was *not* transcribed and the transcript originally attributed to *Mkrn1-ps1* was an overlooked mRNA isoform at the *Mkrn1* locus.[412] Furthermore, in

---

409 Willingham and Gingeras, 2006, p. 1,215.
410 Zheng and Gerstein, 2007.
411 Hirotsune, et al., 2003.
412 Gray, et al., 2006.

the samples studied it was found that the 5'-regions of both *Mkrn1-ps1* alleles were fully methylated, also indicating this pseudogene was likely not transcribed. These "contradictory results underscore the difficulty in evaluating the functional status of a pseudogene."[413]

Because a large number of cell proteins interact as part of life's design, the interaction must be functional, or, at the least, the proteins cannot impede the roles of other proteins to cause adverse reactions. Consequently, a change in one protein often requires a change in a large number of other proteins to ensure that the protein's interactions with all of the other proteins are either neutral or beneficial. Likewise, it now appears that some or many pseudogenes have a function that requires compatibility with the rest of the genome.[414] For this reason, Zheng and Gerstein[415] conclude that the boundary between pseudogenes and other genes is now somewhat ambiguous.

In humans, some pseudogenes may be functional genes that were deactivated as part of their regulation or even possibly as a result of a mutation. Thus, "Pseudogenes may recover the full original function of the genes from which they derive ... by mutagenesis transfection, or in vivo by site-specific (or intermolecular) recombination."[416]

As we learn more details of the role of each gene in a cell, or at least the function of the protein they encode, such as found in the ENCODE project research, we will be better able to ascertain what DNA sequences, if any, are in fact functionless.[417] Only when the entire DNA genome is analyzed in detail will it be possible to determine the percentage, if any, of DNA that is actually non-coding or lacks a function in the genome. As Balakirev and Ayala write:

> How pervasive are "functional" pseudogenes? Many
> pseudogenes have been identified in all sorts of

---

[413] Zheng and Gerstein, 2007, p. 220.

[414] Woodmorappe, 2003; 2003a; 2003b; 2003c.

[415] Zheng and Gerstein, 2007.

[416] Balakirev and Ayala, 2003, p. 137.

[417] The Encode Consortium, 2007.

organisms on the grounds that they are duplicated genes that exhibit stop codons or other disabling mutations in their DNA sequences, so that they cannot have the full function of the original genes from which derived. In many of these cases, however, it remains unknown, because it has not been investigated, whether the pseudogenes, described only on the basis of DNA sequences, may have acquired regulatory or other functions, or play a role in generating generic variability.[418]

Much DNA which does not have a coding function serves other roles in the cell and the goal now is to discover these functions. Although the function of all human DNA is still unknown, it is clear that

there is no evidence for significant stretches of DNA with no function. Frequently, genes with related functions are clustered. These clustered genes are usually transcribed into single expression units (messenger RNA's) containing the information for the synthesis of several functionally related proteins.[419]

This same pattern of gene clustering also exists in the most "primitive" bacteria known.[420]

Even though geneticists have not yet *discovered* a use for many pseudogenes, this does not prove that none exists. It simply shows that we do not yet know the function of many DNA transcripts. Claims that pseudogenes have been proven to be useless cannot refer to the scientific literature for support because evidence for this view "is nowhere to be

---

[418] Balakirev and Ayala, 2003, p. 137.
[419] Zubay, 1995, p. 642.
[420] Zubay, 1995, p. 642. See also the ENCODE research Djebali, et al., 2012.

found."[421] The fact is, "Proving that a gene is totally nonfunctional, and is therefore definitely a pseudogene, is impossible."[422] Balakirev and Ayala concluded "some functionality [of pseudogenes] has been discovered in all cases, or nearly all, whenever this possibility has been pursued with suitable investigations."[423] Pink et al. add that although

> some pseudogenes are transcriptionally silent, others are active, raising the question of whether their non-coding transcripts are a spurious use of cellular energy or instead harnessed by the cell to regulate coding genes. This question is particularly pertinent given the recent flurry of evidence suggesting that long non-coding RNAs play a critical role in regulating genomic function.[424]

This observation explains the fact that some putative pseudogenes are named after the functional gene they resemble. For example, the 4,846 bp pseudogene named the "CEL-like" gene, (CELL), has a "striking homology" to the CEL gene, except the CELL pseudogene lacks exons 2-7 found in the CEL gene.[425] This putative pseudogene, as is true of many other once-labeled pseudogenes, is transcribed.

These examples challenge the original pseudogene definition that they are damaged genes. Rather, experimental verification now suggests that such a definition applies only to a "tiny proportion of the large number of pseudogenes present in a variety of genomes."[426] Some putative pseudogenes are linked together, which also suggests they

---

[421] Behe, 1996, p. 26.

[422] Mounsey, 2002, p. 770.

[423] Balakirev and Ayala, 2003, p. 137.

[424] Pink, et al., 2011, p. 792.

[425] Lidberg, et al., 1992, p. 630.

[426] Zheng and Gerstein, 2007, p. 219.

have a function.[427] Pseudogenes selectively transcribed indicates they were misnamed and should be reclassified.[428]

In short "the list of DNA sequences that have no effect on the organism has steadily decreased as knowledge of the operation of the genome has increased."[429] This research is critical because of the evidence that, for example, pseudogenes are important in cancer causation, and it is known

> that pseudogenes are capable of regulating tumor suppressors and oncogenes by acting as microRNA decoys. The finding that pseudogenes are often deregulated during cancer progression warrants further investigation into the true extent of pseudogene function. In this review, we describe the ways in which pseudogenes exert their effect on coding genes and explore the role of pseudogenes in the increasingly complex web of non-coding RNA that contributes to normal cellular regulation.[430]

Pseudogenes as Evidence of Dysgenetics

Some of the differences found in both genes and pseudogenes can be explained by the accumulation of mutations that have occurred since Creation.[431] The creationist view postulates that the original created organism was mutation-free, and the once-perfect genomic system has since degenerated, leading to some useless DNA sequences and numerous imperfect copies of genes. Mechanisms that could create

---

[427] Lamerdin, et al., 1996; Savelyeva, et al., 1998.; Schutte, et al., 2000.

[428] Zheng and Gerstein, 2007.

[429] Gibson, 1994, p. 104; see especially Djebali, et al., 2012.

[430] Pink, et al., 2011, p. 792.

[431] Woodmorappe, 2004.

pseudogenes include mutations, unequal crossing over that disrupts functional DNA sequences, and transposition errors.

For this reason, the existence of non-functional pseudogenes does not prove the genome was not designed. At most, it proves some designed genes were corrupted as a result of mutations or mistakes in some genetic process. Mistakes in gene copying commonly occur and, although the vast majority are repaired, some well-documented examples of non-corrected genes exist in the medical literature.[432] Up to two-fifths of all pregnancies now result in miscarriages, often because of DNA damage, a problem indicating human DNA is now enormously corrupt compared to the original creation.[433] Evidence that some pseudogenes are damaged genes also includes their involvement in disease.

Although some pseudogenes may not have a function due to genome deterioration, evolution cannot explain how, or why, both pseudogenes, and the entire genome for that matter, originally evolved.

Evolutionists have proposed that in order for pseudogenes to become functional, many complex proteins compatible with the pseudogene evolved. These include proteins that pry apart the two DNA strands and align the copying machinery at the proper location, enzymes that stitch the nucleotides together into the appropriate DNA string, proteins that strengthen the RNA string called "single stranded binding proteins," and other proteins that insert the pseudogene copy back into the chromatin DNA.[434] The creation model explains these examples as a result of genome degeneration.

A Creationist Perspective

The close similarity of the putative damage in pseudogenes in different life-forms, called "shared mistakes," is used to argue for evolution based on the

---

[432] Jorde, et al., 1997.

[433] e.g., see Meisenberg and Simmons, 2006, p. 153.

[434] Adams, et al., 1998.

JERRY BERGMAN, PH.D.

analogy that identical typo errors or other mistakes in printed texts argue for plagiarism from one of those earlier texts. Thus, identical putative errors in genes argues for a mistake in the postulated common ancestor that was passed down to its progeny.[435] In support of this view, Dawkins wrote that the "very existence of pseudogenes—useless, untranscribed genes that bear a marked resemblance to useful genes—is a perfect example of the way animals and plants have their history written all over them."[436]

Neo-Darwinists also argue "God would not create similar non-functional sequences in humans" and other animals, such as chimps, thus a common ancestor is the better explanation.[437] Aside from the difficulty of judging what God would or would not do, a mutation in a similar pseudogene may be in the same location in two different animals for many reasons, such as the gene is actually functional, or because a similar genetic mutation occurred due to the presence of a mutational *hot spot*, i.e., a site of frequent mutations.[438]

Many pseudogenes, such as those lacking promoters, contain evidence of a frame shift, nonsense mutations, or the loss of splice sites, all evidence of genetic degeneration. This evidence conforms to the Genesis account of the Fall as the cause of genetic degeneration, not the Darwinian progression view of evolution. Deterioration is a prediction of the creation model, while evolutionary advancement is a prediction of neo-Darwinism.[439]

As Zheng and Gerstein note, the discovery that some pseudogenes are functional has raised the question:

> how should the concept of 'nonfunctional' be interpreted in defining pseudogenes? How could this finding be amalgamated with the established evolutionary theory, which often uses pseudogenes

---

[435] Woodmorappe, 2004.
[436] Dawkins, 2009, p. 336.
[437] Gibson, 1994, p. 91.
[438] Andersson and Andersson, 2001.
[439] Williams, 1981, pp. 114-119.

as nonfunctional and neutrally evolving DNAs for estimating various parameters in evolution? The scientific community, especially those dealing with molecular evolution and gene or pseudogene annotation, began to ponder these questions.[440]

Possible functions for pseudogenes are reported almost monthly.[441] The title of one article on this topic, "Pseudogenes are Not Pseudo any More" is a good summary of the current state of the research.[442]

Conclusions

Arguing for evolutionary naturalism on the basis of DNA sequences not having a known function is an argument from ignorance.[443] Now that we know that many pseudogenes are transcribed and have been determined to have a function, the most that can be concluded is that the function of many pseudogenes is currently unknown. As the history of the neo-Darwinism vestigial organ argument has documented, the function of many body organs and structures was determined as more knowledge about anatomy and physiology was gained.[444]

Until the entire human genome has been carefully and fully studied, a feat that may still be decades away, it is premature at this early stage of genome research to conclude that any gene or structure is functionless.[445] Already, many examples of clear function have been found, falsifying the "useless junk" gene theory.[446] As noted above, pseudogenes that have been carefully

---

[440] Zheng and Gerstein, 2007, p. 219.
[441] Hernández, et al., 1998; Baertsch, et al., 2008; Cooper and Kehrer-Sawatzki, 2008; Jegga and Aronow, 2008; Pink, et al., 2011.
[442] Wen, 2012, p. 27.
[443] Balakirev and Ayala, 2003.
[444] Bergman and Howe, 1990.
[445] Zheng and Gerstein, 2007.
[446] Sakai, et al., 2008; Sasidharan and M. Gerstein, 2008, pp. 729-1001.

investigated often exhibit functional roles, such as gene expression, gene regulation, [and] generation of genetic (antibody, antigenic, and other) diversity. Pseudogenes are involved in gene conversion or recombination with functional genes. Pseudogenes exhibit evolutionary conservation of gene sequence, reduced nucleotide variability, excess synonymous over non-synonymous nucleotide polymorphism, and other features that are expected in genes or DNA sequences that have functional roles.[447]

As a result, the following conclusion has now been supported by the evidence:

Pseudogenes have long been labeled as "junk" DNA, failed copies of genes that arise during the evolution of genomes. However, recent results are challenging this moniker; indeed, some pseudogenes appear to harbor the potential to regulate their protein-coding cousins. Far from being silent relics, many pseudogenes are transcribed into RNA, some exhibiting a tissue-specific pattern of activation. Pseudogene transcripts can be processed into short interfering RNAs that regulate coding genes through the RNAi pathway.[448]

The latest conclusion is that the research

evidence has shown that pseudogenes are not only transcribed, but also post-transcriptionally modulate their cognate genes by three distinct mechanisms: (1) natural anti-sense RNA suppression; (2) RNA

[447] Balakirev and Ayala, 2003, p. 123.
[448] Pink, et al., 2011, p. 792.

interference by producing siRNAs; and (3) acting as decoys of stabilizing or disabling/inhibiting factors.[449]

Only when the various functions of each gene are fully understood can viable conclusions about uselessness be hypothesized. Even then, as noted above, "proving that a gene unit is totally nonfunctional, and therefore definitely a pseudogene, is impossible."[450] The discovery that some sequences labeled pseudogenes perform genetic functions justifies the assumption that many, if not most, pseudogenes may eventually be found to have a function. Current research continues to support this conclusion. As Zheng and Gerstein concluded, the "diverse ways that a genome sequence can realize its biological function have made it difficult to define a nonfunctional sequence."[451]

The evolutionary view involving mutational and natural selection predicts a mechanism that facilitates, or at least allows, the evolution of the genome. This would involve the transformation from one hypothetical pre-gene into the millions of different genes existing in the living world by known, plausible, naturalistic processes. This evolutionary idea includes a naturalistic means of producing new genes that are functional, and yet not detrimental, to allow some of these genes to confer a survival advantage to the organism.

As more and more animal and plant genomes are sequenced and analyzed, it is becoming increasingly clear that the design view fits the data far better than the Darwinian view. It is clear that a whole "genome is less like a static library of information than an active computer operating system for a living thing."[452] A design view predicts the entire genome was originally functional dominated by information, stability, design, purpose, and order, but has degraded somewhat over time.[453] This complex system is evidence for order, design, and purpose for

[449] Wen, et al., 2012, p. 29.
[450] Mounsey, et al., 2003, p. 772.
[451] Zheng and Gerstein, 2007, p. 222.
[452] Gerstein and Zheng, 2006, p. 49.
[453] Williams, 1981.

most pseudogenes, even in their present post-Fall condition.[454] It is now recognized that the study of functional pseudogenes is just beginning and many questions remain that need

> to be addressed, such as the regulatory elements controlling the cell or tissue specific expression of pseudogenes. But, definitely, the so-called pseudogenes are really functional, not to be considered any more as just "junk" or "fossil" DNA. Surely many functional pseudogenes and novel regulatory mechanisms remain to be discovered and explored in diverse organisms.[455]

The research so far has falsified Dawkins' boast that pseudogenes are useful only for embarrassing creationists. We do not need to stretch our "creative ingenuity to make up a convincing reason why an intelligent designer should have created a pseudogene" as Dawkins claims. We need only to read the scientific literature.

---

[454] Pitman, 2012.

[455] Wen, et al., 2012, p. 31.

References

Adam, E., M.R. Volkert, and M. Blot. 1998. "Cytochrome C biogenesis is involved in the transposon Tn5-mediated bleomycin resistance and the associated fitness effect in *Escherichia coli*." *Molecular Microbiology* 28(1):15-24, April.

Adams, Roger, John Knowler, and David Leader. 1992. *The Biochemistry of the Nuclear Acids*. New York, NY: Chapman and Hall.

Andersson, J.O., and S.G. Andersson. 2001. "Pseudogenes, Junk DNA, and the Dynamics of Rickettsia Genomes." *Molecular Biology and Evolution* 18(5):829-839.

Baertsch, R., M. Diekhans, W. Kent, D. Haussler, and J. Brosius. 2008. "Retrocopy Contributions to the Evolution of the Human Genome." *BMC Genomics* 9:466, October 8.

Balakirev, Evgeniy S., and Francisco J. Ayala. 2003. "Pseudogenes: Are they "Junk" or Functional DNA?" *Annual Review of Genetics* 37(1):123-151.

Behe, Michael J. 1996. *Darwin's Black Box*. New York, NY: Free Press.

_____. 2003. "A Functional Pseudogene?: An Open Letter to Nature." *Discovery.org*, May 13.

Bergman, Jerry. 1994. "Genetic Function of Introns as a Means of Reducing Copying Errors." *Ohio Journal of Science* 94:25.

_____. 2001. "The Functions of Introns: From Junk DNA to Designed DNA." *Perspectives on Science and Christian Faith* 53(3):170-178.

_____. 2006. "Does Gene Duplication Provide the Engine for Evolution?" *Journal of Creation* 20(1):99-104, April.

_____. 2010. "The Pleiotropy Problem for Evolution." *CRSQ* 46(4):284-289.

_____ and George Howe. 1990. *Vestigial Organs are Fully Functional: A History and Evaluation of the Vestigial Organ Origins Concept.* Terre Haute, IN: Creation Research Society Books.

Brown, M.A., C.F. Xu, H. Nicolai, B. Griffiths, J.A. Chambers, D. Black, and E. Solomon. 1996. "The 5' End of the BRCA1 Gene Lies within a Duplicated Region of Human Chromosome 17q21." *Oncogene* 12(12):2,507-2,513, June 30.

Chen, Chingfer, Andrew J. Gentles, Jerzy Jurka, and Samuel Karlin. 2002. "Genes, Pseudogenes, and Alu Sequence Organization across Human Chromosomes 21 and 22." *Proceedings of the National Academy of Sciences of the United States of America* 99(5):2,930-2,935.

Cooper, D.N., and H. Kehrer-Sawatzki (editors). 2008. *Handbook of Human Molecular Evolution*, Volumes 1 and 2. New York, NY: John Wiley & Sons.

Cooper, S. 1999. *Human Gene Evolution.* New York, NY: Academic Press.

Dawkins, R. 2009. *The Greatest Show on Earth: The Evidence for Evolution.* New York, NY: The Free Press.

Djebali, S., et al. 2012. "Landscape of Transcription in Human Cells." *Nature* 489(7414):101-108.

Doolittle, R.R. 1993. "The Comings and Goings of Homing Endonucleases and Mobile Introns." *Proceedings of the National Academy of Science* 90(12):5379-5381.

Elder, John, and Bruce J. Turner. 1995. "Concerted Evolution of Repetitive DNA Sequences in Eukaryotes." *The Quarter Review of Biology* 710(3):297-315.

The Encode Consortium. 2007. *Nature* 447(7146):799-816, June 14.

Fairbanks, Daniel J., and Peter J. Maughan. 2006. "Evolution of the NANOG Pseudogene Family in the Human and Chimpanzee Genomes." *BMC Evolutionary Biology* 6(12), DOI:10.1186/1471-1471-2148-6-12.

Gerstein, Mark, and Deyou Zheng. 2006. "The Real Life of Pseudogenes." *Scientific American* 295(2):48-55, August.

Gibson, L.J. 1994. "Pseudogenes and Origins." *Origins* 21(2):91-108.

Gray, T.A., A. Wilson, P.J. Fortin, and Robert D. Nicholls. 2006. "The Putatively Functional *Mkrn1-p1* Pseudogene is Neither Expressed nor Imprinted, Nor Does it Regulate its Source Gene Trans." *Proceedings of the National Academy of Science* 103(32):12,039-12,044.

Guo, X., Zhaolei Z., M.B. Gerstein, D. Zheng. 2009. "Small RNAs Originated from Pseudogenes: *cis-* or *trans-* Acting?" *PLoS Computational Biology* 5(7):1-15, e1000449.

Hernández, J.M., B. Blat, C. Iruela, F. Vila, and J. Hernández-Yago. 1998. "Identification of Two Processed Pseudogenes of the Human Tom20 Gene." *Molecular & General Genetics* 258(1-2):117-122.

Hirotsune, Shinji, Noriyuki Yoshida, Amy Chen, Lisa Garrett, Fumihiro Suglyama, Satoru Takahashi, Ken-ichi Yagami, Anthony Wynshaw-Boris, and Atsushi Yoshiki. 2003. "An Expressed Pseudogene Regulates the Messenger-RNA Stability of Its Homologous Coding Gene." *Nature* 423(6935):91-96.

Holmes, Bob. 1995. "Did Genetic 'Garbage' Spur Primate Evolution?" *New Scientist.* September 15, p. 18.

Jackers, P., N. Clausse, M. Fernandez, A. Berti, F. Princen, U. Wewer, M.E. Sobel, and V. Castronovo. 1996. "Seventeen Copies of the Human 37 kDa Laminin Receptor Precursor/p40 Ribosome-Associated Protein Gene are Processed Pseudogenes Arisen from Retropositional Events." *Biochimica et Biophysica Acta* 1305(1-2):98-104, February 7.

Jacq, C., J.R. Miller, and G.G. Brownlee. 1977. "A Pseudogene Structure in 5S DNA of Xenopus Laevis." *Cell* 12(1):109-120, September 1.

Jegga, A.G., and B.J. Aronow. 2008. "Evolutionarily Conserved Noncoding DNA." In *Handbook of Human Molecular Evolution*, Volume 1, pp. 853-860. Edited by David N. Cooper and Hildegard Kehrer-Sawatzki. New York, NY: John Wiley & Sons.

Jorde, Lynn, John Carey, and Raymond White. 1997. *Medical Genetics*. St. Louis, MO: Mosby.

Jurka, J. 1989. "Subfamily Structure and Evolution of the Human L1 Family of Repetitive Sequences." *Journal of Molecular Evolution* 29(6):496-503.

Kandul, N.P., and M. Noor. 2009. "Large Introns in Relation to Alternative Splicing and Gene Evolution: A Case Study of *Drosophila bruno-3*." *BMC Genetics* 10(67):1-16.

Lalley, P.A., M.T. Davison, J.A. Graves, S.J. O'Brien, J.E. Womack, T.H. Roderick, N. Creau-Goldberg, A.L. Hillyard, D.P. Doolittle, and J.A. Rogers. 1989. "Report of the Committee on Comparative Mapping." *Cytogenetics and Cell Genetics* 51(1-4):503-532.

Lamerdin, J.E., S.A. Stilwagen, M.H. Ramirez, L. Stubbs, and A.V. Carrano. 1996. "Sequence Analysis of the ERCC2 Gene Regions in Human, Mouse, and Hamster Reveals Three Linked Genes." *Genomics* 34(3):399-409, June.

Lee, Jeannie T. 2003. "Molecular Biology: Complicity of Gene and Pseudogene." *Nature* 423(6935):26-28.

Lidberg, U., J. Nilsson, K. Stromberg, G. Stenman, P. Sahlin, S. Enerback, and G. Bjursell. 1992. "Genomic Organization, Sequence Analysis, and Chromosomal Localization of the Human Carboxyl Ester Lipase (CEL) Gene and a CEL-Like (CELL) Gene." *Genomics* 13(3):630-640.

Meisenberg, Gerhard, and William Simmons. 2006. *Principles of Medical Biochemistry*. Philadelphia, PA: Mosby.

Miller, Kenneth R. 1994. "Life's Grand Design." *Technology Review* 97(2):24-32, February-March. http://millerandlevine.com/km/evol/lgd/index.html.

Mishra, N.C. 2010. *Introduction to Proteomics: Principles and Applications*. Hoboken, NJ: Wiley

Mounsey, A., et al. 2002. "Evidence Suggesting That a Fifth Annotated *Caenorhabditis elgegans* Genes May be Pseudogenes." *Genome Research* 12(5):770-775, May.

Nishikimi, M., R. Fukuyama, S. Minoshima, N. Shimizu and K. Yagi. 1994. "Cloning and chromosomal mapping of the human nonfunctional gene for L-gulono-gamma-lactone oxidase, the enzyme for L-ascorbic acid biosynthesis missing in man." *The Journal of Biological Chemistry* 269(18):13,685-13,688, May 6.

Pearson, H. 2006. "Genetics: What is a Gene?" *Nature* 441(7092):398-401, May 24.

Pink, C., K. Wicks, D. Caley, E. Punch, L. Jacobs, and D. Carter. 2011. "Pseudogenes: Pseudo-Functional or Key Regulators in Health and Disease?" *RNA* 17(5):792-798, May.

Pitman, Sean D. 2002. "Pseudogenes." Unpublished paper. [https://www.creationapologetics.org/editorials/pseudogenes.html, March.]

Sakai, Hiroaki, Takeshi Itoh, and Takashi Gojobori. 2008. "Processed Pseudogenes and Their Functional Resurrection in the Human and Mouse Genomes." *Handbook of Human Molecular Evolution*. London, UK: John Wiley & Sons, pp. 1203-1208.

Sanford, J. 2005. *Genetic Entropy & The Mystery of the Genome*. Lima, NY: Ivan Press.

Sasidharan, R., and M. Gerstein. 2008. "Protein Fossils Live on as RNA." *Nature* 435(7196):729-1,001, June 5.

Savelyeva, L., A. Class, S. Gier, P. Schlag, L. Finke, J. Mangion, M.R. Stratton, and M. Schwab. 1998. "An Interstitial Tandem Duplication of 9p23-24 Coexists with a Mutation in the BRCA2 Gene in the Germ Line of Three Brothers with Breast Cancer." *Cancer Research* 58(5):863-866, March 1.

Schutte, Brian C., Bryan C. Bjork, Kevin B. Coppage, Margaret I. Malik, Simon G. Gregory, Deborah J. Scott, Luci M. Brentzell, Yoriko Watanabe, Michael J. Dixon, and Jeffrey C. Murray. 2000. "A Preliminary Gene Map for the Van der Woude Syndrome Critical Region Derived from 900 kb of Genomic Sequence at 1q32-q41." *Genome Research* 10(1):81-94, February. www.genome.org.

Svensson Ö, L. Arvestad, and J. Lagergren. 2006. "Genome-Wide Survey for Biologically Functional Pseudogenes." *PLOS Computational Biology* 2(5):358-369.

Tam, O., A. Aravin, P. Stein, A. Girard, E. Murchison, S. Cheloufi, E. Hodges, M. Anger, R. Sachidanandam, R. Schultz, and G.. Hannon. 2008. "Pseudogene-derived Small Interfering RNAs Regulate Gene Expression in Mouse Oocytes." *Nature* 453(7194):534-538, April 10.

Thiele, H.M. Berger, A. Skalweit, and B. Thiele. 2003. "Expression of the Gene and Processed Pseudogenes Encoding the Human and Rabbit Translationally Controlled Tumor Protein (TCTP)." *European Journal of Biochemistry* 267:5473–5481.

Wen, Y-Z., L-L. Zheng, L-H. Qu, F.J. Ayala, and Z-R. Lun. 2012. "Pseudogenes are Not Pseudo any More." *RNA Biology* 9(1):27-32.

Willingham, A., and T. Gingeras. 2006. "TUF Love for 'Junk' DNA." *Cell* 125(7):1215-1220, June 30.

Williams, E. 1981. *A Creation Model for Natural Processes in Thermodynamics and the Development Order.* Chino Valley, AZ: Creation Research Society Books.

Woodmorappe, John. 2000. "Are Pseudogenes 'Shared Mistakes' Between Primate Genomes?" *CEN Technical Journal* 14(3):55-71.

_____. 2003a. "Pseudogene Function: Regulation of Gene Expression." *TJ* 17(1):47-52.

_____. 2003b. "Pseudogene Function: More Evidence." *TJ* 17(2):15-18.

_____. 2003c. "Unconventional Gene Behavior and Its Relationship to Pseudogenes." *Proceedings of The Fifth International Conference on Creationism on Creationism.* Edited by Robert L. Ivey, Jr., pp. 505-514. Pittsburgh, PA: Creation Science Fellowship.

_____. 2004. "Potentially Decisive Evidence Against Pseudogene 'Shared Mistakes.'" *TJ* 18(3):63-69.

Yoshikazu Ohya, Y., and A. Yasuhiro. 1989. "Functional Expression of Chicken Calmodulin in Yeast." *Biochemical and Biophysical Research Communications* 158(2):541-547, January 1.

Zheng, Deyou, and Mark B. Gerstein. 2007. "The Ambiguous Boundary Between Genes and Pseudogenes: The Dead Rise Up, or Do They?" *Trends in Genetics* 23(5):219-224, May.

Zubay, Geoffrey L. 1995. *Principles of Biochemistry.* Dubuque, IA: William C. Brown Pub.

LOUIS PASTEUR (1822-1895), A CREATIONIST WHO DISPROVED THE THEORY OF
SPONTANEOUS GENERATION. HIS WORK WAS IMPORTANT IN ESTABLISHING THE
SCIENTIFIC STUDY OF BACTERIA. PHOTOGRAPH BY E. PIROU . COURTESY OF THE
WELLCOME COLLECTION, LONDON

CHAPTER 7

Antibiotic Resistance
and Macroevolution

Introduction

One of the most common arguments against the creation worldview is the well-documented development of antibiotic resistance in pathogenic bacteria that cause infections.[456] Many Darwinists have claimed that the development of antibacterial resistance is one of the strongest evidences for Darwinian evolution. A typical example is in the book *The Evolution Explosion* by Harvard biologist Stephen Palumbi. In this work, according to a recent review, Palumbi discusses in detail the cases in which human's abuse of chemicals have caused

> evolution in other species by changing their environments: his examples include the evolution of antibiotic resistance in bacteria, herbicide resistance in plants, pesticide resistance in insects, and changes in the growth rate of fish caused by overfishing. Remarkably, many people familiar with these phenomena have failed to see that they demonstrate evolution driven by

---

[456] Ayala, 1978.

selection. There is, for example, a public misconception that 'drug resistance' involves not evolutionary change in pathogenic bacteria, but some process whereby a person becomes acclimated to antibiotics.[457]

Other examples of the claim that development of antibiotic resistance proves macroevolution include Greenspan,[458] Crews,[459] Iltis,[460] and Kopaska-Merkel.[461] This chapter focuses on the common claim that the development of bacterial resistance to antibiotics provides evidence for the molecules-to-human evolution via mutations theory.

Development of antibiotic resistance is a major concern for another reason—human health. Infectious diseases historically have killed billions and have caused several of the most devastating chapters in humankind's history.[462] Scientists have been so successful in the past century in preventing and curing infectious diseases that only a few years ago it was incorrectly assumed that modern science had, at last, enabled us to "close the book on infectious diseases."[463]

Recent history has proven this conclusion to be tragically premature.[464] Two major topics of current concern in the fields of communicable diseases are emerging, namely new infectious diseases, such as HIV, Ebola and the Zika virus, and "reemerging" infectious diseases, such as pertussis.[465] The development of resistance must be understood in order to deal with the serious health threat posed by this development.

The modern bacterial resistance problem has many causes, including the misuse of antibiotics and the transfer of resistance

---

[457] Coyne, 2001, p. 586.
[458] Greenspan, 2002.
[459] Crews, 2001.
[460] Iltis, 2000, pp. 44-45.
[461] Levine and Miller, 1994; Kopaska-Merkel, 2000, p. 44.
[462] Marks and Beatty, 1976.
[463] Berkelman and Hughes, 1993, p. 426.
[464] Garrett, 1995; Rothman and Greenland, 1998.
[465] DiSpezio, 1998.

genes from one bacterium to another.[466] This is possible because many bacteria have a built-in natural resistance to a number of antibiotics, and the genes that produce this resistance can be passed on to other bacteria by a variety of means.

Bacteria that have become resistant to several different antibiotics, called multi-drug resistance, as we will explain, are often incorrectly called 'superbugs' by the media.[467] Vancomycin is now the most effective agent for some pathogens, but even it has lost some of its effectiveness in recent years.[468] Resistance can exist at various levels. The low-level is when the antibiotic amount required to kill or inhibit bacteria growth is only slightly above the level that is commonly required to inhibit growth in susceptible non-resistant organisms. High-level resistance is where the antibiotic levels that must be administered can be as high as ten or more times the level required to kill susceptible organisms without harming the host.[469]

The Mechanisms Involved in Antibiotic and Pesticide Resistance

Non-resistant bacteria commonly become resistant by several different methods, most of which have nothing to do with mutations or Darwinism. In most cases, antibiotic resistance results from the fact that persons with certain traits are better able to survive exposure to pathogens. This especially includes health protection traits that are highly variable, such as the natural defenses existing in all organisms.[470]

An important mechanism by which bacteria become resistant to antibiotics is by obtaining one or more specific resistance genes from another bacterium. Most antibiotic-resistant genes in bacteria

---

[466] Finegold, 1979.

[467] Barbour and Restrepo, 2000, pp. 449-457.

[468] Padiglione, et al., 2000; Yan, et al., 2000.

[469] Baquero, 2002, p. 51.

[470] Palumbi, 2001, p. 1,787.

are located on small circular units of DNA called plasmids, that are commonly passed on to other bacteria, and even can be spread from dead to living bacteria.[471] The plasmid-containing genes for drug resistance are called **resistance factors** or **r-factors**.

Bacteria can obtain new genes from other bacteria by several methods, but the most common one is by **conjugation**. Conjugation is a complex system that transfers a copy of a small set of genes in a plasmid from one bacterium cell, called the donor, to another bacterium, called the recipient. Tube-like structures called pili latch onto the recipient and position it in such a way that a conjugation bridge can form, allowing for the transfer of resistance genes.[472] A common example is bacterial resistance to penicillin, acquired by obtaining the gene that produces penicillinase by conjugation. Penicillinase is an enzyme that alters the penicillin molecule in such a way that it is rendered ineffective.

Some antibiotics may be temporarily effective, but cellular repair mechanisms, redundant regulatory systems, or subsequent protein synthesis, later restores vitality to the bacteria. Some pathogenic organisms respond to the antibiotic by producing a significant increase in its metabolism, so that the previous antibiotic level is no longer sufficient to interfere with its metabolic process.

Bacteria also can acquire new genes by two other similar processes. The first is **transduction**, a virus-mediated transfer of DNA from one host to another one. Bacterial viruses, known as **bacteriophages**, sometimes pick up a resistance gene from a naturally resistant bacterium, which they in turn can pass on to non-resistant bacteria. In this case, the bacteria's genome gains new information, but the source is not from mutations. Instead, the new genetic material is from another bacterium that already possessed the resistance gene, or gene set, that confers resistance. This resistance type is obtained by the transfer of resistance plasmids preexisting in the bacterium gene pool.

---

[471] Black, 2014.
[472] Black, 2014.

This plasmid produces an enzyme that either destroys or inactivates the antimicrobial substance.[473]

The second method of transfer is **transformation**, the process in which a bacterium takes up exogenous DNA from its environment. Also, many gene sets called transposons are self-transmissible and can transfer one or more genes from their normal location to other plasmids or chromosomes. Some transferred genes enable the bacteria to become resistant by producing enzymes designed to destroy or inactivate the antibiotic drug.

Another example of transformation is passing genes to bacteria that enable the recipient bacteria to produce a necessary vitamin or other compound whose production is blocked by the antibiotic. For example, sulfonamide works by blocking the bacteria's ability to synthesize folic acid, which is required for growth. If the genes used to manufacture folic acid are acquired from another bacterium, the recipient bacterium can synthesize its own folic acid, rendering the sulfonamide ineffective, or at least far less effective.

Resistance can result from means other than gene acquisition.[474] Sulfonamide resistance is also due to mutations, such as in *Streptococcus pneumoniae* resistance, which is evidently usually due to changes in the gene coding for the enzyme dihydropteroate synthase (DHPS), the enzyme that allows bacteria to synthesize folic acid.[475] Folate co-enzyme studies support the conclusion that mutations in DHPS affect resistance.

Antibiotics Inactivated by Various Other Means

Antibiotics in the periplasm or cytoplasm may be inactivated by bacteria through three mechanisms, **modification**, **isolation**, or **destruction**, none of which are due to mutations, but rather are caused

---

[473] Burton and Engelkirk, 2000, pp. 199-201.
[474] See Maskell, et al., 1997.
[475] Kazanjian, et al., 2000.

by complex innate physiological mechanisms. One example is when bacterially manufactured enzymes alter the antibiotic drug so that it is no longer toxic to the bacteria. That this is not a result of new mutations is documented by the fact that medically prescribed antibiotics usually come from fungi and bacteria, both which have coexisted since creation. This antibiotic is produced naturally by both fungi and bacteria as part of their own defense systems against bacteria. Without their innate defenses, bacteria could not protect themselves from other bacteria, and soon would become extinct.

Most commercial antibiotics were originally produced by fungi or bacteria as part of their own natural defense system. In response to antibiotics, bacteria have many well designed built-in systems to protect and defend themselves. What is commonly referred to as *gaining resistance* to an antibiotic is more accurately understood as a bacterial strain that has *lost sensitivity* to the antibiotic.[476]

Bacteria were resistant to many antibiotics long before humans used them. This has been confirmed by culturing bacteria found on human explorers frozen to death long before human-developed antibiotics existed. A 1988 University of Alberta study of the bacteria found in the bodies of Arctic explorers frozen in ice in 1845 discovered that some of the bacterial strains were resistant to antibiotics.[477] The study, which evaluated six strains of genus *Clostridium* in three men who were buried in permafrost, found that the bacteria were particularly resistant to clindamycin and cefoxitin. Both these antibiotics were marketed over a century after the men died.[478] Clostridia are part of the normal bacteria flora of the human gut.

An antibiotic drug also can be deactivated by modifying a critical part of its molecular structure. An example is **beta-lactamase**, an enzyme that attacks the antibiotic penicillin primarily by damaging its beta-lactam ring. As a result, the antibiotic is no longer functional, and therefore microorganisms that produce beta-lactamase are resistant

---

[476] Rowland, 1987.
[477] McGuire, 1988.
[478] Struzik, 1990, p. 1.

to *all* antibiotics containing the beta-lactam ring. Beta-lactamase is manufactured by a set of genes on R-plasmids that can be passed to other bacteria. In 1982, over 90% of all clinical *Staphylococcus* infections were penicillin-resistant, compared to close to 0% in 1952.[479] The reason for the increase was due largely to the rapid spread of the beta-lactamase plasmid, primarily by conjugation transfer, and *not* evolution by new mutations.

As a result of the ineffectiveness of penicillin, doctors often administer methicillin, a drug that kills bacteria by disabling another bacterial metabolic mechanism. By the 1980s, several important strains of *Staphylococcus* also were resistant, not only to methicillin, but also to another drug known as nafcillin.

A 1990 study found most strains of staphylococci were resistant to many different antibiotics. A research team treated a patient infected with a bacterial strain that was resistant to cadmium, penicillin, kanamycin, neomycin, streptomycin, tetracycline, and trimethoprim. Because all

> of these drugs operated by specific biochemical mechanisms that were used by a host of related drugs, the Australian staph could resist, to varying degrees, some thirty-one different drugs. In a series of test-tube studies, the Australians showed that these various resistance capabilities were carried on different plasmids that could be separately passed from one bacterium to another. The most common mode of passage was conjugation: one bacterium simply stretched out its cytoplasm and passed plasmids to its partner.[480]

In 1992, almost 15% of all *Staphylococcus* in the USA were methicillin-resistant, and by 1993 vancomycin remained the only antibiotic that could kill all strains of the organism.[481]

---

[479] Garrett, 1994.

[480] Garrett, 1995, p. 413.

[481] Garrett, 1994, p. 412.

Staphylococci are everywhere—in the soil, on human skin, and in our oral cavities—and can easily be passed on to other persons by simple body contact. The majority of the almost one-million annual post-surgical infections were due to staphylococcal infections, mostly by the methicillin-resistant staph strain.

A major cause of this situation is overuse of antibiotics that kill the non-resistant strains, allowing the resistant strains to thrive and become more common.

Transporters and Efflux Pumps

Yet another method whereby bacteria can become resistant to antibiotics is by transfer of the genes that manufacture the cell pumps that remove antibiotics from the cell before they can cause harm. These selective pumps can remove many kinds of toxins, including anti-cancer drugs. Efflux pumps use metabolic energy to transfer antibiotics from the cytoplasm to outside of the cell, thereby reducing the effective concentration of the antibiotics inside the cell. These **multi-drug resistant pumps** are often manufactured by a set of genes located on plasmids which can be passed to other bacteria during conjugation.

The pump mechanism attaches a protein label to the antibiotic drug that causes it to be removed from the bacteria by exocytosis. A family of similar mechanisms exists in both prokaryotic and eukaryotic cells. Humans possess a super-family of transporters, such as the human P-glycoprotein that can remove a diverse class of amphipathic drugs from cells. The P-glycoproteins also result in multi-drug resistant cancer cells.[482]

---

[482] Chang and Roth, 2001.

Resistance Due to Mutations

Bacteria can also become resistant as a result of mutations, but all of those mutations studied so far are either *loss* mutations, or gene *expression* mutations that result in speeding up the already existing systems that remove or inactivate antibiotics. None are the result of new cellular innovations but are caused merely by altering the volume control.

Some antibiotics function by binding to certain sites on bacterial cells. A point mutation can alter the geometry of the antibiotic binding site and, as a result, the mutation can protect the bacteria from the antibiotic. A down side is that the mutation can degrade or destroy the function for which the binding site was designed. For example, a neutral mutation in one amino acid that prevents the required antibody-enzyme interaction alters the binding site on the 4-quinolone antibiotic which disables the gyrase enzyme in bacteria.

The classic example of this mechanism is ribosome point mutations that have rendered streptomycin and other mycin antibiotics ineffective.[483] Mycin antibiotics function by attaching to a specific receptor site on the bacteria's ribosomes, thereby interfering with their protein-manufacturing process. As a result, the proteins the bacteria produce are now either non-functional, or are not produced. The result is the bacteria cannot grow, divide, or propagate.

Bacterial mutations cause the bacteria to become streptomycin-resistant if the ribosome site, where the streptomycin attaches, is altered by mutations. As a result, the streptomycin no longer can bind, and therefore no longer interferes with the ribosomal function of producing protein. Mutation-caused changes that enable the bacteria to become mycin-resistant can occur in several different locations on the ribosome.[484]

Mammalian ribosomes do not contain the specific site where myosin drugs attach, and for this reason the drug does not interfere

---

[483] Davies, et al., 1971; Davies and Nomura, 1972.
[484] Didier, et al., 1999.

with mammal ribosome function. Consequently, mycin drugs adversely affect bacterial growth without harming the host. Because fundamental differences exist between prokaryotic (bacterial) and eukaryotic ribosomes, these variations often are exploited in order to produce antibiotics to kill bacteria without harming the host.

In *Mycobacterium tuberculosis* bacteria, an enzyme changes the antibiotic isoniazid into its active form that kills the bacteria. In another example of a mutation-caused resistance, the mutation damages the enzyme which converts the antibiotic into its active form, allowing the antibiotic to remain in its largely inactive and harmless conformation. As a result, it confers antibiotic resistance to the mutant bacteria.[485] While this mutation prevents the antibiotic from killing the bacteria, it also cripples the bacteria, an effect called the "fitness cost."

The Fitness Cost

Mutations that alter a protein resulting in antibiotic resistance are also likely to *weaken* the organism. Thus, when it becomes resistant to a drug, it is likely to become *less fit* in other ways.[486] This is called the *cost of resistance*, or the fitness cost.[487] Often the cost is very high and the mutation renders the resistant strain poorly able to survive in a non-antibiotic environment.[488] Mutations that both confer resistance, and allow the bacteria to survive, do *not* evolve the bacteria because they render them *less able* to survive in an antibiotic free environment.[489]

These mutations render bacteria less-fit in the wild because the mutant strain is less able to compete with the wild type. Numerous empirical studies have confirmed the conclusion that mutations which confer resistance *decrease* the fitness of bacteria in environments

[485] Wieland, 1994, p. 5.
[486] Spetner, 1997, p. 144.
[487] Lenski, 2002, p. 1,009.
[488] Baquero, 2002, p. 51.
[489] Wieland, 1994, p. 6.

without antibiotics. One negative result is that they do not reproduce as quickly as non-resistant bacteria. One study that compared multi-drug resistant tuberculosis bacteria with non-resistant strains, found the multi-drug-resistant strain had significantly decreased fitness compared to the drug-susceptible strain.[490] The research also indicates the same is true of viruses.[491]

When the drug is no longer part of the environment, the non-resistant type is typically much better adapted than resistant types. In a relatively sterile hospital environment, however, the resistant strain has a clear advantage in patients given antibiotics because it can render many antibiotics useless. The classic example is a patient who develops resistance to antibiotics in a hospital, but when sent home, the infection clears because the resistant bacteria cannot compete with non-resistant normal flora.[492]

For example, streptomycin-resistant bacteria are weaker in the wild for several reasons. The major reason is that the ribosome specificity is lowered in bacteria that become streptomycin resistant. As a result, the ribosomes' ability to translate certain RNA transcripts into protein is less effective because protein regulation, speed, and efficiency are all adversely effected.[493] Although reduction of binding affinity does not always result in the loss or reduction of all binding specificity, the specificity for the proteins required for efficient ribosome function are usually decreased. As a result, the bacteria is now partly, or largely, immune to the antibiotic.

Other mutations that can help a bacterium survive in an antibiotic environment interfere with the regulation of various bacterial functions. For example, *Staphylococcus* can become penicillin-resistant as a result of damage to a control gene that leads to unregulated production of penicillinase, the enzyme that breaks down penicillin. In the presence of penicillin, these mutants have a clear survival advantage. However,

---

[490] Davies, et al., 2000.
[491] Martinez-Picado, et al., 1999.
[492] Wieland, 1994, p. 6.
[493] Gartner and Orias, 1966.

these bacteria that overproduce penicillinase waste many needed nutrients.

Apart from those affecting the ribosome, other mutations also have been found to render bacteria streptomycin-resistant.[494] In all of these cases, the mutation that causes the resistance results either from the degradation or the *loss* of genetic information by gene damage, resulting in a gene product that is no longer functional.

In the host, natural resistance to pathogens is due to normal immune system function such as from vaccination or prior exposure. Resistance resulting from mutations, however, always carries a fitness cost.

An example is the sickle cell anemia mutation in humans that confers resistance to malaria. Sickle cell anemia carries a major fitness cost. However, although "infectious disease is assumed to be an important cause of natural selection in humans, strong selection in favor of alleles that confer resistance to disease has been demonstrated only in the case of malaria."[495] The same observation has been confirmed in other structurally complex animals. The resistance due to mutations is evidently largely, but not exclusively, confined to viruses, bacteria, and insects.[496]

Cell Surface Receptors and Antibiotic Resistance

The outer membrane of gram-negative bacteria, a bacteria type with a cell wall that resists staining with certain dyes, serves as a barrier to the outside world to protect the bacterial cell. Specific proteins known as *porins* located in the bacteria's outer membrane serve as diffusion channels or gateways for certain hydrophilic molecules, such as certain antibiotics. Loss of certain *porins* due to loss mutations *increases* the bacteria's resistance to some antibiotics because the small amounts

---

[494] Gartner and Orias, 1966.

[495] Schliekelman, et al., 2001, p. 545.

[496] Tananka, et al., 1984; Sabourault, et al., 2001; Cooper, et al., 2002.

of antibiotic that are able to enter the cell are insufficient to kill the bacteria.

Another mutation that may confer some resistance are those that control gene duplication levels. If the antibiotic attacks a protein normally produced in high amounts, a larger dose of an antibiotic may be required to be effective. A mutation that allows restoration of the normal metabolic level that existed in the bacteria before the antibiotic entered it, or at least a level allowing survival, confers resistance to the antibiotic. In this case, new and different genes are not created, but only the regulation level is changed. Consequently, this mutation is *not* an example of evolution. Furthermore, in normal environments the overproduction is often harmful, again illustrating the fitness cost.

Changes in the Cellular Target of Cell Surface Molecules

In order to enter a bacterial cell, an antibiotic first must bind to cell surface proteins called binding sites.[497] Mutations cause many bacteria to become resistant to antibiotics by altering the cell surface proteins that enable the antibiotic to enter the cell. This mutation type is also a loss mutation, resulting in the loss of a protein or proteins. Both binding and subsequent transport of antibiotics typically involve the same protein or protein complex. Some resistance may occur as a result of one or more alterations of these drug-binding sites on the cell surface, preventing the antibiotic or other drug from binding. Consequently, the antibiotic is prevented, or hindered, from entering the cell and, therefore, cannot as readily accumulate to toxic levels.

Another method whereby bacteria acquire resistance is via alterations, caused by mutations, that modify the cellular target in such a way as to render the antibiotic ineffective. Specific trans-membrane transporters serve to import into a cell various target molecules

---

[497] Penrose, 1998.

including nutrients, but also may import some antibiotics, such as metabolic analogues. A mutation to, or a loss of, the transporter may decrease the antibiotic levels entering the cell and, consequently, it will be less effective. However, it will also interfere with the bacteria's ability to take in nutrients.

Resistance also can occur as a result of membrane *permeability* alterations or other cell surface alterations that prevent, or interfere, with the drug binding to, and thus entering, the cell.[498] This mutation also renders the organism less fit in a natural environment because the damaged receptor also is less able to take in substances that it normally brings into the cell needed for survival.

Hydrophobic molecules can diffuse through the membrane itself, but some mutations involving outer membrane biochemistry can have an adverse impact on these diffusion rates; thus, these mutations potentially *increase* drug resistance.[499] These mutations also evidently slow the infusion of certain nutrients and other needed materials. As a result, these resistant bacteria are normally *less* fit than the wild type of bacteria.

In bacteria with cell walls, the antibiotic must pass through both the bacterial cell wall and the cell membrane in order to enter a cell. If the bacterial cell membrane- permeability level is altered, and the antibiotic is no longer able to pass through, it cannot reach its target to cause cell damage or block cell reproduction, such as by binding to DNA or to a cell's ribosomes. However, this drug-resistant organism now is also less able to survive in the wild. Most resistance-conferring mutations in bacteria are loss mutations that render the organism less fit to survive in an antibody-free environment. One example of this is that bacteria develop

> resistance to the viruses that infect them, and the
> bacteria often become resistant by mutations in the

---

[498] Cohen, 1992; Gentry, 1991.

[499] Domenech-Sanchez, et al., 1999; Chevalier, et al., 2000; De, et al., 2001; Wong, et al., 2001.

genes that encode surface receptors to which the viruses attach to initiate the infection. However, some of the same receptors are used by the bacteria to transport nutrients into the cell or to maintain the structural integrity of their cell wall. Consequently, mutations that make the bacteria resistant to viral infection are often deleterious when viruses are absent from the environment.[500]

In summary, the problem of bacterial resistance does *not* provide evidence for macroevolution, but instead supports intelligent design. In no case has a mutation been found that resulted in new functional information, such as one that produced a new, different gene.

The problem of antibiotic resistance today is a result of several factors, including the use of antibiotics that either are not needed, such as those given to treat viral diseases, or are not given in the correct dosage or for the proper duration. In addition, under-use of prevention and vaccination, important but often ignored methods for fighting bacteria, contribute to the problem.

Mycobacterium tuberculosis and *Staphylococcus* Strains

Development of antibiotic resistance is central in the reemergence of many diseases. Examples include multiple resistance in *Mycobacterium tuberculosis*, vancomycin resistance of some gram-positive cocci, and penicillin resistance in *Pneumococcus* and *Staphylococcus*.[501]

An excellent example of the increase in resistant strains of bacteria is the organism that causes tuberculosis (TB), *Mycobacterium tuberculosis*. This organism is of major concern because about eight million new cases of active TB are reported annually, causing

---

[500] Lenski, 2002, p. 1,009.

[501] Udo, et al, 1990; Willingham, et al., 2001.

approximately three-million deaths worldwide. In the United States alone, about 27,000 new cases and over 2,000 deaths occur annually. Patients who cannot be treated with any drug or drug combination often are treated by removing a lung section, resulting in many fatalities.

Other multi-drug resistant bacteria include *Staphylococcus aureus* and *Staphylococcus epidermidis*. These are of special concern because *S. aureus* is the second most common cause of nosocomial infections in hospitals.[502] Specifically, such infections take the form of skin and wound bacterial infections and lower respiratory tract infections. Between 60 and 90 percent of all coagulase-negative staphylococci are now methicillin- resistant.

Some bacteria are now resistant to every FDA-approved drug except vancomycin, and there is concern that resistance to vancomycin ultimately will lead to vancomycin-resistant *S. aureus* and *S. epidermidis*. Up to 25 percent of hospital-acquired infections are caused by antibiotic-resistant *S. aureus*.[503] These strains require treatment with the drug Zyvox, marketed only since 1999. Vancomycin itself was developed to treat methicillin-resistant bacteria that became resistant to penicillin.

One of the latest examples involves *Staphylococcus aureus* resistance to one of the newest modern antibiotics noted above, vancomycin. The *S. aureus* builds its cell wall out of tightly cross-linked strands. A bacterial gene codes for the enzyme that constructs a "cap" on the strand ends used to help produce the cross linking needed to build a "strong tough wall that contains and protects the cell's contents."[504] Vancomycin binds to the strand end and, as a result, stops further cell wall formation.[505]

The resultant uncrossed linked areas allow water to enter by osmosis, causing the cell to balloon out, bursting it, and killing the bacteria. A specific mutation makes an altered enzyme that produces

[502] Medeiros, 2001.
[503] Palumbi, 2001.
[504] Postlethwait and Hopson, 2003, p. 220.
[505] Mulichak, et al., 2001.

an altered cap that is unaffected by vancomycin. In this case, the mutation clearly provides the bacteria with a survival advantage, but only in an abnormal environment. In a normal environment, the

> mutant cap leads to a *weaker* cell wall than normal, and so populations of these mutant cells grow more slowly than normal cells. The environment now becomes key. In a regular cellular environment with no antibiotics present, staph cells with the normal gene grow quickly, cap their strand ends, crosslink them into strong cell walls, and outcompete staph cells with the mutant gene.[506]

Another antibiotic resistance system that does not lend support to evolution is the rise of antibiotic resistance as a result of mutations which *reduce* or *damage* the function of preexisting systems. Examples include protein binding effectiveness reduction, cell transport systems damage, or regulatory control disruption. It usually requires only a single mutation (i.e., a point mutation) to reduce or eliminate a system already present in the bacterium cell. These mutations are easily acquired, and is why the resulting new phenotypes are rapidly produced. For example, within a decade or less after a new insecticide is introduced, many insects become resistant to it.

For example, DDT was discovered in 1939 but, ironically, resistance to it was reported in house flies even before its developer, Paul Müller, received the Nobel Prize for his work.[507] The same is true for bacteria and other organisms. The only apparent exception is in yeasts.[508]

Conversely, mutations that *add* new systems, such as a new regulatory system, energy-generating system, or transport system, are all unknown. Darwinists posit eons for them to develop, and they have never been documented to happen. Mutations increasing certain

---

[506] Postlethwait and Hopson, 2003, p. 220; emphasis added.
[507] Palumbi, 2001, p. 1,786.
[508] Palumbi, 2001.

enzyme affinity may be beneficial, but often occur rapidly, indicating that design is involved. For example, mutations affecting hemoglobin-oxygen affinity help the host to acclimatize to a high altitude, but the same mutation can also cause polycythemia, a rare blood cancer in which bone marrow produces too many red blood cells.

Major Causes of the Current Drug-Resistance Problem

The main solution to the drug-resistant bacteria problem is to, as far as possible, reduce the use of antimicrobial agents, and to insist patients take the proper dosages for the recommended time period to prevent resistant organisms from once again gaining a foothold in the body.[509] Many patients stop taking a drug when their symptoms have abated and, as a result, the more resistant or virulent bacteria are able to regain a foothold in the patient's body. Taking the drug for the *entire* duration helps to insure that *all* of the bacteria of concern are killed, and none are again able to gain a foothold in the patient's body.[510]

Surveys indicate that at least half of all current antibiotic use is inappropriate for various reasons, including antibiotics that are either not indicated, such as in the case of a viral infection, or are prescribed at an incorrect dosage or duration of use.[511] Antibiotics often are prescribed for upper respiratory infections such as colds and bronchitis. However, these are usually viral, thus not affected by antibiotics. When patients visit their physician, many expect some type of treatment. Doctors often comply and prescribe antibiotics unnecessarily. Antibiotics may be prescribed in some cases because viral infections sometimes are accompanied by bacterial infections; thus physicians often prescribe antibiotics to ensure the most effective and rapid treatment possible.[512]

---

[509] Palumbi, 2001.
[510] Neu, 1992.
[511] Burton and Engelkirk, 2000, p. 203.
[512] Arakawa, 2000; Raloff, 2001; Nicolaou, et al., 2001.

Some people also take antibiotics for prophylactic reasons to avoid, for example, traveler's diarrhea. Antibiotics used in this way may *increase* the chance of developing problems because all antibiotics kill off some indigenous intestinal flora, making it easier for pathogens to gain a foothold in the person's system.[513]

Physicians in most cases should prescribe *only* narrow-spectrum drugs that kill the specific pathogen of concern. Prolonged use of broad-spectrum antibiotics often destroy the normal body flora, especially in the intestine, mouth, or vaginal area. As a result, a person will lack the protection conferred by indigenous microbial flora, and thus become more susceptible to opportunistic organisms or secondary invaders.[514] This produces what is called a **superinfection**, which can cause diarrhea and other problems.[515] An example is the vaginal yeast infection that often follows antibacterial therapy. Bacteria confer vaginal protection because they help to control the indigenous yeast *Candida albicans,* and killing those bacteria allows the yeast, a single-celled fungus, to flourish.

Greater use of vaccines also can enable more persons to be protected against various viruses and bacteria, often negating the need for antibiotics. Other highly recommended practices to achieve a reduction in the use of antibiotics are infection prevention and control. Such practices include frequent hand washing, and avoiding promiscuous sex, tattooing, and body piercing. An additional concern is that antibiotics are now used in livestock feed for prophylactic purposes.[516] Although often sub-therapeutic levels of antibiotics are used involving only a few antimicrobial types, several of these are ionophores used in human medicine, including tetracycline and macrolides, which are able to reversibly bind and transport particular ions across lipid cell membranes.[517]

---

[513] Lappé, 1982.
[514] Gibbons, 1992; Levy, 1992; Chin, 2000.
[515] Finegold, 1979.
[516] Palumbi, 2001.
[517] Anderson, 2002.

Summary

The recent development of bacteria and insect resistance *does not* support classically defined neo-Darwinism, which postulates evolution due to the natural selection of mutations. Macroevolution requires information-building mechanisms that add new information to DNA. In virtually all cases, bacteria or insect resistance is a result of the damage to an existing system, or a transfer of genes.[518] In the rare cases where a mutation is involved, development of resistance involves only loss mutations, such as the mutation that produces a deformed ribosome-active site.

This is confirmed by the fact that resistance is acquired very rapidly, in far too brief a period for evolutionary emergence of complex biochemical or physiological systems. Mutation-caused resistance results in less viability in the wild, and as a result the resistant strains cannot effectively compete in the non-antibiotic environment.

The multi-drug resistance problem is not small—and now results in tens of thousands of deaths annually.[519] Human uses and abuses of antibiotics are the major cause, not Darwinian evolution. The acquisition of antibiotic resistance does not provide evidence for evolution, but rather for intelligent design,[520] and only by understanding the mechanisms involved can the resistance problem be ameliorated.[521]

---

[518] Beenman, 1982
[519] Chang and Roth, 2001.
[520] Cornaglia, et al., 2000.
[521] Thompson, 1994.

References

Anderson, Kevin. 2002. Letter to Author.

Arakawa, Y., Y. Ike, M. Nagasawa, N. Shibata, Y. Doi, K. Shibayama, T. Yagi, and T. Kurata. 2000. "Trends in Antimicrobial-Drug Resistance in Japan." *Emerging Infectious Diseases* 6(6):572-575.

Ayala, Francisco. 1978. "The Mechanisms of Evolution." *Scientific American* 239(3):56-69.

Baquero, Fernando. 2002. "Antibiotic Resistance: Origins, Mechanisms, and Extent of Resistance." In *Encyclopedia of Evolution*, Volume 1, pp. 50-54. Mark Pagel (editor). New York: Oxford University Press.

Barbour, A.G., and B.I. Restrepo. 2000. "Antigenic Variation in Vector-Borne Pathogens." *Emerging Infectious Diseases*. 6(5):449-457.

Beeman, Richard. 1982. "Recent Advances in Mode of Action of Insecticides." *Annual Review of Entomology*. 27(1):253-281.

Berkelman, Ruth, and James Hughes. 1993. Editorial: "The Conquest of Infectious Diseases: Who are We Kidding?" *Annals of Internal Medicine* 119(5):426-427.

Black, Jacqueline. 2014. *Microbiology: Principles and Explorations*. New York, NY: John Wiley and Sons.

Burton, Gwendolyn, and Paul Engelkirk. 2000. *Microbiology for the Health Sciences*. Philadelphia, PA: Lippincott Williams and Wilkins.

Chang, Geoffrey, and Christopher B. Roth. 2001. "Structure of MsbA from *E. coli*: A Homolog of the Multidrug Resistance ATP Binding Cassette (ABC) Transporters." *Science* 293(5536):1,793-1,800.

Chevalier, J., J.M. Pages, A. Eyraud, and M. Mallea. 2000. "Membrane permeability modifications are involved in antibiotic resistance in *Klebsiella pneumoniae.*" *Biochemical and Biophysical Research Communications* 274(2):496-499.

Chin, James (editor). 2000. *Control of Communicable Diseases Manual*, 17ᵗʰ Edition. Washington, D.C.: American Public Health Association (APHA).

Cohen, Mitchell L. 1992. "Epidemiology of Drug Resistance: Implications for a Post-Antimicrobial Era." *Science* 257(5073):1050-1055.

_____. 2002. "Antibiotic Resistance: Epidemiological Considerations." In *Encyclopedia of Evolution*, Volume 1, pp. 54-57. Mark Pagel (editor). New York: Oxford University Press.

Cooper, K., M. Burd, and K.S. Lefevere. 2002. "Correlated Response of Autogeny to Selection for Adult Starvation Resistance in the Blowfly, *Lucilia cuprina.*" *Heredity* 88(1):35-38.

Cornaglia, G., A. Mazzariol, and R. Fontana. 2000. "The Astonishing Complexity of Antibiotic Resistance." *Clinical Microbiology Infect* 6(Supplement 3):93-94.

Coyne, Jerry. 2001. "The Case of the Missing Carpaccio." *Nature* 412(6847):586-587.

Crews, Frederick C. 2001. "Saving Us from Darwin." *The New York Review of Books*, October 4.

Davies, A.P., O.J. Billington, B.A. Bannister, W.R. Weir, T.D. McHugh, and S.H. Gillespie. 2000. "Comparison of Fitness of Two Isolates of Mycobacterium Tuberculosis, One of Which Had Developed Multi-Drug Resistance During the Course of Treatment." *Journal of Infection* 41(2):184-187, September.

Davies, J., M. Brzezinska, and R. Benveniste. 1971. "R factors: Biochemical Mechanisms of Resistance to Aminoglycoside Antibiotics." *Annals of the New York Academy of Science* 182(1):226-233.

Davies, J., and M. Nomura. 1972. "The Genetics of Bacterial Ribosomes." *Annual Review of Genetics* 6(1):203-234.

De, E., A. Basle, M. Jaquinod, N. Saint, M. Mallea, G. Molle, and J.M. Pages. 2001. "A new mechanism of antibiotic resistance in Enterobacteriaceae induced by a structural modification of the major porin." *Molecular Microbiology* 41(1):189-198.

Didier, E.S., D.C. Bertucci, and L. Leblanc. 1999. "Inhibition of Microsporidia Growth in vitro." *Abstracts of the General Meeting of the American Society for Microbiology* 99:11.

DiSpezio, Michael. 1998. *The Science, Spread and Therapy of HIV Disease*. Shrewsbury, MA: Science Publishers.

Domenech-Sanchez, A., S. Hernandez-Alles, L. Martinez-Martinez, V.J. Benedi, and S. Alberti. 1999. "Identification and characterization of a new porin gene of *Klebsiella pneumoniae*: Its role in beta-lactam antibiotic resistance." *Journal of Bacteriology* 181(9):2,726-2,732.

Finegold, S.M. 1979. "Antimicrobial Therapy of Anaerobic Infections: A Status Report." *Hospital Practice* 14(10):71-81.

Garrett, Laurie. 1995. *The Coming Plague: Newly Emerging Diseases in a World Out of Balance*. New York, NY: Farrar, Straus, and Giroux.

Gartner, T., and E. Orias. 1966. "Effects of Mutations to Streptomycin Resistance on the Rate of Translation of Mutant Genetic Information." *Journal of Bacteriology* 91(3):1,021-1,028.

Gentry, L.O. 1991. "Bacterial Resistance." *Orthopedic Clinics of North America* 22(3):379-388.

Gibbons, A. 1992. "Exploring New Strategies to Fight Drug-Resistant Microbes." *Science* 257(5073):1036-1038.

Greenspan, Neil S. 2002. "Not-So-Intelligent Design." *The Scientist*16(5):12, March 4.

Iltis, Hugh. 2000. "Letters to the Editor." *Reports of the National Center for Science Education* 20(5):44-45, September-October.

Kazanjian, P., W. Armstrong, P.A. Hossler, W. Burman, J. Richardson, C.H. Lee, L. Crane, J. Katz, and S.R. Meshnick. 2000. *"Pneumocystis carinii* Mutations are Associated with Duration of Sulfa or Sulfone Prophylaxis Exposure in AIDS Patients." *Journal of Infectious Diseases* 182(2):551-557.

Kopaska-Mentel, David. 2000. "Letters to the Editor." *Reports of the Natural Center for Science Education* 20(5):44, September-October.

Lappé, M. 1982. *Germs That Won't Die.* Garden City, NY: Anchor Press.

Lenski, Richard E. 2002. "Cost of Resistance." In *Encyclopedia of Evolution,* Volume 2, pp. 1008-1010. Mark Pagel (editor). New York: Oxford University Press.

Levine, Joseph, and Kenneth Miller. 1994. *Biology: Discovering Life.* Lexington, MA: D.C. Heath and Company.

Levy, S.B. 1992. *The Antibiotic Paradox.* New York, NY: Plenum Press.

McGuire, Rick. 1988. "Eerie: Human Arctic Fossils Yield Resistant Bacteria." *Medical Tribune,* December 29, pp. 1, 23.

Marks, Geoffrey, and William K. Beatty. 1976. *Epidemics.* New York, NY: Charles Scribner's Sons.

Martinez-Picado, J., A.V. Savara, L. Sutton, and R.T. D'Aquila. 1999. "Replicative Fitness of Protease Inhibitor-Resistant Mutants of Human Immunodeficiency Virus Type 1." *Journal of Virology* 73(5):3,744-3,752.

Maskell, et al. 1997. "Mechanism of Sulfonamide Resistance in Clinical Isolates of Streptococcus Pneumonia." *Antimicrobial Agents and Chemotherapy* 41(10):2121-2126.

Medeiros, Antone. 2001. "Nosocomial Outbreaks of Multiresistant Bacteria: Extended-Spectrum Beta-Lactamases Have Arrived in North America." *Annals of Internal Medicine* 119(5):428-430.

Mulichak, A.M., H.C. Losey, C.T. Walsh, and R.M. Garavito. 2001. "Structure of the UDP-Glucosyltransferase GtfB that Modifies the Heptapeptide Aglycone in the Biosynthesis of Vancomycin Group Antibiotics." *Structure* 9(7):547-557.

Neu, H.C. 1992. "The Crisis in Antibiotic Resistance." *Science* 257(5073):1064-1073.

Nicolaou, K., and Christopher N.C. Boddy. 2001. "Behind Enemy Lines." *Scientific American* 284(5):56-61.

Padiglione, A.A., E.A. Grabsch, D. Olden, M. Hellard, M.I. Sinclair, C.K. Fairly, and M.L. Grayson. 2000. "Fecal Colonization with Vancomycin-Resistant Enterococci in Austria." *Emerging Infectious Diseases* 6(5):534-536.

Pagel, Mark (editor). 2002. *Encyclopedia of Evolution*, Volume 2. New York: Oxford University Press.

Palumbi, Stephen R. 2001. "Evolution—Humans as the World's Greatest Evolutionary Force." *Science* 293:1,786-1,790, September 7.

Penrose, Eric. 1998. "Bacterial Resistance to Antibiotics—A Case of Un-Natural Selection." *Creation Research Society Quarterly* 35:76-83.

Postlethwait, John H., and Janet L. Hopson. 2003. *Explore Life*. Boston, MA: Brooks/Cole Thomson Learning.

Raloff, J. 2001. "Antibiotic Resistance is Coming to Dinner." *Science News* 159(21):325.

Rothman, Kenneth J., and Sander Greenland. 1998. *Modern Epidemiology*, 2nd Edition. Philadelphia, PA: Lippincott-Raven Publishers.

Rowland, M. 1987. "Fitness of Insecticide Resistance." *Nature* 327(6119):194, May.

Sabourault, C., V.M. Guzov, J.F. Koener, C. Claudianos, F.W. Plapp, Jr., and R. Feyereisen. 2001. "Overproduction of a P450 that Metabolizes Diazinon is Linked to a Loss-of-Function in the Chromosome 2 Ali-Esterase (MdalphaE7) Gene in Resistant House Flies." *Insect Molecular Biology,*10(6):609-618.

Schliekelman, Paul, Chad Garner, and Montgomery Slatkin. 2001. "Natural Selection and Resistance to HIV; A Genotype that Lowers Susceptibility to HIV Extends Survival at a Time of Peak Fertility." *Nature.* 411(6837):545-546.

Spetner, Lee. 1997.*Not by Chance.* Brooklyn, NY: The Judaica Press.

Struzik, Ed. 1990. "Ancient Bacteria Revived." *Sunday Herald,* September 16, p. 1.

Tananka K., J. Scott, and F. Matsumura. 1984. "Picrotoxinin Receptor in the Central Nervous System of the American Cockroach; Its Role in the Action of Cyclodiene-Type Insecticides." *Pesticide Biochemistry and Physiology* 22:117-127.

Thompson, Bert. 1994. "Bacterial Antibiotic Resistance—Proof of Evolution?" *Reason and Revelation*14(8):61-63.

Udo, E.E., and W.B. Grubb. 1990. "Transfer of Resistance Determinants from a Multi-Resistant *Staphylococcus aureus* Isolate." *Journal of Medical Microbiology* 35(2):72-79.

Wieland, Carl. 1994. "Antibiotic Resistance in Bacteria." *Cen Tech J.* 8(1):5-6.

Willingham, F.F., T.L. Schmitz, M. Contreras, S.E. Kalangi, A.M. Vivar, L. Caviedes, E. Schiantarelli, P.M. Neumann, C. Bern, and R.H. Gilman. 2001. "Hospital Control and Multidrug-Resistant

Pulmonary Tuberculosis in Female Patients, Lima, Peru." *Emerging Infectious Diseases* 7(1):123-127.

Wong, K.K., F.S. Brinkman, R.S. Benz and R.E. Hancock. 2001. "Evaluation of a structural model of *Pseudomonas aeruginosa* outer membrane protein OprM, an efflux component involved in intrinsic antibiotic resistance." *Journal of Bacteriology* 183(1):367-374.

Yan, H., Q. Zhao, J. Yuan, X. Cheng, and B. He. 2000. "Affinity Adsorbents for the Vancomycin Group of Antibiotics." *Biotechnology and Applied Biochemistry* 31(Part 1):15-20.

RUDOLF CLAUSIUS (1822-1888) FORMULATED THE SECOND LAW OF THERMODYNAMICS AND IS CREDITED ON PAGE 117. NEW YORK, NY: D. APPLETON.

CHAPTER 8

Matter, Energy, and Entropy

The laws of physics provide several of the most convincing evidences for the Creator's existence. One of the most important proofs of a creator is the fact that, as Einstein demonstrated, matter is a form of energy. Every time energy is changed from one form into another (such as when electrical energy is converted into light energy in a light bulb) some useful energy is lost (in a light bulb, for example, much energy is lost as heat). The *total quantity* of energy never changes, but it is in a less usable form. The heat produced by a light bulb is not usable unless one uses the light bulb to heat a house. Thus, the level of energy (i.e., the quantity) is constant in the entire universe but the level of *usable* energy (i.e., the quality) decreases with time. Most of the wasted energy dissipates as heat that cannot be reused.

For this reason, the universe can be described as being in a state of qualitative decay (meaning that the amount of *usable* energy in the total universe decreases with time). As a result, the universe is running down and will eventually achieve a state of total equilibrium (perfect entropy), unless a force outside the universe intervenes.

The Earth has an excellent supply of outside energy—the Sun—which everyday showers us with enormous levels of usable energy. The amount of energy supplied by the Sun in a day is greater than the amount of energy used by humans in a whole year. We also have use of the energy stored in so-called fossil fuels. But this energy, as ecologists are well aware of, is now being rapidly converted into non-renewable forms (mostly heat and waste products). Eventually, unless more energy is obtained from other sources, we will run out of petroleum, coal, and other energy sources.

The law of inertia, which is that matter will do nothing different in terms of position and motion unless acted on by an outside force, is one of many other evidences of a creator. A piece of stationary matter will remain motionless forever—it will move only if and when it is pushed by an outside force. If moving, it will *continue* to do so forever unless, and until, it is acted on by an outside force. For example, a ball, when thrown up in the air by an outside force, inevitably interacts with various forces such as gravity, wind resistance, or other objects in the air (such as dust), until it eventually stops its upward journey and returns to the ground.

The law of the *conservation of energy*, i.e., energy is never lost, only converted from one type to another, requires hypothesizing *a first mover* (often called the prime mover) to start the whole process. If matter simply "existed" in the universe, it would remain motionless forever unless acted upon by some outside force. Where did that original outside force come from? For eons, humans have accepted the view that matter has eternally existed and, some argue, eternally moved (had energy from the start). To conclude that it has always existed, though, ignores the problem that, in order to exist, matter and energy must have come from *somewhere*—its origin is actually unanswered by this evasion. It is now recognized that matter could not always have existed.

For this reason, an "origin of the universe" theory must not only explain the *origin of matter*, but the origin of the *forces* that act on matter to produce movement (and must explain the forces that bind matter together as well).

The nature of matter is such that order and energy from outside of the universe must *continue* to organize it, or decay—which is actually a flow towards a state of uniformity—will eventually produce a state of perfect randomness. The energy needed to build any complex system must almost be *continually supplied* in a deliberate, complex maintenance program designed to counter and resist decay. Otherwise, both the various natural forces that act on the system and the random movement of the molecules within it will eventually cause its collapse.

The end result is always the total breakdown and decay (entropy) of a system. Entropy describes not only the limitations of heat engines but "the behaviors inherent within matter and energy."[522] For example, in spite of elaborate precautions, nails eventually rust (oxidize), and slowly weaken a building's structure. Wind, temperature changes, chemical reactions, and plant growth weaken the bonds in the wood, concrete, and other building materials, eventually causing the house to fall apart. Many of the parts will then become indistinguishable from the outside environment. This may take much time but, as any householder knows, continued maintenance is necessary in order to resist or counteract this from happening.

All of the molecules in the universe are, as a unit, constantly moving toward a state of complete equilibrium—*small individual isolated sections can gain order, but only at the expense of the total system.*

For example, assume that a barrel could be constructed to permanently contain all of the molecules inside of it, and was also both prevented from decaying and was totally uninfluenced by outside forces. Even differential sorting of molecules by mass (causing the denser molecules to move to, and remain, at the bottom and, in the process, forcing the lighter ones towards the top) requires an *outside* force called gravity. It is thus an **open system.**

In a **closed system,** *no* outside forces, such as gravity, could act upon the molecules inside. If wood, rubber, air, glass, steel, water, and plastic were all placed into the barrel in a closed system, after many thousands of years its contents would break down so that *all of the molecules would distribute themselves equally inside of the container* and would also never gain or lose their momentum. The energy would

---

[522] Benton, 1990, p. 1.

continually be transferred from one molecule to another and no energy would be lost. Eventually, an equal number of glass, air, wood, plastic, and metal molecules would exist in any given cubic centimeter, and, on the average, each cubic centimeter would contain an equal level of energy.[523]

In reality, only the universe as a whole constitutes such a system. The energy in the system is continually being transferred downhill from one part into another, moving towards total energy and mass equilibrium. Only because of its vastness does this process take much time. Thus, energy tends to be contained within an area only because of time constraints. Newtonian physics states that, in normal physical or chemical reactions, neither matter nor energy can be created or destroyed, but only transferred. Einsteinian physics theorizes that matter and energy can be interchanged—but again, neither one can be *created* or *destroyed* by natural processes.

The Origin(s) of the Universe

The only reasonable explanation for the existence of the natural world are: 1) that some outside agency created *both* energy and matter; 2) it has always existed; or 3) it created itself. The last hypothesis is probably the most difficult to defend in view of the fact that the natural laws only support, and we are only able to visualize, transformations caused by a force that is outside of that which is acted upon; *self-creations* or self-movement never occurs. All creations require some type of a creator just as all moving requires a force to cause movement.

The second hypothesis, the idea that matter and energy have *always* existed, contradicts the evidence that the universe and everything in it had a beginning.

If matter has *always* existed, we would expect to find a certain state of affairs. For example, certain isotopes of uranium would all have

---

[523] Parker, 1983.

decayed long ago into thorium, continuing through each successive element in its decay chain until a stable isotope of lead was formed.[524] All of the radium would have trans-mutated into radon, the radon into polonium, etc.[525] The fact that all of these radioactive isotopes have not yet decayed indicates that matter has not only *not* been in existence forever, but in fact came into existence a relatively short time ago. The idea of nucleosynthesis has been proposed as a solution to this problem, but this only moves the creation of matter farther back in time.

Of course, we could hypothesize that certain uranium isotopes are presently being naturally created, but from what and how can only be speculated. The only evidence that we have today is that a certain uranium isotope is decaying into thorium, all thorium into protactinium or another element, etc. *All other radioactive elements also* are decaying into baser, lighter elements.[526] Although well-known scientists have researched this question, debate still exists largely because faith and belief are very important in determining which theory one accepts.

The most popular view advocated today by scientists, the big bang theory, hypothesizes a *beginning* of all that exists except the first matter from which all physical reality supposedly arose. This first matter is hypothesized to have been a primordial "egg" smaller than the period at the end of this sentence. The evidence for this position includes the presupposition that the universe is expanding and, if the expansion rate can be estimated, the time it may have begun can be hypothesized by extrapolating backward. From this theory, the common explanation is that the elements "naturally" came into existence during the big bang or from supernovas, but this hypothesis, however logical, has only the support of armchair reasoning, not direct empirical verification (which is impossible because the origin of the elements is history).

As with all theories, one can explain away much (or even most) of the evidence that contradicts one's own personal beliefs.

---

[524] Monroe and Jackson, 1977.
[525] Dorin, 1984.
[526] Poppy and Wilson, 1973.

As most scientists are fairly bright, they are often superior to non-scientists in rationalizing contradictions in their theories. For this reason, while scientists may have the intelligence that helps them to discover and understand the natural world, this same intelligence may also enable, and even cause them to create a "good" reason to hold answers that they "believe" are true, *regardless of whether it is actually so.*

In the living world, we know that only life produces life. Likewise, intelligence *must* come from intelligence, specifically a superior intelligence. Just as humans have not been able to produce anything more intelligent than ourselves, for intelligent humans to exist, a vastly superior intelligence must have created us, thus must have preceded us. There are no known examples of something able to produce something else *more* intelligent than the producer. Only by biological reproduction and education can equal intelligence result. For example, humans can build bridges or other structures much larger than ourselves, but this is not an example of creating something superior. Rather, it is using mechanical advantages to build a system that results in a structure that humans can utilize to serve us.

Implications for a Creation Worldview

This brief discussion helps us to understand that science has empirically demonstrated, albeit unwittingly, that an outside force is required to create not only matter and energy, but also to sustain the universe as well. Awareness of this reality should humble us before our Creator, and force us to be more aware of our dependence on Him.

All of this well-known and accepted information has enormous implications for demonstrating the existence of a creator. The fact that the universe is running down proves that there was a time when it was "wound up." An ending proves a beginning, and only that which never ends could never have begun. In the infinity of time, we cannot imagine something not having a beginning. Most scientists accept this and thus hypothesize that the "big bang," in essence, involves the spontaneous creation of the universe. Creationists recognize that the creation of the universe implies a creator (or some orderer) who brought our orderly universe into existence, proving the existence of an orderer. Studying the order (i.e., design) in the universe tells us a great deal about the orderer. We know from a study of the creation that the creator-designer of the universe has incredible wisdom and loves complexity. Thus God, as we know him in the Scriptures, is demonstrated to exist from a study of His creation.

It is axiomatic that *something* must be eternal, or at least a chain of causative occurrences must be eternal. One cannot logically argue that matter brought itself into being from nothing. How can *nothing* bring *something* into being? Until matter existed, it was nonexistent, and something nonexistent cannot bring something else into existence.

The uncaused first cause, some deduce, must be God—Who always existed and always will exist. This answers the question, "Who created God?," but does not explain *why* God has always existed. This "why" question is only one of numerous others that we cannot answer except to conclude: "It just is." Why does gravity exist? Either God created it or "it just exists," are the only answers. Why does matter exist? Either "God created it" or "it just exists," is also our best answer. Scientists hypothesized that either matter always existed, or resulted from the tremendous "explosion" called the Big Bang—and the conclusion that matter always existed is held by very few scientists today. Again, the same question must be asked—"Why does matter exist today?"—a question not answered by the conclusion that it at one time did not exist. Why (or how) did the "primordial cosmic egg" appear and produce the changes in the universe that produced the big bang? Where did this wonder, with the potential to produce our entire universe, come from? In one way this evolutionary concept, if merged with theism, makes the idea of creation more acceptable in that the creation of life is *less* of a miracle: In this view, God started the evolutionary process and, in essence, guides it, in order to eventually produce humans. On the other hand, this accommodationist idea of "theistic evolution" also makes God *less* God and more of a tinkerer. In the end, it is more rational to believe that God, and *not* evolution, is the more than capable First Cause, indeed the *only* cause, of Creation, and to therefore just accept God *as GOD.*

References

Benton, Dudley J. 1990. "A Microscopic Perspective on Availability and Irreversibility." A presentation at the Tennessee Valley Authority, ASME (American Society of Mechanical Engineers) Winter Annual Meeting, 26-30 December 1989. Norris, TN/Houston, TX: Engineering Laboratory, January.

Culver, Roger B. 1993. *Facets of Physics: A Conceptual Approach.* Minneapolis/St. Paul, MN: West Publishing Company.

Dorin, Henry. 1984. *Unified Chemistry.* Fairfield, NJ: CEBCO (The County Employee Benefits Consortium of Ohio).

Monroe, James, and Bonnie Jackson. 1977. *Physical Science: An Inquiry Approach.* New York, NY: Canfield Press.

Parker, Sybil P. (editor in chief). 1983. *McGraw Hill Encyclopedia of Physics.* New York, NY: McGraw-Hill.

Poppy, Willard, and Leland Wilson. 1973. *Exploring the Physical Sciences.* Englewood Cliffs, NJ: Prentice-Hall.

RUDOLF LUDWIG CARL VIRCHOW (1821-1902), GERMAN PHYSICIAN AND
FOUNDER OF THE CELLULAR PATHOLOGY THEORY. HE IS CALLED "THE FATHER OF
MODERN PATHOLOGY" AND THE FOUNDER OF SOCIAL MEDICINE. VIRCHOW WAS
ARGUABLY THE PREEMINENT LIFE SCIENTIST IN NINETEENTH-CENTURY GERMANY.
HE ALSO STRONGLY OPPOSED DARWINISM. PHOTOGRAPH OF UNKNOWN DATE,
PUBLISHED IN BERLIN IN 1885. ILLUSTRATION COURTESY OF THE WELLCOME
COLLECTION, LONDON

CHAPTER 9

The Failure of Endosymbiosis to Bridge the Gap Between Eukaryotes and Prokaryotes

Introduction

All cells can be divided into two major types, **prokaryotes**, cells without organelles, and **eukaryotes**, cells with them. An enormous gap exists between the two basic cell types that has not, and *cannot*, be bridged by transitional forms. The most popular effort to bridge the gap is the theory of endosymbiosis popularized by Lynn Margulis. This theory postulates that some of the eukaryote organelles evolved from other organisms which took residence in primitive prokaryotic cells. Many major problems with this hypothesis were reviewed, leading to the conclusion that it is widely accepted not because of empirical evidence but only by default because it is the most plausible naturalistic hypothesis.

Only two naturalistic theories of organelle formation still exist. These two theories are (1) the autogenous, or "self-generated," hypothesis which concludes that organelles evolved by "progressive differentiation of descendants via mutations of many kinds and their natural selection" and (2) **endosymbiosis.**[527]

Endosymbiosis—also called serial endosymbiosis (SET) or the *xenogenour hypothesis* —is the idea that organelles (in particular mitochondria, chloroplasts, and flagella) were once free-living bacteria that were engulfed by other bacteria, and then evolved inside of their host to take on specialized functions, including producing ATP as an energy source for the host.[528]

The common endosymbiosis scenario is that animals which were once free-living have "joined together" in cooperative communities, which we now call cells, that later became part of multicellular organisms. Within these organisms, groups of cells have taken on specialized roles—some becoming muscle, others brain, bone, skin and so on.[529] This theory was developed in greatest detail by Lynn Margulis, and this paradigm has moved from an obscure, poorly accepted idea to the most widely acknowledged theory of organelle development today partly through her work and influence.[530]

This theory concludes that the mitochondria lost many of their genes in adapting to life inside of eukaryotes. If this were the case, we would expect that different cell lines would have lost different genes. Yet so far all mitochondria for a given organism type have close to identical genes. Since mtDNA, the DNA found in mitochondria, is significantly smaller than even the DNA in small bacteria, those who hold this view have looked for evidence of large mtDNA in the mitochondria of eukaryotic organisms. The best example they have been able to find is the mitochondrial DNA of the freshwater protozoan, *Reclinomonas americana*, which has 69,034 base pairs, the largest number of genes so far identified in any mtDNA.[531]

These examples, though, are of little help because they all still show

---

[527] Margulis, 1971a, p. 230.
[528] Palmer, 1997.
[529] Hoagland and Dodson, 1995, p.72.
[530] Margulis, 1971b.
[531] Lang, et al., 1997, p. 493.

major differences between mitochondria and bacteria. For example, even for this best example, enormous differences exist between the 69-kbp *R. americana* mtDNA, the 580-kbp genome of the eubacterium *Mycoplasma genitalium,* and the 1,830 kbp *Haemophilus influenzae* genome, the two genomes that have been compared to mtDNA. *R. americana* mtDNA has a total of 97 protein-coding genes compared with the 470 protein-coding regions in the eubacterium *Mycoplasma genitalium* and the 1,743 protein-producing genes in the *Haemophilus influenzae* genome. Furthermore,

> Comparison of the *Mycoplasma* and *Haemophilus* genomes suggested that their different gene contents reflect . . . profound differences in physiology and metabolic capacity between these two organisms. . . . In this context, the *Reclinomonas* mitochondrial genome may be viewed as an extreme example of eubacterial genome reduction, such that the only genes remaining are related to mitochondrial gene expression (transcription, RNA processing and translation) and biogenesis of the protein complexes required for electron transport and coupled oxidative phosphorylation (including components implicated in mitochondrial protein transport and biosynthesis).[532]

The theory also argues that after multicellular organisms evolved, groups of their eukaryotic cells later assumed specialized roles—some becoming muscle cells, others brain cells, bone cells, skin cells, and so on.[533] In other words, the free-living symbionts that joined with single cells, now called eukaryotic cells, later evolved into over 250 types of specialized cells that make up modern multicellular organisms.

---

[532] Lang, et al., 1997, p. 496.
[533] Lang, et al., 1997, p.72.

The History of the Theory

Evidently endosymbiosis was first proposed in 1883 by Schimpler for plastids and later Russian biologist Merezhkovsky developed the idea to explain the origin of chloroplasts. Then, in 1922, an endosymbiosis theory for mitochondria was presented by Walin. Endosymbiosis was developed in the greatest detail, by far, by Lynn Margulis.[534] It was partly through her persistence, and influence as the wife of the late Carl Sagan, that the theory has moved from an obscure, poorly-accepted idea to the most widely accepted organelle development hypothesis today.

Although the endosymbiosis origin of mitochondria and chloroplasts is now textbook orthodoxy, proposals that "other cellular compartments are the result of symbiosis are not so widely accepted."[535] The endosymbiosis theory of organelle evolution is widely accepted not because of empirical evidence but because no other theory is even remotely plausible. Thus Battley describes endosymbiosis as "tentative at best."[536] The theory relies very heavily on the homology between organelles and bacteria. For example:

1. Mitochondria and chloroplasts are similar in both size and shape to prokaryotes.
2. Mitochondria, in contrast to other organelles, are not manufactured by the direction of nuclear genes but arise from preexisting mitochondria, and chloroplasts arise from preexisting chloroplasts. Mitochondria and chloroplasts divide by fission, as do prokaryotes.
3. Mitochondria, chloroplasts, and prokaryotes all have their own DNA, their DNA lacks histone proteins, are circular, and are attached to the inner cell or organelle membrane.

---

[534] Cavalier-Smith, 1997, p. 46; Margulis, 1971b.
[535] Behe, 1996, p. 189.
[536] Battley, 1996, p. 276.

4. Organellar ribosomes are more similar in size to prokaryotic ribosomes than eukaryotic types.

5. The outer membrane of both chloroplasts and mitochondria has structural and chemical similarities to the eukaryote cell membrane. This fits the conclusion that it would have been synthesized by the original "host" cell and used to engulf the endosymbiotic bacteria that became the mitochondria.

In spite of these superficial similarities, major differences exist.

Endosymbiosis Does Not Solve the Organelle Origins Problem

Endosymbiosis is recognized by most researchers as an implausible explanation of the origin of most organelles. For example, evidence to support the theory that spirochete bacteria gave rise to flagella does not exist. Tubulin (the primary component of microtubules) has not been found in any prokaryote, and DNA has never been found in the flagella. For this reason, most evolutionary biologists reject the idea that flagella (and most other structures) originated by symbiosis.

Furthermore, examination finds that it is even an inadequate explanation for the three organelles that are usually claimed to have originated this way: the mitochondria, the chloroplast, and the flagellum. A major scientific problem with the endosymbiosis hypothesis, which was recognized when the theory was first proposed, is that the theory still remains untestable. [537] It is actually less plausible today because so much more is known about cell organelles, especially mitochondria, and bacteria.

Since no physical evidence exists for this theory, armchair reasoning is used as support. It is reasoned that because mitochondria, and their analog in plants (the chloroplasts), contain a small plasmid

---

[537] Margulis, 1971a, p. 230.

ring of DNA which superficially *in some ways* resembles the DNA of prokaryotes more than eukaryotes, that the theory is supported. However, in *other ways* the DNA used by organelles is *more similar* to that of eukaryotic nuclear genes. A well-known example is that some organelle genes possess introns that are similar to eukaryotic nuclear genes and are quite different from prokaryotic genes.

The theory leaves unanswered the questions, "What prevented the host cell from digesting the invading organism?," and "Where did the many other structures required for a eukaryotic cell to survive come from?" For example, microtubules, which are critical for cell division and motility in eukaryotic cells, are not explained by the theory. DeDuve notes that nothing is known about the development of the cytoskeleton system which required a large number of authentic innovations to function. Endosymbiosis at best explains the origin of two organelles, but in order for a eukaryote cell to function, a whole new set of structures is required, all of which must exist concurrently for functional integrity.

The most common argument for the endosymbiosis theory of organelle origin is the fact that the chloroplasts and mitochondria have ribosomes and rRNA that are "distinctly different" from those manufactured by nuclear DNA and in some ways resemble those of prokaryotes.[538] This DNA difference, though, can be adequately explained by the role of DNA in mitochondria, which is to control oxidative metabolism.

Mitochondria

The mitochondria are critically important cell structures because they contain the machinery and enzymes necessary to convert food into energy-carrying molecules called **adenosine triphosphates** (ATP). They can process fats, sugars, and protein and are found in all cells

---

[538] Mears, et al., 2006.

except mature red blood cells. Called the **powerhouse** of the cell, we now know that the more-active cells such as muscle, liver, and kidney tubule cells contain large numbers of mitochondria, and the less-active cells, such as the mucous-secreting cells, contain few of them.

Specifically, the enzymatic process by which the mitochondria convert food to ATP is called **oxidative phosphorylation.** The end process involves converting adenosine diphosphate (ADP) to adenosine triphosphate (ATP), a higher energy molecule. Other functions of the mitochondria are regulatory in nature including helping to control the calcium level in the cytoplasm. They are also involved in specific kinds of lipid synthesis.

The mitochondrium is a unique organelle because it contains its own DNA (mtDNA) in the form of plasmids. The mtDNA is usually located in the mitochondria's matrix compartment, although it is sometimes attached to the inner mitochondrial membrane. The human mtDNA has been completely sequenced and has 16,569 base pairs.[539] The mitochondrial DNA is used exclusively for the organelle's own functions, specifically to enable it to have *some* control, although not complete control, over its own replication.

Structurally, the mitochondria have an outer and inner membrane. The inner membrane has numerous plate-like folds called **cristae** (a fold or crest) that possess membranous sacks containing enzymes. The cristae produce many small rooms inside of this often "hot-dog" or spherical-shaped, double-membraned structure. Cristae can be either exclusively lamellar or exclusively tubular, and some mitochondria contain both types. The inner membranes contain a large set of enzymes that cause the conversion of food into ATP by a series of reactions called the **Krebs** or **citric acid cycle** that produces oxidative phosphorylation. The inner area called the **matrix** is filled with gel containing scores of different kinds of enzymes. The inner and outer membranes differ in enzymatic activity and also lipid composition.

---

[539] Darnell, et al., 1986, p. 926.

Some of the enzymes such as **ATPase** are permanently fixed in the mitochondrial membrane.

Mitochondria have the structures needed to manufacture protein, but they are very different from those used by bacteria. They are described as "undersized," mini- ribosomes, mini-RNA polymerase, and even mini-DNA.[540] Thus they are very different from bacteria.

Actually, the vast majority of genes controlling mitochondria and chloroplasts are located in the central nucleus and not in the organelles themselves.[541] Thus a transfer of genes from the organelles to the host nucleus has to be postulated. This problem is not minor: "the migration of genes from endosymbionts to the nucleus is remarkable because it seems to have raised more difficulties than it solved."[542] The analogy is not unlike hypothesizing moving a small house into a larger house as a means of explaining the rooms when they can be explained more easily, even from an evolutionary stand point, by hypothesizing their individual separate construction. This concern is significant in that the endosymbiosis of mitochondria and chloroplasts are the major evidence for the theory.

From a Darwinist standpoint the hypothesis which endosymbiosis replaced, where the host cells form the organelles and nucleus inside the cell by a process of ingrowing membranes, seems more possible and thus still has its adherents. As the problems with endosymbiosis accumulate, no doubt the "in-growing membrane" hypothesis will again be invoked. [543]

The genetic code that is used in human mitochondria is in many ways different from those used by *all* prokaryotic genes and eukaryotic nuclear genes.[544] Mitochondria produce fully 90 percent of the cell's energy, and their impairment causes a disease that most readily affects

---

[540] Kamenetskii, 1997, p. 68.

[541] Heider, 1997, p. 6.

[542] deDuve, 1996, p. 57.

[543] Heider, 1997, p. 6.

[544] Darnell, et al., 1986.

the central nervous system.[545] A single mitochondrion has a total of 16,569 base pairs which code for 37 genes that specify the structure of only 13 proteins and 24 RNA molecules. This is only a *few* of the genes needed by mitochondria, 99 percent of which are in the nucleus, indicating a level of integration that argues, even from an evolutionary world view, that endosymbiosis is less tenable than competing theories.

Because the human mitochondria "must import 99 percent of their proteins from the cytoplasm,"[546,] the law of parsimony would conclude that it would be far simpler to evolve mitochondria from scratch than to incorporate an independent organism which required 1) the loss of most of its genes, 2) the evolution of new ones, and 3) that most of the genes it needed to function would evolve in the nucleus. Furthermore, the double-set gene system requires the evolution of extremely complex import machinery involving complex surface receptors, binding relays, and target signaling systems.[547]

The most difficult problem is that the mitochondria have a code of their own, which is different from both bacterial and eukaryotic codes by 4 codons. Furthermore, in yeast mitochondria, leucine codes beginning with "CU" code for threonine so that 8 codes exist to code for threonine while AGH and AGG code for arginine.

If the code was the same as bacteria and different than eukaryotes that would support endosymbiosis. However, while some theorize that the mitochondrial code could have evolved separately, the difference has forced some evolutionists to hypothesis that the mitochondrial code is more "primitive" and the bacteria code more evolved. Actually, evidence exists that the mitochondrial code is designed for the needs of mitochondria and to *prevent* exchange of mtDNA genes with nuclear genes.

Another major problem with the endosymbiosis theory of organelle origins, as is true of the panspermia theory, is that it does not solve the

---

[545] Wallace, 1997.
[546] Schatz, 1997, p.121.
[547] Dietmeier, et al., 1997.

problem of organelle evolution but instead avoids the problem because it *starts* with the existence of complex functioning systems which it cannot explain:

> For purposes of argument, however, let's suppose that the symbiosis Margulis envisions was in fact a common occurrence throughout the history of life. The important question for us biochemists is, can symbiosis explain the origin of complex biochemical systems? Clearly it cannot. The essence of symbiosis is the joining of two separate cells, or two separate systems, *both of which are already functioning.* In the mitochondrion scenario, one preexisting viable cell entered a symbiotic relationship with another such cell. Neither Margulis nor anyone else has offered a detailed explanation of how the preexisting cells originated. Proponents of the symbiotic theory of mitochondria explicitly assume that the invading cells could already produce energy from foodstuffs; they explicitly assume that the host cell already was able to maintain a stable internal environment that would benefit the symbiont.[548]

Margulis and Sagan propose that the earliest eukaryotic cells were the **protoctists:** the amoebas, diatoms, giant kelps, and red seaweeds.[549] These animals, though, are all still eukaryotes and are in most ways very similar to "higher" level eukaryotes. They are markedly different from prokaryotes and do not even begin to bridge the gap. Even though the endosymbiosis theory does not fit the facts very well, it is periodically recycled when alternative theories are shown to be wrong, and no doubt it will be recycled again.[550]

---

[548] Behe, 1996, p. 189.

[549] Margulis, 1995, p. 91.

[550] Helder, 1997.

Why Organelle Evolution Is Impossible

Behe argues that the gap existing between the eukaryotic and prokaryotic cell types cannot ever be bridged because of **irreducible complexity**. In order for a machine to work, the complexity of even a simple machine can be reduced only so far—below this, the machine cannot function. A classic example is a standard mouse trap which must have a minimum of five major parts to operate: a platform, a holding bar, a hammer, a catch, and a spring.

As Behe convincingly argues, a mouse trap will not function until *every* one of its necessary parts is in place, each of which must be designed properly to articulate with the other parts. Some have suggested that some of these parts can be eliminated by various methods such as nailing the trap to the floor. This approach does not eliminate a part but replaces its function with another part. Likewise, organelles will not function unless *every* needed, designed, and manufactured part exists, and *all* of them are assembled to form an operating unit. [551]

Organelles are complex structures, many consisting of multi thousands of smaller complex parts, and the irreducible complexity concern *also* is true of each individual part in each organelle type. A cell cannot survive without ribosomes, each of which contains thousands of parts, all of which must be manufactured to exact specifications. It is for this reason that an animal cannot live until all of its billions of parts are manufactured and properly assembled. Even though DNA is described as having "massive intelligence . . . by itself [it has] neither a future nor a present. DNA without a cell to sustain and express it has no physiologic meaning."[552]

Few scientists have even endeavored to speculate on what these transitional forms may have been like, let alone endeavor to present evidence for the multi-millions of transitional forms necessary to create any reasonable scenario which could bridge the free living cells and the cells used in multicellular organisms.

---

[551] Behe, 1996.
[552] Kornberg, 1989, p. 316.

The cell's transport system is another example that illustrates how the concept of irreducible complexity makes organelle evolution impossible. After proteins are manufactured, they do not float around freely inside the cell, but must be transported by an appropriate mechanism to where they are needed. The three common mechanisms of transporting proteins are **gated transport, vesicular transport**, and **transmembrane transport**. Gated transport requires the construction of a door mechanism in the cell membrane and a chemical sensor (a protein which has the correct identification tag). When the protein package approaches the sensor, it causes the gate to open, allowing the protein to pass through.

This control mechanism that allows classes of proteins to leave the cell requires the protein to contain the proper identification tag and a gate that is programmed to open for that tag. The gate itself also contains many parts, thus introducing another level of irreducible complexity. Each of these gated transport components is extremely complex and at the molecular level consists of multi thousands of parts, *all* of which must exist for the gated transport system to function properly.

The vesicular transport system uses a set of sensors. But instead of a gate, the proper identification tag causes the compartment membrane to bulge outward, pinching off and forming a vesicle that totally surrounds the protein. The transport vesicle, which has its own identification tag, then travels to a specific destination. Once there, if the vesicle tag and the identification sensor match, another sensor recognizes the vesicle and allows it to merge with the compartment. Then the pinching off process is reversed to allow the proteins to be carried inside the new compartment.

The irreducible complexity of the system would include two complex sensor systems, two identification tags as well as the vessel itself. At a level beyond this, each sensor identification tag and the carrier vessels are likewise at the molecular level constructed from thousands of parts, each of which is also an example of irreducible complexity. The vesicle must contain all of the structures that allow it to bud off from the original compartment and to unite with another compartment.[553]

---

[553] Behe, 1996.

The Origin of the Nucleus

The nucleus is also theorized to have originated by endosymbiosis. As noted by Hartman and Fedorou:

> A major problem in the formation of the eukaryotic cell is the origin and evolution of the nucleus. Mereschowsky proposed in 1910 that the nucleus was formed from bacteria that had found a home in an entity that was composed of "amoebaplasm" and was not a bacterium. [554]

There now exists two major competing theories for the endosymbiotic origin of the nucleus. The first one claims that the eukaryotic cell originated as a result of a fusion of an archaeon with a bacterium (and the archaeon became a nucleus). Several variants of this idea exist that have major differences. One of the many major difficulties with this conjecture is that

> the prokaryotic host cell must have been able to engulf its future symbiont.

> The engulfing of other cells requires a complex internal cytoskeleton, which interacts with the plasma membrane. This cellular configuration, in the absence of a cell wall, allows phagocytosis to take place. Prokaryotes, whether they are Archaea or Bacteria, do not have a complex internal cytoskeleton and, in general, they do have a cell wall, and therefore they are incapable of phagocytosis. [555]

Endosymbiosis is "complicated further by the fact that a whole set of new cellular structures (i.e., endoplasmic reticulum, spliceosome, etc.)

---

[554] Hartman and Fedorov, 2002, p. 1420.
[555] Hartman and Fedorov, 2002, p. 1420.

other than the cytoskeleton had to be constructed from prokaryotes that lacked them."[556]

An enormous gap exists between prokaryotic (bacterial and cyanobacterial) cells and eukaryotic (protist, plant, and animal) cells:

> prokaryotes and eukaryotes are profoundly different from each other and clearly represent a marked dichotomy in the evolution of life... The organizational complexity of the eukaryotes is so much greater than that of the prokaryotes that it is difficult to visualize how a eukaryote could have arisen from any known prokaryote.[557]

These differences include the fact that prokaryotes lack organelles, a cytoskeleton, and most of the other structures present in eukaryotic cells. Consequently, in bacteria, the functions of most organelles and other ultrastructure cell parts must be carried out by the bacteria's cell membrane and its in-foldings called "mesosomas."

The Four Major Methods of Producing ATP

A crucial difference between prokaryotes and eukaryotes is the means they use to produce ATP. All life produces ATP by three basic chemical methods only: oxidative phosphorylation, photophosphorylation, and substrate-level phosphorylation.[558]

In prokaryotes, ATP is produced both in the cell wall and in the cytosol by glycolysis. In eukaryotes, most ATP is produced in chloroplasts (for plants), or in mitochondria (for both plants and animals). No means of producing ATP exists that is intermediate between these four basic methods and no transitional forms have ever

[556] Hartman and Fedorov, 2002, p. 1420.
[557] Hickman, et al., 1997, p. 39.
[558] Lim, 1998, p. 149.

been found that bridge the gap between these four different forms of ATP production. The machinery required to manufacture ATP is so intricate that viruses are not able to make their own ATP. They require cells to manufacture it and viruses have no source of energy apart from cells.

In prokaryotes, the cell membrane takes care of not only the cell's energy-conversion needs, but also nutrient processing, synthesizing of structural macromolecules, and the secretion of the many enzymes needed for life.[559] The cell membrane must for this reason be compared with the *entire* eukaryote cell ultrastructure which performs these many functions. No simple means of producing ATP is known and prokaryotes are not by any means simple. They contain over 5,000 different kinds of molecules and can use sunlight, organic compounds such as carbohydrates, and inorganic compounds as sources of energy to manufacture ATP.

Another example of the cell membrane in prokaryotes assuming a function of the eukaryotic cell ultrastructure is as follows: their DNA is physically attached to the bacteria cell membrane and DNA replication may be initiated by changes in the membrane. These membrane changes are in turn related to the bacterium's growth. Further, the mesosome appears to guide the duplicated chromatin bodies into the two daughter cells during cell division.[560]

In eukaryotes, the mitochondria produce most of the cell's ATP (anaerobic glycolysis also produces some) and, in plants, the chloroplasts can also serve this function. The mitochondria produce ATP in their internal membrane system called the cristae. Since bacteria lack mitochondria, and hence their internal membrane system, they must produce ATP in their cell membrane, which they accomplish by two basic steps. The bacterial cell membrane contains a unique structure designed to produce ATP and no comparable structure has been found in *any* eukaryotic cell.[561]

---

[559] Talaro and Talaro, 1993, p. 77.
[560] Talaro and Talaro, 1993.
[561] Jensen, Wright, and Robinson, 1997.

The ATPase and the electron transport chains are located in bacteria *inside* the cytoplasmic membrane between the hydrophobic tails of the phospholipid membrane inner and outer walls. Breakdown of sugar and other food causes the positively charged proteins on the *outside* of the membrane to accumulate to a much higher concentration than they are on the membrane *inside*. This creates an excess positive charge on the outside of the membrane and a relative negative charge on the inside.

The result of this charge difference is a dissociation of HOH molecules into H+ and OH- ions. The H+ ions that are produced are then transported outside of the cell membrane and the OH- ions remain on the inside. This results in a potential energy gradient similar to that produced by charging a flashlight battery. The potential energy gradient produces a force called a **proton motive force** that can accomplish a variety of cell tasks including converting ADP into ATP.

In some bacteria, such as *Halobacterium,* this system is modified by use of *bacteriorhodopsin*, a protein similar to the sensory pigment rhodopsin used in the vertebrate retina.[562] Illumination causes the pigment to absorb light energy, temporarily changing rhodopsin from a *trans* to a *cis* form. The trans-to-cis conversion causes deprotonation and the transfer of protons across the plasma membrane to the periplasm.

The protein gradient that results is used to drive ATP synthesis by use of the ATPase complex. This modification allows bacteria to live in regions of low oxygen but rich light. This anaerobic ATP manufacturing system, which is unique to prokaryotes, uses a chemical compound other than oxygen as a terminal electron acceptor.[563] The location of the ATP producing system is only one of many major contrasts that exists between bacteria cell membranes and mitochondria.

Another sign of problems for the endosymbiosis idea is the widespread disagreement by researchers about the idea's mechanism.

---

[562] Lim, 1998, p. 166.
[563] Lim, 1998, p. 168.

For example, Margulis and Sagan note that archaebacteria have been renamed "Archaea" by Carl Woese and this terminology is now accepted by many.[564] This classification rejects endosymbiosis and is a "denial of their bacterial nature" because it results in elevating "the group 'Archaea' to parallel status with other bacteria and all eukaryotes."[565] The result is a classification of three fundamental groups of life which contradicts the endosymbiont theory.

Chloroplasts

Chloroplasts are double-membraned, ATP-producing organelles found only in plants. Inside their outer membrane is a set of thin membranes organized into flattened sacs stacked up like coins called **thylakoids** (Greek, *thylac* or sack, and *oid* meaning like). The disks contain chlorophyll pigments that absorb solar energy, which is the ultimate source of energy for all the plant's needs including manufacturing carbohydrates from carbon dioxide and water via *photosynthesis*.[566] The chloroplasts first convert the solar energy into ATP stored energy, which is then used to manufacture storage carbohydrates that can be converted back into ATP when energy is needed.

The chloroplasts also possess an *electron transport system* for producing ATP. The electrons that enter the system are taken from water. During photosynthesis carbon dioxide is reduced to a carbohydrate by energy obtained from ATP.[567]

Photosynthesizing bacteria (cyanobacteria) use yet another system. Cyanobacteria do not manufacture chloroplasts but use chlorophyll bound to cytoplasmic thylakoids. Once again plausible transitional

---

[564] Margulis and Sagan, 2002, p. 154; see Lewis, 2003.

[565] Margulis and Sagan. 2002. *Acquiring Genomes. A Theory of the Origins of Species.* New York, NY: Basic Books, p. 154.

[566] Mader, 1996, p. 75.

[567] Mader, 1996, p. 12.

forms have never been found that can link these two ATP producing forms of photosynthesis.

The two most common evolutionary theories of the origin of the mitochondria-chloroplast ATP-production systems are 1) endosymbiosis of mitochondria and chloroplasts from the bacterial membrane system, and 2) the gradual evolution of the prokaryote cell membrane system of ATP production into the mitochondria and chloroplast systems. Believers in endosymbiosis teach that mitochondria were once free-living bacteria, and that "early in evolution ancestral eukaryotic cells simply ate their future partners."[568] Both the gradual conversion and endosymbiosis theory require many transitional forms, while each new form must provide the animal with a competitive advantage compared with the unaltered animals.

The many contrasts between the prokaryotic and eukaryotic means of producing ATP, some which were noted above, are strong evidences against the endosymbiosis theory. No intermediates to bridge these two systems have ever been found and arguments put forth in the theory's support are all highly speculative. These and other problems have recently become more evident as a result of new major challenges to the standard endosymbiosis theory.

The standard theory has recently been under attack from several fronts, and some researchers are now arguing for a new theory to explain "how the first complex cell came together." These scientists argue that this "new idea could solve some nagging problems with the prevailing theory." They admit that, although the new theory of endosymbiosis is "elegantly argued, ... there are an awful lot of things the hypothesis doesn't account for." They also concluded that the old theory was one of the most just-so stories ever concocted. According to the old theory, the origin of the

> mitochondrion was a lucky accident. First, the ancestral cell—probably an archaebacterium, recent genetic analyses suggest—acquired the ability to engulf and

---

[568] Vogel, 1995, p. 1933; Tuszynski, 2007, p. 207.

digest complex molecules. It began preying on its microbial companions. At some point, however, this predatory cell didn't fully digest its prey, and an even more successful cell resulted when an intended meal took up permanent residence and became the mitochondrion. For years, scientists had thought they had examples of the direct descendants of those primitive eukaryotes: certain protists that lack mitochondria. But recent analysis of the genes in those organisms suggests that they, too, once carried mitochondria but lost them later (*Science*, 12 September 1997, p. 1,604). These findings hint that eukaryotes might somehow have acquired their mitochondria before they had evolved the ability to engulf and digest other cells.[569]

Is the new theory of endosymbiosis really any better? Both theories argue that "early in evolution ancestral eukaryotic cells simply ate their future partners."[570]

Conclusions

Two major classes of organisms exist, prokaryotes and eukaryotes, and no intermediates have ever been found between them. What is found when analyzing their cells is either an absence of organelles, as in the prokaryotes, or fully-functional and fully-developed organelles, as in the eukaryotes. The fact is, "No missing links between eukaryotes and bacteria exist, either in the fossils or in life."[571]

The common scenario used to explain the existence of multicellular organisms is that cells which were once free-living have "joined together in cooperating communities we call multicellular organisms,

---

[569] Vogel, 1998, p. 1633.
[570] Tuszynski, 2007, p. 207.
[571] Tuszynski, 2007, p. 207.

and within these organisms groups of cells have taken on special roles—becoming muscle, brain, bone, skin, and so on."[572] For this to be true, billions of transitional forms must have existed not only between the non-organelle life system of the prokaryotes and the organelle life system of eukaryotes, but also further billions of transitional forms also must have existed between the original prokaryote and all the hundreds of specialized tissues and cell kinds, including nerve, muscle, the rods and cones of the retina, and other cell types.

The endosymbiosis idea is popular not because of the empirical evidence, but because no other hypothesis is even remotely plausible in the face of the complete absence of fossil and other evidence. Thus, Professor Edwin H. Battley of The State University of New York (Stony Brook, NY,) described the endosymbiosis theory as "tentative at best."[573] A major problem with endosymbiosis is that it has always been, and still is, untestable. [574] More research and knowledge has motivated one researcher at the forefront of this field to conclude that:

> Data published over the past two or three years, much of them from genome-sequencing projects, have hinted that it is time for a new theory. In particular, it is turning out that eukaryotic nuclear genomes carry many genes of bacterial (sometimes -proteobacteria) origin which have nothing to do with mitochondrial functions. Moreover, mitochondrion-free eukaryotes that we had come to think of as direct descendants of ancient proto-eukaryotes carry mitochondrial genes in their nuclear genomes.[575]

The endosymbiosis theory has also come under attack from many other quarters, and no doubt this attack will continue.

---

[572] Hoagland and Dodson, 1995, p.72.
[573] Battley, 1996, p. 276.
[574] Margulis, 1971a, p. 230.
[575] Doolittle, 1998, p. 15.

References

Alberts, Bruce, et al. 1989. *Molecular Biology of the Cell.* New York, NY: Garland Publishing.

Battley, Edwin H. 1996. Review of B.D. Dyer and R.A. Obar. 1994. *Tracing the History of Eukaryotic Cells: The Enigmatic Smile.* New York, NY: Columbia University Press in *The Quarterly Review of Biology* 71(2):275-276.

Behe, Michael. 1996. *Darwin's Black Box: The Biochemical Challenge to Evolution.* New York, NY: Basic Books.

Cavalier-Smith T. 1997 "Our Symbiotic Origins?" *The Sciences* 37(4):46-47.

Chown, Marcus. 1996. "Seeds, Soup and the Meaning of Life." *New Scientist.* 2043(151):6.

Darnell, James, Harvey Lodish, and David Baltimore. 1986. *Molecular Cell Biology.* New York, NY: W,H, Freeman and Company.

da Silva, Wilson. 1997. "Ancestral Bacterium Keeps DNA Locked Apart." *New Scientist* 154(2082):19, May 17.

Dayton, Leigh. 1992. "Bizarre bacterium in a class of its own." *New Scientist* 133(1805):26.

deDuve, Christian. 1996. "The Birth of Complex Cells." *Scientific American* 274(4):50-57.

DeSalle, Rob, and David Lindley. 1997. *The Science of Jurassic Park and the Lost World.* New York NY: Basic Books.

Dietmeier, Klaus, et al. 1997. "Tom5 functionally links mitochondrial preprotein receptors to the general import pore." *Nature* 388(6638):195-200, July.

Dyer, Betsey, and Robert Alan Obar. 1994. *Tracing the History of Eukaryotic Cells: The Enigmatic Smile.* New York, NY: Columbia University Press.

Frank-Kamenetskii, Maxim. 1997. *Unraveling DNA: The Most Important Molecule of Life.*

Reading, MA: Perseus Books.

Fuerst, John, and Richard Webb. 1991. "Membrane-bounded nucleoid in the eubacterium *Gemmata obscuriglobus.*" *Proceedings of the National Academy of Sciences, USA.* 88(18):8,184-8,188, September 15.

Grimaldi, David. 1996. *Amber: Window to the Past.* New York, NY: Harry N. Abrams, Inc.

_____.2004. "Captured in Amber." *Scientific American* 14(2s):84-91.

Hartman, Hyman, and Alexei Fedorov. 2002. "The Origin of the Eukaryotic Cell: A Genomic Investigation." *PNAS* 99(3):1,420-1,425.

Helder, Margaret. 1997. "Endosymbiotic Theory." *Creation Dialogue* 24(4):6.

Herrmann, Bernd, and Susanne Hummell (ed.). 1994. *Ancient DNA.* New York, NY: Springer Publishing.

Hickman, Jr., Cleveland P., Larry S. Roberts, and Allan Larson. 1997. *The Biology of Animals.* New York, NY: WCB/McGraw Hill.

Hoagland, Mohlon, and Burt Dodson. 1995. *The Way Life Works.* New York, NY: Random House.

Kornberg, Arthur. 1989. *For Love of Enzymes.* Cambridge, MA: Harvard University Press.

Lang, B. Franz, Gertraud Burger, Charles O'Kelly, Robert Cedergren, G. Brian Golding, Claude Lemieux, David Sankoff, Monigue Turnel, and Michael Gray. 1997. "An Ancestral Mitochondrial DNA Resembling a Eubacterial Genome in Miniature." *Nature* 387(6632):493-497, May.

Lewin, Benjamin. 1997. *Genes IV.* Oxford, England: Oxford University Press.

Lindsay, Margaret, Richard Webb, and John Fuerst. 1997. "Pirellulosomes: A new type of membrane-bounded cell compartment in planctomycete bacterial of the genus *Pirellula.*" *Microbiology* 143(3):739-748.

Margulis, Lynn. 1971a. "The Origin of Plant and Animal Cells." *American Scientist* 59(2):230-235, March-April.

_____. 1971b. *Origin of Eukaryotic Cells.* New Haven, CT: Yale University Press.

_____, Lynn, and Dorion Sagan. 1995. *What is Life?* New York, NY: Simon and Schuster.

_____, Lynn, and Dorion Sagan. 2002. *Acquiring Genomes: A Theory of the Origins of Species.* New York, NY: Basic Books.

Mathieu, Leo, and Sorin Sonea. 1995. "A Powerful Bacterial World." *Endeavor* 12(3):112117.

Mears, J.A., et al. 2006. "A structural model for the large subunit of the mammalian mitochondrial ribosome." *Journal of Molecular Biology* 358(1):193–212, April.

Palmer, Jeffrey. 1997. "Genome Evolution: The Mitochondrion That Time Forgot." *Nature* 387(6632):454-455, May 29.

Schatz, Gottfried. 1997. "Just Follow the Acid Chain." *Nature* 338(6638):121-122.

Starr, Cecie. 1997. *Biology: Concepts and Applications.* Belmont, CA: Wadsworth Publishing Company.

Terzaghi, E.A., A.S. Wilkins, and D. Penny. 1984. *Molecular Evolution: An Annotated Reader.* Boston, MA: Jones and Bartlett.

Tuszynski, Jack A. 2007. *Molecular and Cellular Biophysics*. Boca Raton, Fl: CRC Press.

Vogel, Gretchen. 1998. "Did the First Complex Cell Eat Oxygen?" *Science* 279(5357): 1,633-1,634, March 13.

Wallace, Douglas. 1997. "Mitochondrial DNA in Aging and Disease." *Scientific American* 277(2):40-47.

Woods, Michael. 1996. "Research Gets Rise From Yeast." *The Toledo Blade*: Toledo, Ohio, Monday, June 3.

Zubay, Geoffrey, William Parson, and Dennis Vance. 1995. *Principles of Biochemistry*. Dubuque, IA: William C. Brown Publishing.

CHAPTER 10

Summary

Work by a large number of scientists have largely falsified Darwinian evolution and the secular creation story of the big bang. Most people are aware of the Jewish, Christian, and Muslim belief that God, who exists outside of time, created the Earth and all life on it. The courts have consistently ruled that this worldview cannot be taught in government schools. Only the secular worldview can. The most eminent cosmologist of our century, Cambridge University Lucasian Professor of Physics, Stephen Hawking, wrote an excellent book titled *Brief Answers to the Big Questions* which I will extensively quote from to explain the secular creation story that this book, and the first book on this topic titled *The Three Major Pillars of Darwinism Demolished*, has falsified.

Hawking explained that random forces first produced simple organic molecules by which "somehow, some . . . atoms came to be arranged in the form of molecules of DNA . . . . As DNA reproduced itself, there would have been random errors, many of which would have been harmful, and . . . a few errors would have been favorable to the survival of the species—these would have been chosen by Darwinian natural selection" (pp. 73, 75). Eventually, multi-cellular organisms which, after more millions of years, by mistakes called mutations, evolved into fish that, after millions more years, evolved into mammals and, after a few hundred more million years, evolved into humans (pp. 75-76). Thus, he concludes, humans and all life are the result of chance and billions of mistakes. Since Hawking concluded that science has proven the origin of all life was by evolution, the last question left for religion was how the universe began. This question, Hawking assures us, has also been answered by the Big Bang which *ultimately* produced the creation of everything from nothing. The first something that appeared from nothing was "smaller than a proton" (p. 34). Then, from this smaller-than-a-proton-object space, visible matter, stars, and planets followed. Thus, the Big Bang explains the origin of space, matter, energy, and time, all of which appeared from nothing (pp. 29-31). His book, called stunningly brilliant by reviewers, has earned thousands of glowing reviews on Amazon and elsewhere.

Hawking explains, thanks to the Big Bang, that "you can get a whole universe for free" because "the fantastically enormous universe of space and energy can materialize out of nothing" (pp. 31-32). Thus, Hawking writes, "the universe itself, in all its mind-boggling vastness and complexity, could simply have popped into existence . . . [and] we do not need a God to set it up so that the Big Bang could bang" (p. 34). Hawking rejected theism because, he concluded, God is not needed to explain the existence of either the universe or life. As this work and many others have shown, the science is very clear. *Nothing has not, and cannot, produce our universe and lead to the Solar System and life as it exists on Earth.*

Reference

Hawking, Stephen. 2018. *Brief Answers to the Big Questions*. New York, NY: Bantam Books.

Printed in the United States
by Baker & Taylor Publisher Services